Meridian Documents of American History

GEORGE F. SCHEER, *General Editor*

The Confederacy

edited by ALBERT D. KIRWAN

MERIDIAN BOOKS, INC. *New York*

University, where he received his doctorate. Since
1938 he has taught at the University of Kentucky, becoming Professor of History in 1954. Mr. Kirwan is the
author of REVOLT OF THE RED NECKS (1951), and editor
of JOHNNY GREEN OF THE ORPHAN BRIGADE (1956).
He is married and the father of two sons.

M

First published by Meridian Books, Inc., September 1959
First printing August 1959

to Denny and Brit

CONTENTS

General Editor's Preface 9

Introduction 13

I *It Begins* 21

II *Farms and Factories* 54

III *Churches and Schools* 74

IV *The Muses* 97

V *Inflation* 117

VI *Invasion* 141

VII *"Stitch, Stitch, Stitch"* 168

VIII *Discontent* 197

IX *King Cotton* 225

X *The Fifth Column* 263

XI *It Ends* 282

Notes 293

Bibliography 303

Index 316

GENERAL EDITOR'S PREFACE

The purpose of the multivolume Meridian Documents of American History series is to provide for the student, scholar, and general reader, in an attractive and inexpensive format, a comprehensive and well-rounded collection of the principal documents of American history. While the volumes are not intended to serve as narrative histories, the documents are furnished with enough background to make a continuous story for the reader who may wish to peruse them without reference to other works. The primary aim of the editors is to show in a series of supplementary readers the American past as it was recorded by those who lived it.

The significance of documents is no recent discovery, nor is their compilation a new historical enterprise. In 1779, midway through the War for Independence, Elbridge Gerry moved, though unsuccessfully, in the Continental Congress that each state appoint an official to collect before they were lost "Memorials of the Rise and Progress and Termination of the Revolution." Already well-known was Thomas Hutchinson's pioneer publication, *A Collection of Original Papers Relative to the History of the Colony of Massachusetts-Bay*. A few years later, as the new nation took shape, such scholars as Ebenezer Hazard, Jonathan Elliot, Jared Sparks, Peter

Force, and John Brodhead, to name a few, began marshaling volumes of historical documents.

The object of these labors, which proliferated astonishingly after the Civil War, was generally "a body of authentic materials ready prepared" for the hand of the future historian. And for a long time the prodigious works of these early compilers and their successors, such men as B. F. Stevens, Worthington C. Ford, Paul L. Ford, Edmund C. Burnett, and others, remained largely the province of the professional historian. From them he constructed broad histories and narrow monographs. Against them as touchstones he tested the validity of historical statements and judgments.

However, as early as 1822, Hezekiah Niles recognized another value in documents. In the preface to his *Principles and Acts of the Revolution in America* he stated that he was presenting documentary evidence "to show the *feelings* that prevailed in the revolution, not to give a *history of events*." The Meridian series has been undertaken with the similar conviction that contemporary testimony establishes for its reader an identification with the past vastly excelling in immediacy and reality the most accomplished secondhand retelling.

In the Meridian volumes, documents are considered to be anything written, printed, or otherwise recorded which may be regarded as contemporary evidence. In fitting them together, the editors have eschewed the traditional approach (introductory paragraphs that summarize the documents, appraise them, and supply bibliographical details) for a technique that endeavors to present them as major elements in a continuing narrative. Evaluations of the documents are foregone in favor of evaluations of the persons and the times that together brought forth the documents.

Although the broad principles governing the series apply to all volumes, freedom has been allowed each individual editor to present the documents in the field of his specialty as he himself thinks they may best be exhibited. One editor has decided to handle his materials topically; another as "problems" in his particular field; another, chronologically. Another feels that his documents tell a cohesive and lucid story of themselves, so he has added little interpretive tissue, except for enlightening queries, while another has felt that the intricacies of his field demand extensive explication. Thus the series does not consist of rigidly styled documentaries, but rather of books developed individually as their subjects dictate.

In this volume, Mr. Kirwan's own excellent and provocative introduction speaks for his intentions. He has elected to explore topically the political, diplomatic, economic, and social aspects of life in the Confederate states, while adhering as closely as possible to a chronology within each topic. That there are definite omissions, he points out. Some of them are unavoidable, as in the case of slave and Negro opinion. Others are deliberate. For example, the best in Confederate poetry and song is already familiar and the majority of the fiction read was imported; most of the locally produced poetry, music, drama, and literature possessed, to say the least, very little distinction. There is considerably more to be gained, therefore, from the publication of contemporary critical commentary that not only mirrors the Confederate arts but also reflects the Confederacy's own estimate of them than there is from a toilsome journey through bad poems, awkward musical lyrics, and grotesque bits of fiction. In such areas as these, Mr. Kirwan has succeeded in creating a valuable dual image of the Confederate as he was and as he envisioned himself.

Altogether, drawing upon a variety of fresh sources, Mr. Kirwan has painted with documents a remarkably balanced, human portrait of an age and a people who lived tragically but fully for a brief time in the American past.

George F. Scheer

April 1959

In the four years from 1861 to 1865 the American nation struggled through the supreme crisis of its existence. Southern delusions that states could step peaceably out of the Federal Union as an exercise of a right; that a new nation of 5,500,000 whites and 3,500,000 slaves spread over a third of the land area of the Union could not be conquered and subjugated by an emotionally and politically divided North; that unlimited agricultural resources and industrial supplies from a friendly Europe would provide all necessary prerequisites to defense, were swept away in the storm of places like Shiloh and Gettysburg and Atlanta. Northern delusions that the whole business would be settled in ninety days were shattered by the pitiful dead of a hundred fields.

In the endless literature of that celebrated war the fortitude and valor of the Confederate soldier has become part of the national heritage—and deservedly so if records, official and unofficial, are to be credited. However, no more than a few hundred thousand Confederates were ever in service at any one time—a small fraction of the total population of the South. What of the rest of the people? Neglected in song and story, the civilian and the life he led must be studied if we would understand the Confederacy.

Life behind the lines, though drastically affected by the war, went on its inevitable way. Whether the armies won victories or suffered defeats, the people at home had to live; and living they knew joy and hope, suffered pain and despair, sought consolation in religion or amusement, sang paeans to their leaders when things went well and railed against them when things went bad.

But what was life like in the Confederacy? Did this great tragic experience produce poets who wrote in heroic verse of their supreme adventure? If not, were Southern critics aware of the new nation's literary limitations? Was there hope for creation of a national literature? What did religious leaders have to say about slavery, and what stand did they take on secession? What of education? Were Southerners content with the less than adequate schools of their region, or did they hope to do something about them? What of graphic arts, of agriculture, of manufacturing?

How did the people keep body and soul together when flour sold for $300 a barrel and bacon for $10 a pound? How did they clothe themselves when overcoats sold for $1,000 and boots for $250 a pair? How deep did patriotism run? Were there many who took advantage of neighbor and country by demanding exorbitant prices for necessities, or did most dedicate themselves to victory? Northern speculators connived, with their government's approval, to purchase cotton at handsome prices. Were Southerners seduced into this illegal trade?

What of politics? Was it a mistake to choose Jefferson Davis to lead the new government? Would things have gone better under an abler man, such as, perhaps, Robert Toombs or Howell Cobb? Or was independence an unattainable dream and Davis the best available man, as Robert E. Lee seemed to think he was? Alexander Stephens may have contributed to the final collapse by his public denunciation of administration policy and his personal attacks on Davis; was it a mistake, in the name of unity, to elect a reluctant secessionist like Stephens to office? Would it have been better to let men who had led the revolution head the new government? Davis surrounded himself with some counselors who had little popular support, or were considered mediocrities who simply carried out instructions from their chief; was he wise in loyally sustaining these officials despite the opposition they provoked? Did Judah P. Benjamin, for all his intellectual powers, strengthen or weaken the administration? Was conscription, under the circumstances, the best way to raise an army, or was Joseph E. Brown right in denouncing it as unnecessary and unconstitutional? Did Davis injure the cause by interfering with his generals, or would it have been better, as one of his critics thought, if "some honest planter" who did not think of himself as a military genius had headed the government? Was it stubbornness that induced Davis to support Braxton Bragg after he had lost the confidence of rank and file? Many charged that favoritism influenced choice of army officers and civil officials as well. Was it bad judgment or pettiness or both that caused Davis to remove Joseph E. Johnston as commander of the Army of Tennessee before Atlanta in July 1864?

Hindsight suggests that the government was unwise in its cotton policy—that in order to build up foreign credit it should have exported cotton before the blockade became effective. But would foreign credit have been of great value in 1863 and later when the Union navy was cutting imports to a fraction of the need? The Confederate Congress was roundly denounced for causing inflation by failure to tax and by deciding to fight the war on borrowed money; was the Congress at fault, or was the constitutional restriction on taxation, together with popular opposition to taxes, the real cause?

The all-pervading influence during the years of the Confederacy was, of course, the war itself. It crowded into all facets of the day-by-day life of the citizen. It made

its way to his table and devoured the food he had husbanded for his wife and children; it sat beside his hearth
and consumed the warmth that should have driven the
chill from his house; it reached its hand into his pocket
and took the coin that would have purchased necessities;
it accompanied him into the market place and gathered
up the goods that would have been abundant; it went
with him to church where he prayed for victory or heard
sermons condemning the invaders; it sat beside him in the
theater; it pushed into his sick chamber and snatched
away his medicines; and at night it lay down beside him
in his bed, wrapped itself in his blanket, and left him
only a few hours of cold and comfortless sleep.

The Confederacy did not use all its resources, either
human or material, in fighting the war, but it probably
came as close to doing so as any nation since Carthage. To
have conducted the war properly, the government would
have had to centralize control of the economy. Conscription, detailing, licensing, and price-fixing were attempts
at this, but they met such opposition that their effect was
largely nullified. Could the administration, public opinion
being what it was, have gone further than it did toward
centralization? In other words, was State rights compatible
with the facts of nineteenth-century life?

Finally, there is the matter of foreign policy. From the
outset, influential people in England and France favored
recognition of the Confederacy, and even intervention.
Aid from abroad might have insured the Confederacy's
independence, and no efforts should have been spared by
the Davis government to obtain it. One factor working
against recognition was the seeming inability of the South
to launch a successful military offensive. A single military
victory on Northern soil might well have brought diplomatic dividends out of all proportion to sacrifices such a
campaign would entail. Only a few more divisions made
available to Lee in the summer of 1862 might have made
the abortive Maryland campaign a brilliant success. Could

not these divisions have been drawn from North Carolina or Tennessee? What doomed the Confederacy to the use of three-quarter measures at such a time?

Another deterrent to foreign recognition of the Confederacy was its "peculiar institution." Of course, slavery was the underlying cause of secession, and perhaps the idea of emancipation was unthinkable to the South in the early years of the war. Yet, a few months before the end, the Confederate government offered Britain emancipation in return for recognition. Although the time had long passed when there was any prospect of British recognition, might not the offer two years earlier have borne fruit?

In this book I have tried to furnish some answers to these and other questions. One hundred and fifty-odd items from contemporary documents will, I hope, give a many-sided and accurate picture of the Confederacy. The document is, of course, history in the raw. From materials such as these the historian normally writes his text. He searches, selects, analyzes, and then presents his conclusions about the evidence to his readers. Here I perform only the first two of these services, leaving to the reader the interpretation of the document. In this way, and to this extent, the reader becomes his own historian.

Eyewitness accounts of battles have been omitted. The military history of the Confederacy is a separate story in itself and has been covered adequately elsewhere. But even in depicting life in the Confederacy in its social, cultural, and political manifestations, arbitrary decisions had to be made. Should documents pertaining to Kentucky and Missouri be included? The Confederate government considered them full-fledged members of the Confederacy; they were represented in the Confederate Congress, and they furnished large numbers of troops to the Confederate army. Yet, even if secession be considered a constitutional act, the manner in which it was effected in those states was irregular. Therefore, they have not been considered here as among the member states.

Source material on the Confederacy is voluminous, but not evenly balanced. People in all walks of life were conscious that they were living in a period of high drama, and diaries, journals, and latter-day memoirs were written in great numbers. Everyone wrote about economic conditions—high prices and shortages and makeshifts. To a man who is hungry nothing is so important as food; accordingly, a hundred documents on high prices and scarce commodities exist for every one on education or religion or the fine arts. Material is abundant on political questions, on conscription, *habeas corpus,* state versus Confederate authority, on criticisms of the administration; in these areas are dozens of first-rate narratives for every incident that took place. But the ordinary observer did not write about religion, education, literature, or the theater, and the investigator must plow deeper if he is to find evidence on those subjects. Then, too, Negro slaves constituted almost forty per cent of the population of the Confederacy. If there were any common denominator among them, it would be important to know what the slaves thought about matters. The overwhelming majority of them were illiterate, but a few could write. Some of them must have written letters, and some, perchance, kept diaries. The white man wrote copiously about the slave, and a few Negroes outside the South were fluent and prolific writers, but if there is any body of material written by slaves during this period, I do not know of it.

So, while I have tried to include all phases of life in the Confederacy and to keep them in proper perspective, I cannot pretend that I have wholly succeeded. I have selected those materials that seemed most authentic and had the most literary appeal. Where possible I have selected contemporary materials—diaries and letters—rather than later recollections. The value of the contemporary document is obvious. It may give a distorted or untrue picture in the light of later knowledge. It may reflect bias or partisanship. But, even in so doing, it breathes the living spirit of the times, and the reader soon learns to detect and make allowance for its lack of objectivity.

Where given names and official rank are missing in the original document, I have supplied them in the customary brackets on their first appearance. Excessively long paragraphs have been broken at convenient places, and although in a few instances I have carefully followed the spelling and punctuation of the original for its picturesque flavor, in general I have edited spelling and punctuation to conform with modern practices and to make for easier reading. In all but one document, I have capitalized the word "Negro" wherever it was not originally so. In no case have I made any change whatever in grammar or meaning. All words or phrases that ordinarily would be italicized appear in the documents in small capitals. This is to avoid any confusion with my commentary, which is set in italic type throughout.

Most of the items are excerpts. I have indicated omissions within documents, but have not indicated omissions at the beginning or end of the excerpt. The sources of all documents are in the Notes.

I wish to express my thanks to many people for aid: to the staff of the University of Kentucky Library; to the Duke University Library, and especially to its archivist, Miss Mattie Russell; to the Library of Congress; Harvard University Library; University of Virginia Library; the Union Theological Seminary Library; and the Valentine Museum Library. I am especially indebted to Mr. George F. Scheer for astute editorial advice. His wise suggestions and careful editing have smoothed many transition passages. I am grateful to the University of Kentucky Research Fund for a grant used in preparing the manuscript. I am indebted to my colleague Professor Thomas D. Clark for many kindnesses. It was he who urged me to undertake this assignment, and he has relieved me of other duties in order that I might fulfill it. My wife, Betty Kirwan, and my sister, Mrs. Coleman McDevitt, have with great patience typed the manuscript not once but several times. They have also advised me frequently in the selection and arrangement of documents, and their generous and thoughtful aid made the preparation of the book a pleasant project indeed.

Albert D. Kirwan

March 1959

WE THE PEOPLE OF SOUTH CAROLINA IN CONVENTION AS-
SEMBLED DO DECLARE AND ORDAIN AND IT IS HEREBY DE-
CLARED AND ORDAINED That the ordinance adopted by us in
convention on the twenty-third of May in the year of our
Lord one thousand seven hundred and eighty-eight
whereby the Constitution of the United States of America
was ratified and also all acts and parts of acts of the General Assembly of this state ratifying amendments of the said
Constitution are hereby repealed; and that the union now
subsisting between South Carolina and other states under
the name of the "United States of America" is hereby dissolved.[1]

*It was December 20, 1860, at seven o'clock, and
Charleston's Institute Hall was brilliantly illuminated by
chandelier and candelabrum. As the last of the 169 delegates of the special convention called by the South Carolina Legislature signed his name to the document, President D. F. Jameson held it aloft for delegates and specta-
tors to see. Outside cannon began to boom. Bonfires
sprang up. Ebullient military units paraded. South Carolina had seceded from the Union, and her people danced
in the streets as though a great victory had been won.*

*South Carolina had not come to this fateful decision
without considerable forethought. Almost three decades*

before, she had nullified the tariff bill of 1832 and had armed herself to resist the army that Andrew Jackson proposed to march against her. In the debates over the Compromise measures of 1850 the celebrated John C. Calhoun had warned that unless the North should respect Southern rights the South must in self-defense secede, and a few months later, at the Nashville Convention, South Carolina delegates had openly argued for secession.

Thus, South Carolina early established a reputation as a firebrand in opposing the authority of the national government. And this reputation tended to obscure the fact that at one time or another many states in other sections had given rein to similar inclinations.

In 1811, for instance, Josiah Quincy of Massachusetts urged secession of his state if Louisiana should be admitted into the Union. Three years later, unhappy over the second war with Britain, New Englanders openly talked of nullification, and their resolutions adopted at Hartford carried at least a suggestion of secession should the national government not treat their demands favorably.

In truth, the doctrine of State rights—as state opposition to national authority came to be known—was a minority doctrine, to be espoused or denied as local interests might dictate. And those who advocated it were as inconsistent as were their shifting interests. By the 1850's, when the South as a section had generally embraced the philosophy, it still thought it eminently proper for the national government to act as a slave-catcher and take by force fugitive slaves who were being protected by state law in the North. At the same time Northern states, while denouncing the theory of state interposition, were actually nullifying the Fugitive Slave Act.

But by 1860 the South had become, it appeared, a permanent minority, and South Carolina and other Southern states were firmly committed to the doctrine of State rights. The reason for this position was that slavery had become the central issue in American politics; and the South feared that a strong national government in the hands of a Northern majority hostile to its "peculiar institution" might destroy its way of life.

The doctrine of State rights had philosophical as well as historical antecedents. The theory, as expressed by Jefferson in the Kentucky Resolutions of 1798, was that the states had created the national government. They had, therefore, given it what authority it had and this authority was explicitly limited by the Constitution. All other authority was reserved to the states, who were also to decide when the national government exceeded its powers. In such event a state might declare an act of the national government null and void.

It was not a long step from nullification to secession. State righters argued that the Union had been formed as a compact between the states, each state agreeing to abide by the Constitution as a consideration of the other states so behaving. But, they maintained, since the states had come voluntarily into the Union they had a right to withdraw if the compact was violated by the other parties. And this was a constitutional right, not a revolutionary one.

And so, with the triumph, in 1860, of a party dedicated to the containment of slavery in its present boundaries in defiance, it seemed to South Carolina, of the Constitution, the time for separation had come.

In imitation of their forefathers of Revolutionary days the Carolinians, upon seceding, appointed a committee to draw up a "Declaration of the Immediate Causes which . . . justify the Secession of South Carolina from the Federal Union." Chairman of the committee was C. G. Memminger. German-born, Memminger had come to Charleston as an orphan and been adopted at the age of eleven by Thomas Bennett, a former governor of the state, who educated him for the law. Success in law and merchandising followed and gained him a reputation as a grave and businesslike financier. He was not one of the *original secessionists; instead he had urged delay in the movement until co-operation could be obtained from other states. Small of stature and undistinguished in appearance, his blue-gray, calm eyes reflected no emotion as he stood before the Secession Convention and read:*

And now the state of South Carolina having resumed her separate and equal place among nations deems it due to herself, to the remaining United States of America, and to the nations of the world that she should declare the immediate causes which have led to this act. . . .

We affirm that [the] ends for which this government was instituted have been defeated, and the government itself has been destructive of them by the action of the nonslaveholding states. Those states have assumed the right of deciding upon the propriety of our domestic institutions; and have denied the rights of property established in fifteen of the states and recognized by the Constitution; they have denounced as sinful the institution of slavery; they have permitted the open establishment among them of societies whose avowed object is to disturb the peace of and eloign the property of the citizens of other states. They have encouraged and assisted thousands of our slaves to leave their homes; and those who remain have been incited by emissaries, books, and pictures to servile insurrection.

For twenty-five years this agitation has been steadily increasing until it has now secured to its aid the power of the common government. Observing the FORMS of the Constitution, a sectional party has found within that article establishing the Executive Department the means of subverting the Constitution itself. A geographical line has been drawn across the Union, and all the states north of that line have united in the election of a man to the high office of President of the United States whose opinions and purposes are hostile to slavery. He is to be entrusted with the administration of the common government because he has declared that "Government cannot endure permanently half slave, half free," and that the public mind must rest in the belief that slavery is in the course of ultimate extinction.

This sectional combination for the subversion of the Constitution has been aided in some of the states by elevating to citizenship persons who, by the supreme law of the land, are incapable of becoming citizens; and their votes have been used to inaugurate a new policy hostile to the South and destructive of its peace and safety.

On the 4th of March next this party will take possession of the government. It has announced that the South shall be excluded from the common territory, that the judicial tribunal shall be made sectional, and that a war must be waged against slavery until it shall cease throughout the United States.

The guarantees of the Constitution will then no longer exist; the equal rights of the states will be lost. The slave-holding states will no longer have the power of self-government or self-protection, and the Federal government will have become their enemy. . . .

We, therefore, the people of South Carolina, by our delegates in convention assembled, appealing to the Supreme Judge of the world for the rectitude of our intentions, have solemnly declared that the Union heretofore existing between this state and the other states of North America is dissolved, and that the state of South Carolina has resumed her position among the nations of the world as a separate and independent state with full power to levy war, conclude peace, contract alliances, establish commerce, and to do all other acts and things which independent states may of right do.[2]

South Carolina had moved with such assurance because she was confident that other states would follow her. Meeting in Washington on January 5, 1861, the senators from Georgia, Florida, Alabama, Mississippi, Arkansas, Louisiana, and Texas

RESOLVED, 1. That in our opinion each of the Southern

states should, as soon as may be, secede from the Union.

RESOLVED, 2. That provision should be made for a convention to organize a Confederacy of the seceding states, the convention to meet not later than the 15th of February at the city of Montgomery.[3]

By February 1 all six states had joined South Carolina, and upon invitation of Alabama, delegates of the seceded states assembled in Montgomery on February 4 to form a new union.

A Provisional Constitution was unanimously adopted on February 8, creating a government quite similar to that of the United States. By it the Convention was given the additional responsibility of legislating for the provisional government, and thus became temporarily a one-house Congress. The Convention also was given the power to choose a provisional president and vice-president, and to these offices it elected Jefferson Davis of Mississippi and Alexander H. Stephens of Georgia.

This government was supported by an act of the Congress designed to preserve law and order and legal procedure during the transition period.

BE IT ENACTED BY THE CONFEDERATE STATES OF AMERICA IN CONGRESS ASSEMBLED, That all the laws of the United States of America in force and in use in the Confederate States of America on the first day of November last, and not inconsistent with the Constitution of the Confederate States, be, and the same are hereby continued in force until altered or repealed by the Congress.[4]

The government created by the Provisional Constitution was only a stop gap, to be replaced within one year by a permanent one, and the Convention started at once preparing a permanent constitution. On March 11, 1861, the Constitution of the Confederate States of America was unanimously adopted by the Convention.

The form, as well as the language, of this Constitution was almost identical with that of the United States. This is not surprising, for Southerners on the whole had no

*complaint against the older document. Indeed, it was their
contention that Northern disregard for the Federal Constitution had driven them to secede. The Confederate
Constitution provided for a national government of three
branches, legislative, executive, and judicial. The legislative branch was divided into a House of Representatives
and a Senate whose powers were quite similar to those
of the United States Congress. Methods of election and
qualifications were also similar. The executive branch consisted of a president and vice-president chosen by an Electoral College and with powers and qualifications parallel-
ing those of their counterparts in Washington. The judiciary was to consist of a supreme court and such inferior
courts as Congress might create, but Congress failed to
implement this provision, and a supreme court was never
established. The preamble to the Confederate Constitution emphasized state sovereignty, but on the right of
secession it was silent as was the United States Constitution. The twelve amendments to the latter were worked in
at appropriate sections in the new instrument.[5]*

*Despite the remarkable similarity between the two con-
stitutions, there were some notable differences. Article I,
Section 6, of the Confederate Constitution provided:*

Congress may by law grant to the principal officer in
each of the Executive Departments a seat upon the floor
of either House with the privilege of discussing any measures appertaining to his department. . . .

*It has been suggested that this was a step in the
direction of cabinet government; but, actually, Congress
never enacted a law providing for this innovation.*

*Article I, Section 7, gave the Confederate president an
important legislative power for which many presidents of
the United States, before and since, have yearned.*

The President may approve any appropriation and dis-
approve any other appropriation in the same bill. In such
case he shall, in signing the bill, designate the appropria-
tions disapproved; and shall return a copy of such ap-

propriations, with his objections, to the House in which
the bill shall have originated; and the same proceedings
shall then be had as in case of other bills disapproved by
the President.

*At the same time, the term of the chief executive was
limited.*

Article II, Section 1, 1. The executive power shall be
vested in a President of the Confederate States of America. He and the Vice-President shall hold their offices for
the term of six years; but the president shall not be re-
eligible.

*Southerners had long been opposed to protective tariffs,
subsidies, and pork-barrel legislation for the improvement
of rivers, harbors, and canals. Accordingly, they placed
restrictions on the taxing power of Congress.*

Article I, Section 8. The Congress shall have power—

1. To lay and collect taxes, duties, imposts, and excises
for revenue necessary to pay the debts; provide for the
common defense and carry on the Government of the
Confederate States; but no bounties shall be granted from
the Treasury, nor shall any duties or taxes on importations
from foreign nations be laid to promote or foster any
branch of industry. . . .

3. To regulate commerce with foreign nations and among
the several states and with the Indian tribes; but neither
this nor any other clause contained in the Constitution
shall ever be construed to delegate the power to Congress
to appropriate money for any internal improvement intended to facilitate commerce, except for the purpose of
furnishing lights, beacons, and buoys, and other aids to
navigation upon the coasts, and the improvement of harbors and the removing of obstructions in river navigation;
in all which cases such duties shall be laid on the navigation facilitated thereby as may be necessary to pay the
costs and expenses thereof. . . .

Section 10, 3. No state shall, without the consent of Congress, lay any duty on tonnage, except on seagoing vessels,

for the improvement of its rivers and harbors navigated by the said vessels; but such duties shall not conflict with any treaties of the Confederate States with foreign nations; and any surplus revenue thus derived shall, after making such improvement, be paid into the common treasury.

The United States Post Office had been used since Jackson's time to provide jobs and fat contracts to political adherents of the party in power. Confederate constitution-makers sought to prevent this.

Article I, Section 8, 7. [Congress shall have power] To establish post-offices and post routes; but the expenses of the Post-Office Department, after the 1st day of March in the year of our Lord eighteen hundred and sixty-three, shall be paid out of its own revenues.

Basic in State rights philosophy was a strict limitation of the powers of the central government. The "implied powers" clause had opened a Pandora's box of troubles in the old Union. Yet, the Confederate Constitution contained the identical clause.

Article I, Section 8, 18. [Congress shall have power] To make all laws which shall be necessary and proper for carrying into execution the foregoing powers and all other powers vested by this Constitution in the Government of the Confederate States or in any department or officer thereof.

Furthermore, Article VI made it clear that the new Constitution, like the old, was the "supreme law of the land."

Article VI, Section 3. This Constitution and the laws of the Confederate States made in pursuance thereof, and all treaties made or which shall be made under the authority of the Confederate States shall be the supreme law of the land; and the judges in every state shall be bound thereby, anything in the constitution or laws of any state to the contrary notwithstanding.

Section 4. The Senators and Representatives before mentioned and the members of the several state legislatures and all executive and judicial officers, both of the Confederate States and of the several states, shall be bound by oath or affirmation to support this Constitution.

Export duties were prohibited in the United States Constitution, but the Confederacy permitted them by a two-thirds majority vote of Congress, so that the government might derive a revenue from the export of cotton and other staples.

An interesting and unique restriction on Congressional appropriation of money was provided by Article I, Section 9.

Congress shall appropriate no money from the Treasury except by a vote of two-thirds of both Houses, taken by yeas and nays, unless it be asked and estimated for by some one of the heads of departments and submitted to Congress by the President; or for the purpose of paying its own expenses and contingencies; or for the payment of claims against the Confederate States, the justice of which shall have been judicially declared by a tribunal for the investigation of claims against the Government, which it is hereby made the duty of Congress to establish.

And the very next clause struck at the old Washington custom of rescuing government contractors who had shaved their bids too close.

Section 10. All bills appropriating money shall specify in Federal currency the exact amount of each appropriation and the purposes for which it is made; and Congress shall grant no extra compensation to any public contractor, officer, agent, or servant, after such contract shall have been made or such service rendered.

The Founding Fathers, in 1787, had carefully avoided use of the term "slave." Indeed, the word would have looked incongruous in a document written by men who had led a revolution based on the Rights of Man. Confederate statesmen, however, had no such inhibitions, and the word appears frequently in their Constitution.

Article I, Section 9, provided:

1. The importation of Negroes of the African race from any foreign country other than the slaveholding states or territories of the United States of America is hereby forbidden; and Congress is required to pass such laws as shall effectually prevent the same.

2. Congress shall also have power to prohibit the introduction of slaves from any state not a member of, or territory not belonging to, this Confederacy. . . .

4. No bill of attainder, EX POST FACTO law, or law denying or impairing the right of property in Negro slaves shall be passed.

Also, Article IV, Section 2, provided:

1. The citizens of each state . . . shall have the right of transit and sojourn in any state of this Confederacy, with their slaves and other property; and the right of property in said slaves shall not be thereby impaired.

New states might be admitted into the Confederacy, but only by a two-thirds vote of both houses of Congress. Meanwhile, no Wilmot Proviso would restrict the expansion of slavery into new territories that might be acquired. Article IV, Section 3.

3. The Confederate States may acquire new territory; and Congress shall have power to legislate and provide governments for the inhabitants of all territory belonging to the Confederate States lying without the limits of the several states; and may permit them, at such times and in such manner as it may by law provide, to form states to be admitted into the Confederacy. In all such territory the institution of Negro slavery, as it now exists in the Confederate States, shall be recognized and protected by Congress and by the territorial government; and the inhabitants of the several Confederate states and territories shall have the right to take to such territory any slaves lawfully held by them in any of the states or territories of the Confederate States.

The amending process did not follow either of the methods outlined in the old constitution, and, on its face, it would seem that the Confederate Constitution was the easier to amend.

Article V, Section 1, 1. Upon the demand of any three states legally assembled in their several conventions, the Congress shall summon a convention of all the states to take into consideration such amendments to the Constitution as the said states shall concur in suggesting at the time when the said demand is made; and should any of the proposed amendments to the Constitution be agreed on by the said convention—voting by states—and the same be ratified by the legislatures of two-thirds of the several states, or by conventions in two-thirds thereof—as the one or the other mode of ratification may be proposed by the general convention—they shall thenceforward form a part of this Constitution. But no state shall, without its consent, be deprived of its equal representation in the Senate.

Amendments were discussed during the life of the Confederacy, but none was made.

Finally, the Constitution provided for the transition from the provisional to the permanent government.

Article VII, Section 2, 2. When five states shall have ratified this Constitution in the manner before specified, the Congress under the Provisional Constitution shall prescribe the time for holding the election of President and Vice-President, and for the meeting of the Electoral College, and for counting the votes, and inaugurating the President. They shall also prescribe the time for holding the first election of members of Congress under this Constitution and the time for assembling the same. Until the assembling of such Congress the Congress under the Provisional Constitution shall continue to exercise the legislative powers granted them, not extending beyond the time limited by the Constitution of the Provisional Government.

By the first of June this Constitution had been ratified by the original six states, as well as by Texas, Virginia,

North Carolina, Tennessee, and Arkansas. Congress then
provided for elections in November to choose a president
and vice-president, and also a new Congress for the
permanent government. At that time Davis and Stephens
were elected without opposition and were inaugurated on
Washington's Birthday 1862.

Meanwhile, south from Philadelphia hurried a man
named J. B. Jones, a moderately successful writer of West-
ern adventure novels. A native of Baltimore, married to a
Virginia woman, he had moved to Philadelphia in 1857
and was publishing a weekly called the Southern Monitor
when he learned of the relief expedition for Sumter. At
fifty-one he thought himself too old to fight, but he was
determined to aid the South he loved. He was zealous and
patriotic, but his primary concern was to gather material
for "a full and authentic Diary of the transactions of the
Government." Jones was credulous, prejudiced, and spite-
ful. He hated Jews, the British, and Yankees, and he
seemed to feel that everyone should be in the army, except
his own able-bodied son, who worked with him as a clerk.
But his Diary was accurate and all-inclusive. He made an
entry for every day of the war, commenting on politics,
economics, military and foreign affairs. He was in Mont-
gomery that fateful spring of 1861 and called on the new
President.

Was introduced to the President today. He was over-
whelmed with papers and retained a number in his left
hand, probably of more importance than the rest. He received me with urbanity; and while he read the papers I
had given him, as I had never seen him before I en-
deavored to scrutinize his features, as one would naturally
do. . . . His stature is tall, nearly six feet; his frame is
very slight and seemingly frail; but when he throws back
his shoulders he is as straight as an Indian chief. The
features of his face are distinctly marked with character;
and no one gazing at his profile would doubt for a moment
that he beheld more than an ordinary man. His face is

handsome, and his thin lip often basks a pleasant smile. There is nothing sinister or repulsive in his manners or appearance; and if there are no special indications of great grasp of intellectual power on his forehead and on his sharply defined nose and chin, neither is there any evidence of weakness or that he could be easily moved from any settled purpose. I think he has a clear conception of matters demanding his cognizance and a nice discrimination of details. As a politician he attaches the utmost importance to CONSISTENCY—and here I differ with him. I think that to be consistent as a politician is to change with the circumstances of the case. . . .

When the President had completed the reading of my papers, and during the perusal I observed him make several emphatic nods, he asked me what I wanted. I told him I wanted employment with my pen, perhaps only temporary employment. I thought the corespondence of the Secretary of War would increase in volume, and another assistant besides Major [John] Tyler would be required in his office. He smiled and shook his head, saying that such work would be only temporary indeed; which I construed to mean that even HE did not then suppose the war to assume colossal proportions.

Two days later Jones secured a clerkship in the War Department. This gave him the opportunity he sought— close association with important men and events. On May 20 he wrote:

Mr. [Leroy Pope] Walker, the Secretary of War, is some forty-seven or -eight years of age, tall, thin, and a little bent; not by age, but by study and bad health. He was a successful lawyer, and having never been in governmental employment is fast working himself down. He has not yet learned how to avoid unnecessary labor, being a man of the finest sensibilities and exacting with the utmost nicety all due deference to the dignity of his official position. He stands somewhat on ceremony with his brother officials and accords and exacts the etiquette natural to a sensitive gentleman who had never been broken on the wheel of office. I predict for him a short career. The only hope for his continuance in office is unconditional submission to the President, who, being once Secretary of War of the United States, is familiar with all the wheels of the department. But soon, if I err not, the President will be too much absorbed in the fluctuations of momentous campaigns to give much of his attention to any one of the departments. Nevertheless, Mr. Walker, if he be an apt scholar, may learn much before that day; and Congress may simplify his duties by enacting a uniform mode of filling the offices in the field. The applications now give the greatest trouble; and the disappointed class give rise to many vexations.

MAY 21st.—Being in the same room with the Secretary, and seen by all his visitors, I am necessarily making many new acquaintances; and quite a number recognize me by my books which they have read. Among this class is Mr. [Judah P.] Benjamin, the Minister of Justice, who today informed me that he and Senator [James A.] Bayard had been interested at Washington in my "Story of Disunion." Mr. Benjamin is, of course, a Jew, of French lineage, born, I believe, in Louisiana, a lawyer and politician. His age may be sixty, and yet one might suppose him to be less than forty. His hair and eyes are black, his forehead capacious, his face round and intellectual as one of that shape can be and Mr. B. is certainly a man of intellect, education, and extensive reading, combined with natural abilities of a tolerably high order. Upon his lips there seems to bask an eternal smile; but if it be studied it is not a smile—yet it bears no unpleasing aspect.

MAY 22nd.—Today I had in our office a specimen of Mr. Memminger's oratory. He was pleading for an installment of the claims of South Carolina on the Confederacy; and Mr. Walker, always hesitating, argued the other side merely for delay. Both are fine speakers with most distinct enunciation and musical voices. The demand was audited and paid, amounting, I believe, to several hundred thousand dollars.

And I heard and saw Mr. [Robert] Toombs today, the Secretary of State. He is a portly gentleman, but with the pale face of the student and the marks of a deep thinker. To gaze at him in repose the casual spectator would suppose from his neglect of dress that he was a planter in moderate circumstances and, of course, not gifted with extraordinary powers of intellect; but let him open his mouth and the delusion vanishes. At the time alluded to he was surrounded by the rest of the cabinet in our office, and the topic was the policy of the war. He was for taking the initiative and carrying the war into the enemy's country. And as he warmed with the subject the MAN seemed to vanish and the GENIUS alone was visible. He was most emphatic in the advocacy of his policy and bold almost to rashness in his denunciations of the merely defensive idea. He was opposed to all delays as fraught with danger; the enemy were in the field, and their purposes were pronounced. Why wait to see what they meant to do? If we did that they would not only invade us but get a permanent foothold on our soil. We must invade or be invaded, and he was for making the war as terrible as possible from the beginning. It was to be no child's play, and nothing could be gained by reliance upon the blunders and forbearance of the Yankees. . . .

The Secretary of War well knew how to parry these thrusts; he was not responsible. He was as ultra a man as any, and all he could do was to organize and arm the troops authorized by Congress. Some thirty-odd thousand were mustered in already, and at least five thousand volunteers were offering daily. Mr. Toombs said five hundred thousand volunteers ought to be accepted and for the war. We wanted no six or twelve months' men. To this the Secretary replied that the Executive could not transcend the limits prescribed by Congress.

These little discussions were of frequent occurrence,

and it soon became apparent that the Secretary of War was destined to be the most important man among the cabinet ministers. His position afforded the best prospect of future distinction—always provided he should be equal to the position and his administration attended with success. I felt convinced that Toombs would not be long chafing in the cabinet but that he would seize the first opportunity to repair to the field.[6]

Also in Montgomery at the time was T. C. De Leon, member of a Charleston family of Spanish antecedents. He was named for the celebrated State righter President Thomas Cooper of South Carolina College, a close friend of his father. His oldest brother, David, was surgeon-general of the Confederacy; and another brother, Edwin, was sent by the Confederacy as a diplomatic agent to Europe. De Leon served in the Confederate army throughout the war, but he seems to have been more interested in social than military events. He kept notes of his observations and after the war expanded them into a vivid account of life in the Confederacy. He never married and seems to have been inclined toward a Bohemian life; his writings are graphic and recapture the spirit of the times. He was twenty-two in May 1861, when he wrote the following.

On the whole the effect of Montgomery upon the arrival was rather pleasing, with a something rather provincial, quite in keeping with its location inland. Streets, various in length, uncertain in direction and impractical as to pavement, ran into Main Street at many points; and most of them were closely built with pretty houses, all of them surrounded by gardens and many by handsome grounds. Equidistant from the end of Main Street and from each other stood, in these cradle days, the two hotels of which the capital could boast. Montgomery Hall, of bitter memory—like the much-sung "Raven of Zurich" for uncleanliness of nest and length of bill—had been the resort of country merchants, horse- and cattle-men; but now the Solon of the hour dwelt therein, with the possible hero of many a field. The Exchange—of rather more pretensions and vastly more comfort—was at that time in the hands of a Northern firm who "could keep a hotel." The latter was political headquarters—the President, the Cabinet, and a swarm of the possible great residing there.

Montgomery was Washington over again, only on a smaller scale and with the avidity and agility in pursuit of the spoils somewhat enhanced by the freshness of scent.

"The President is at this house?" I queried of the ex-member of Congress next me at dinner. "But he does not appear, I suppose?"

"Oh, yes: he's waiting here till his house is made ready. But he doesn't have a private table; takes his meals like an everyday mortal, at the ladies' ordinary."

He had scarcely spoken when Mr. Davis entered by a side door and took his seat with only an occasional stare of earnest, but not disrespectful, curiosity from the more recent arrivals.

Even in the few weeks since I have seen him, there was a great change. He looked worn and thinner; and the set expression of the somewhat stern features gave a grim hardness not natural to their lines. With scarcely a glance around he returned the general salutations, sat down absently and was soon absorbed in conversation with General [Samuel] Cooper, who had recently resigned the adjutant-generalship of the United States army and accepted a similar post and a brigadier's commission from Mr. Davis. . . .

Little ceremony or form hedged the incubating government; and perfect simplicity marked every detail about Mr. Davis. His office, for the moment, was one of the parlors of the hotel. Members of the Cabinet and high officials came in and out without ceremony to ask questions and receive very brief replies; or for whispered consultation with the President's private secretary, whose desk was in the same room. Casual visitors were simply announced by an usher and were received whenever business did not prevent. Mr. Davis's manner was unvarying in its quiet and courtesy, drawing out all that one had to tell and indicating by brief answer, or criticism, that he had extracted the pith from it. At that moment he was the very idol of the people; the grand embodiment to them of their grand cause; and they gave him their hands unquestioning, to applaud any move soever he might make. . . .

The government was to consist, after the President, of a Vice-President and secretary for each of the departments of State, War, Navy, Treasury, Post-Office, and Justice; the latter being a combination of the responsibilities of the Interior Department and the Attorney-General's office.

Alexander H. Stephens of Georgia had been elevated to the vice-presidency, as reconciling the oppositions of "original secession" and "anti-secession." He had long been a prominent politician, was thoroughly acquainted with all the points of public life, and was, at this time, quite popular with people of all sections, being generally regarded as a man of exceptional capacity and great independence.

The portfolio of State was in the hands of another Georgian, Robert Toombs. In the present posture of affairs little could be expected from it, as until the nations of Europe should recognize the South she could have no foreign policy. The honorable Secretary himself seemed fully to realize how little onerous was his position. One of the ten thousand applicants for any and every position approached him for a place in his department and exhibited his letters of recommendation.

"Perfectly useless, sir!" responded Mr. Toombs with a thunderous oath. Let us whisper that the honorable secretary was a profound swearer.

"But, sir," persisted the place-hunter, "if you will only look at this letter from Mr. ——, I think you can find something for me."

"Can you get in here, sir?" roared the secretary fiercely, taking off his hat and pointing into it—with a volley of sonorous oaths—"That's the Department of State, sir!"

The Post-Office and Department of Justice were, as yet, about as useful as the State Department; but to the War Office every eye was turned, and the popular verdict seemed to be that the choice there was not the right man in the right place. Mr. Leroy Pope Walker, to whom its administration was entrusted, was scarcely known beyond the borders of his own state; but those who did know him prophesized that he would early stagger under the heavy responsibility that would necessarily fall upon him in event of war. Many averred that he was only a man of straw to whom Mr. Davis had offered the portfolio, simply that he might exercise his own well-known love for military affairs and be himself the DE FACTO Secretary of War.

The selection of Mr. [Stephen R.] Mallory of Florida for the Navy Department was more popular and was, as yet, generally considered a good one. His long experience as chairman of the committee on naval affairs in the United States Senate, and his reputation for clearness of reasoning and firmness of purpose made him acceptable to the majority of politicians and people. Of Mr. [John H.] Reagan the people knew little; but their fate was not in his hands, and just now they were content to wait for their letters.

The Treasury Department was justly supposed to be the key to national success. It was at least the twin, in importance, with the War Office. Mr. Memminger of South Carolina was a self-made man who had managed the finances of his state and had made reputation for some financiering ability and much common sense. He had, moreover, the advantage of being a new man; and the critics were willing to give him the benefit of common law until he should prove himself guilty. Still, the finance of the country was so vital and came home so nearly to every man in it that, perhaps, a deeper anxiety was felt about its management than that of any other branch.

The Attorney-General, or chief of the Department of Justice, had a reputation as wide as the continent—and as far as mental ability and legal knowledge went there could be no question among the growlers as to his perfect qualifications for the position. Mr. Judah P. Benjamin was not only the successful politician who had risen from obscurity to become the leader of his party in the Senate and its exponent of the constitutional questions involved in its action, [but] was known as a ripe and cultivated scholar. So the people who shook their heads at him—and they were neither few nor far between—did it on other grounds than that of incapacity.

This was the popular view of that day at the new capital. The country at large had but little means of knowing the real stuff of which the Cabinet was made. It is true four of the six were old and thoroughly broken party horses, who had for years cantered around the Washington arena till the scent of its sawdust was dear to their nostrils. But the people knew little of them individually and took their tone from the politicians of the past. So—as it is a known fact that politicians are never satisfied—the Cabinet and Congress, as tried in the hotel alembic, were not found pure gold.

So the country grumbled. The newspapers snarled, criticized, and asserted with some show of truth, that things were at a dead standstill, and that nothing practical had been accomplished. . . .

The states went out of the Union separately and at different periods by the action of conventions. These were naturally composed of men who had long been prominently before the people urging the measures of secession. As a matter of course the old political workers of each section, by fair means and foul, were enabled to secure election to these conventions; and, once there, they so fevered and worked upon the public mind, amid rapidly succeeding events, that its afterthought could neither be reasonable nor deliberate. The act of secession once consummated, the state connected itself with the Confederacy and representatives had to be sent to Montgomery. Small wonder that the men most prominent in the secession conventions should secure their own election, as little regard to fitness as ability being had by the excited electors.

The House of Representatives at Montgomery looked like the Washington Congress, viewed through a reversed opera-glass. The same want of dignity and serious work; the same position of ease, with feet on desk and hat on head; the same buzzing talk on indifferent subjects; often the very same men in the lobbies—taking dry smokes from unlit cigars; all these elements were there in duplicate, if somewhat smaller and more concentrated. No point in Montgomery was remote enough—no assemblage dignified enough—to escape the swoop of the lobby vulture. His beak was as sharp and his unclean talons as strong as those of the traditional bird which had blinked and battened so long on the eaves of the Washington edifice. When "the old concern" had been dismembered, limbs had been dragged whole to aid in the construction of the new giant; and scenting these from afar he hastened hither fierce for his fresh banquet.

Glancing down from the gallery of the House, many were the familiar faces peering over the desks; and even where one did not know the individual it was easy to recognize the politician by trade among the rosy and uncomfortable novices. It was constant food for wonderment to thoughtful men that the South had, in most cases, chosen party hacks to legislate for and to lead her in this great crisis, rather than transfused younger blood and steadier nerves into her councils; rather than grafted new minds upon the as yet healthy body. The revolution was properly accepted as the result of corruption and aggressions which these very men had been utterly helpless to correct or to prevent; even had they not been able actors in them. Yet, worn-out politicians—who had years before been "promoted from servants to sovereigns and had taken back seats"—floated high upon the present surge. Men hot from Washington, reeking with the wiles of the old House and with their unblushing buncombe fresh upon them, took the lead in every movement; and the rank old Washington leaven threatened to permeate every pore of the new government.

It is small wonder that the measures of such a congress, when not vacillating, were weak. If the time demanded anything that demand was the promptest organization of an army with an immediate basis of foreign credit to arm, equip, and clothe it. Next to this was the urgent need for a simple and readily managed machinery in the different departments of the government.

Neither of these desiderata could be secured by their few earnest and capable advocates, who thrust them forward over and over again only to be pushed aside by the sensation element with which the popular will of the new nation—or the want of it—had diluted her councils. There were windy dissertations on the color of the flag or on the establishment of a patent office; and members made long speeches bearing on no special point but that most special one of their own re-election. There were bitter denunciations of "the old wreck"; violent diatribes on the "gridiron" flag; with many an eloquent and manly declaration of the feelings and the attitude of the South. But these were not the bitter need. Declarations sufficient had already been made; and the masses—having made them and being ready and willing to maintain them— stood with their hands in their pockets, open-mouthed, eager, but inactive. They were waiting for some organization, for some systematized preparation for the struggle even they felt to be surely coming. Not one in three of the congressmen dared look the real issue directly in the face; and these were powerless to accomplish anything practical. But their constant pressure finally forced from the reluctant legislature a few first steps toward reduction of the chaos.[7]

By the time young De Leon penned his impressions of Montgomery and the new government, the main issue— peaceable withdrawal from the Federal Union or the establishment of revolution by arms—had been decided by an incident in Charleston harbor. Upon their withdrawal the several states had seized Federal forts, arsenals, mints, and other properties within their borders, with the exception of three forts off Florida and one at Charleston, avowing their intention of settling with the United States for their value. On December 26, 1860, Major Robert Anderson, commander of the Union garrison at Fort Moultrie, at Charleston, clandestinely moved his men to Fort Sumter, a less vulnerable post in the harbor. The South Carolinians angrily regarded his action as a violation of what they regarded as a "truce" agreed upon by President James Buchanan before the Secession Ordinance had been passed. Buchanan not only rebuffed a new demand that the troops be removed, but also dispatched a relief vessel, Star of the West, to Sumter. Star of the West was fired upon and driven off by land batteries, manned by Citadel cadets, and hotheaded Governor Francis W. Pickens of South Carolina wrote Major Anderson.

Official information has been communicated to the government of the United States that the political connection heretofore existing between the state of South Carolina and the states which were known as the United States had ceased, and that . . . South Carolina had resumed all the power it had delegated to the United States under the compact known as the Constitution of the United States. The right which . . . South Carolina possessed to change the political relations which it held with other States . . . has been solemnly asserted by the people of this state in convention, and now does not admit of discussion.

In anticipation of the Ordinance of Secession, of which the President of the United States has received official notification, it was understood by him that sending any reinforcement of the troops of the United States in the harbor of Charleston would be regarded by . . . South Carolina as an act of hostility, and at the same time it was understood by him that any change in the occupation of the forts in the harbor of Charleston would in like manner be regarded as an act of hostility. . . .

After the secession of . . . South Carolina Fort Sumter continued in the possession of the troops of the United States. . . . It will suffice to say that the occupancy of that fort has been regarded by . . . South Carolina as the first act of positive hostility committed by the troops of the United States within the limits of this state, and was in this light regarded as so unequivocal that it occasioned the termination of the negotiations then pending at Washington between the Commissioners of . . . South Carolina and the President of the United States.

The attempt to reinforce the troops now at Fort Sumter, or to retake and to resume possession of the forts within the waters of this state which you abandoned after spiking the guns placed there and doing otherwise much damage cannot be regarded by the authorities of the state as indicative of any other purpose than the coercion of the state by the armed force of the government. To repel such an attempt is too plainly its duty to allow it to be discussed. But while defending its waters the authorities of the state have been careful so to conduct the affairs of the state that no act, however necessary for its defense, should lead to a useless waste of life. Special agents, therefore, have been off the bar to warn all approaching vessels . . . having troops to reinforce the forts on board not to enter the harbor of Charleston, and special orders have been given to the commanders of all forts and batteries not to fire at such vessels until a shot fired across their bows would warn them of the prohibition of the state.

Under these circumstances the STAR OF THE WEST, it is understood, this morning attempted to enter this harbor with troops on board, and having been notified that she could not enter was fired into. The act is perfectly justified by me. In regard to your threat in regard to vessels in the harbor, it is only necessary to say that you must judge of your own responsibilities. Your position in this harbor has been tolerated by the authorities of the state, and while the act of which you complain is in perfect consistency with the rights and duties of the state, it is not perceived how far the conduct which you propose to adopt can find a parallel in the history of any country or be reconciled with any other purpose of your government than that of imposing upon this state the condition of a conquered province.[8]

More celebrated as a Civil War diarist than even the famous War Clerk was Mary Boykin Chesnut. She was the daughter of Governor Stephen D. Miller and the wife of James Chesnut, one of the great planters of South Carolina. Her husband was a United States Senator when South Carolina seceded and the first Southerner to resign when the crisis came. He was elected to the Secession Convention and was a member of the committee which drafted the Ordinance of Secession.

Mary Chesnut, though a loyal Southern woman, never let her patriotism blind her to the realities of the difficulties facing her country any more than to the realities of slavery, which she deplored. Almost alone she seemed to doubt from the beginning the lightning victory that others foresaw; and she, much earlier than most, despaired of her country's future. Nor did her conscience require her to abstain from all luxury and frivolity during the time of travail. At the same time she wrote with real poignancy. She was in Charleston, staying at the Mills House, when the Sumter episode was at its climax, and she wrote:

APRIL 8TH . . . We came home [from Miss Pinckney's],

and soon Mr. Robert Gourdin and Mr. [William Porcher] Miles called. Governor [John L.] Manning walked in, bowed gravely, and seated himself by me. Again he bowed low in mock-heroic style, and with a grand wave of his hand, said: "Madame, your country is invaded." When I had breath to speak I asked: "What does he mean?" He meant this: there are six men-of-war outside the bar. Talbot and Chew have come to say that hostilities are to begin. Governor Pickens and [General] Beauregard are holding a council of war. Mr. Chesnut then came in and confirmed the story. [Ex-Senator Louis T.] Wigfall next entered in boisterous spirits, and said: "There was sound of revelry by night." In any stir or confusion my heart is apt to beat so painfully. Now the agony was so stifling I could hardly see or hear. The men went off almost immediately. And I crept silently to my room where I sat down to a good cry.

Mrs. Wigfall came in and we had it out on the subject of civil war. We solaced ourselves with dwelling on all its known horrors, and then we added what we had a right to expect with Yankees in front and Negroes in the rear. "The slaveowners must expect a servile insurrection, of course," said Mrs. Wigfall, to make sure that we were unhappy enough.

Suddenly loud shouting was heard. We ran out. Cannon after cannon roared. We met Mrs. Allen Green in the passageway with blanched cheeks and streaming eyes. Governor [J. H.] Means rushed out of his room in his dressing-gown and begged us to be calm. "Governor Pickens," said he, "has ordered in the plentitude of his wisdom, seven cannon to be fired as a signal to the Seventh Regiment. Anderson will hear as well as the Seventh Regiment. Now you go back and be quiet; fighting in the streets has not begun yet."

So we retired. Dr. [R. W.] Gibbes calls Mrs. Allen Green Dame Placid. There was no placidity today, with cannon bursting and Allen on the Island. No sleep for anybody last night. The streets were alive with soldiers, men shouting, marching, singing. Wigfall, the "stormy petrel," is in his glory, the only thoroughly happy person I see. Today things seem to have settled down a little. One can but hope still. Lincoln, or Seward, has made such silly advances and then far sillier drawings back. There may be a chance for peace after all. Things are happening so fast. My husband has been made an aide-de-camp to General Beauregard.

Three hours ago we were quickly packing to go home. The Convention has adjourned. Now he tells me the attack on Fort Sumter may begin tonight; depends upon Anderson and the fleet outside. . . .

Today at dinner there was no allusion to things as they stand in Charleston Harbor. There was an undercurrent of intense excitement. There could not have been a more brilliant circle. In addition to our usual quartet (Judge Withers, Langdon Cheves, and [William H.] Trescott), our two ex-Governors dined with us, Means and Manning. These men all talked so delightfully. For once in my life I listened. That over, business began in earnest. Governor Means had rummaged a sword and red sash from somewhere and brought it for Colonel Chesnut, who had gone to demand the surrender of Fort Sumter. And now patience—we must wait.

Why did that green goose Anderson go into Fort Sumter? Then everything began to go wrong. Now they had intercepted a letter from him urging them to let him surrender. He paints the horrors likely to ensue if they will not. He ought to have thought of all that before he put his head in the hole.

APRIL 12TH.—Anderson will not capitulate. Yesterday's was the merriest, maddest dinner we have had yet. Men were audaciously wise and witty. We had an unspoken foreboding that it was to be our last pleasant meeting. Mr. Miles dined with us today. Mrs. Henry King rushed in saying: "The news, I come for the latest news. All the men of the King family are on the Island," of which fact she seemed proud.

While she was here, our peace negotiator, or envoy, came in—that is, Mr. Chesnut returned. His interview with Colonel Anderson had been deeply interesting, but Mr. Chesnut was not inclined to be communicative. He wanted his dinner. He felt for Anderson and had telegraphed to President Davis for instructions—what answer to give Anderson, etc. He has now gone back to Fort Sumter with additional instructions. When they were about to leave the wharf, A. H. Boykin sprang into the boat in great excitement. He thought himself ill-used, with a likelihood of fighting and he to be left behind!

I do not pretend to go to sleep. How can I? If Anderson does not accept terms at four, the orders are, he shall be fired upon. I count four, St. Michael's bells chime out, and I begin to hope. At half-past four, the heavy booming of a cannon. I sprang out of bed, and on my knees prostrate I prayed as I never prayed before.

There was a sound of stir all over the house, pattering of feet in the corridors. All seemed hurrying one way. I put on my double-gown and a shawl and went, too. It was to the housetop. The shells were bursting. In the dark I heard a man say: "Waste of ammunition." I knew my husband was rowing about in a boat somewhere in that dark bay and that the shells were roofing it over, bursting toward the fort. If Anderson was obstinate Colonel Chesnut was to order the fort on one side to open fire. Certainly fire had begun. The regular roar of the cannon, there it was. And who could tell what each volley accomplished of death and destruction?

The women were wild there on the housetop. Prayers came from the women and imprecations from the men. And then a shell would light up the scene. Tonight they say the forces are to attempt to land. We watched up there, and everybody wondered that Fort Sumter did not fire a shot. . . .

Last night, or this morning truly, up on the housetop I was so weak and weary I sat down on something that looked like a black stool. "Get up, you foolish woman. Your dress is on fire," cried a man. And he put me out. I was on a chimney and the sparks had caught my clothes. Susan Preston and Mr. Venable then came up. But my fire had been extinguished before it burst out into a regular blaze.

Do you know, after all that noise and our tears and prayers, nobody has been hurt; sound and fury signifying nothing—a delusion and a snare. . . .

APRIL 13TH.—Nobody has been hurt after all. How gay we were last night. Reaction after the dread of all the slaughter we thought those dreadful cannon were making. Not even a battery the worse for wear. Fort Sumter has been on fire. Anderson has not yet silenced any of our guns. So the aides, still with swords and red sashes by way of uniform, tell us. But the sound of those guns makes regular meals impossible. None of us go to table. Tea-trays pervade the corridors going everywhere. . . .

Not by one word or look can we detect any change in the demeanor of these Negro servants. Lawrence sits at our door, sleepy and respectful, and profoundly indifferent. So are they all, but they carry it too far. You could not tell that they even heard the awful roar going on in the bay, though it has been dinning in their ears night and day. People talk before them as if they were chairs and tables. They make no sign. Are they stolidly stupid? or wiser than we are; silent and strong, biding their time . . . ?

The war-steamers are still there, outside the bar. And there are people who thought the Charleston bar "no good" to Charleston. The bar is the silent partner, or sleeping partner, and in this fray it is doing us yeoman service.

APRIL 15TH.—I did not know that one could live such days of excitement. Some one called: "Come out! There is a crowd coming." A mob it was, indeed, but it was headed by Colonels Chesnut and Manning. The crowd was shouting and showing these two as messengers of good news. They were escorted to Beauregard's headquarters. Fort Sumter had surrendered! Those upon the housetops shouted to us: "The fort is on fire." That had been the story once or twice before.

When we had calmed down, Colonel Chesnut, who had taken it all quietly enough, if anything more unruffled than usual in his serenity, told us how the surrender came about. Wigfall was with them on Morris Island when they saw the fire in the fort; he jumped in a little boat and with his handkerchief as a white flag rowed over. Wigfall went in through a porthole. When Colonel Chesnut arrived shortly after and was received at the regular entrance, Colonel Anderson told him he had need to pick his way warily, for the place was all mined. As far as I can make out the fort surrendered to Wigfall. But it is all confusion. Our flag is flying there. Fire-engines have been sent for to put out the fire. Everybody tells you half of something and then rushes off to tell something else or to hear the latest news.[9]

Following President Lincoln's call for volunteers to put down the "insurrection," the Confederate Congress resolved:

Whereas, the earnest efforts made by this government to establish friendly relations between the government of the United States and the Confederate States and to settle all questions of disagreement between the two governments upon principles of right, justice, equity, and good faith, have proved unavailing by reason of the refusal of the government of the United States to hold any intercourse with the commissioners appointed by this government for the purpose aforesaid, or to listen to any proposal they had to make for the peaceful solution of all causes of difficulty between the two governments; and,

Whereas, the President of the United States of America

has issued his proclamation making requisition upon the states of the American Union for 75,000 men for the purpose, as therein indicated, of capturing forts and other strongholds within the jurisdiction of, and belonging to the Confederate States of America, and has detailed naval armaments upon the coasts of the Confederate States of America, and raised, organized, and equipped a large military force to execute the purpose aforesaid, and has issued his other proclamation announcing his purpose to set on foot a blockade of the ports of the Confederate States; and . . .

Whereas, by the acts and means aforesaid, war exists between the Confederate States and the government of the United States . . . Therefore,

SECTION 1. THE CONGRESS OF THE CONFEDERATE STATES OF AMERICA DO ENACT, That the President of the Confederate States is hereby authorized to use the whole land and naval force of the Confederate States to meet the war thus commenced.[10]

And Governor John Letcher of Virginia, complying with an ordinance of the Virginia Convention, issued

A PROCLAMATION

The delegates of the people of Virginia in Convention assembled having by their ordinance passed April 25, 1861, adopted and ratified the Constitution of the provisional government of the Confederate States of America, ordained and established at Montgomery, Alabama, on February 8, 1861, and the state of Virginia having been, by an act of the Confederate States passed May 7, 1861, admitted as a state into the Confederate government, and the President being, under the Constitution of the provisional government of the Confederate States, the Commander-in-Chief of the army and navy of the Confederate States and of the militia of the several states when called into the service of the Confederate States:

Now, therefore, I, John Letcher, governor of Virginia, by

and with the advice of the executive council, do hereby transfer to the authorities of the Confederate States, by regiments, all the volunteer forces which have been mustered into the service of Virginia, and do order a like transfer by regiments, battalions, squadrons, and campanies, of all volunteers of militia, as the same shall be formed and their service may be required.

I further hereby transfer to the authorities of the Confederate States the command of all the officers, seamen, and marines of the Provisional Navy of Virginia for service in the Confederate States.

I do further order that all officers of the Virginia service now on duty in any of the departments of the staff continue to discharge their respective functions under the direction and control of the President until otherwise ordered; and that all quartermaster's, commissary, and medical stores belonging to the state and in charge of said officers, to be turned over for the use of the Confederate States. . . .

I do hereby authorize the use of all public property, munitions of war, etc., captured from the United States, the machinery at Harper's Ferry excepted, by the President or those acting under his authority for the common defense.

Given under my hand as governor, and under the seal of the State, at Richmond, this 6th day of June, A.D. 1861, and in the eighty-fifth year of the Commonwealth.[11]

Thus was the Confederacy committed to strife and bloodshed. The eventful months that followed were to determine its fate. Meanwhile, revolutionary social and economic changes were in the making.

II: FARMS AND FACTORIES

*King Cotton had brought more than slavery to the South.
By blind obeisance to the King, the South was to find itself in another dilemma. In the spring of 1861, the*
Southern Cultivator, *one of the most influential journals of
the South had this to say:*

We have been suddenly brought into a position which
suggests grave probabilities of war. We are therefore
arming. But we labor under a greater deficiency than the
want of arms. IT IS THE WANT OF BREAD. The State of Georgia has not now grain enough within her limits to feed her
population and domestic animals until the gathering of
the next crop. It is presumed that the rest of the Cotton
States are in a similar condition. Last year we obtained
our supplies from the Northwest. It may be that our currency will be in a condition to prevent this supply, except
at ruinous sacrifices. It may be that we shall be cut off
from it altogether. This is probable, unless these supplies
are immediately procured. The subject is worthy of the
immediate attention of the authorities of the different
plantation states.

A part of this deficiency in breadstuffs is accidental,
arising from the drought of the past summer. But it is
much more owing to our defective system of agriculture.
As an illustration, in 1859 upwards of five millions of

dollars worth of provisions of Western growth were brought over the Western and Atlantic Railroad from Chattanooga to Atlanta. This sum did not include horses and mules. It did not include the hogs, sheep, and beef cattle driven into the state, nor provisions landed at Savannah from the North.

The deficiency is then a natural result of our system of agriculture. We are presenting in Georgia, at this moment, the anomalous spectacle of a people having upwards of twenty millions of dollars worth of the earth's products for sale, yet requiring a large proportion of the results of sale to buy the common necessaries of life, which are also the products of the soil.

If we were to write until doomsday in advocacy of a mixed husbandry we could not utter language so forcible as that which is uttered by the present crisis. We are surprised. We are caught unprepared. We have much to sell, nobody to buy, and little to eat and wear.

It has been the cotton planter's rule to make all the cotton he can and as much provisions as is not inconsistent with the largest possible cotton crop. Our present position teaches him exactly to reverse it. To be certain to make enough of bread and meat, and afterwards as much cotton as possible. He is then independent in prices. The fluctuations of the market affect him slightly. If drought or war come he is still surrounded by plenty. And beyond this, this system, instead of exhausting his capital, the source of his wealth and subsistence—the soil—is adding daily to its power of remunerative returns.

Except so far as the people are concerned—their patriotism, their courage, their capacity of endurance, and their skill in arms—never were a people suddenly overtaken by an emergency in a worse state of preparation in other respects than the people of the South at this moment; and if it comes to the worst we shall feel it fearfully.

Let the voice of this crisis to the planters of the South

be heard and heeded. Let us begin at once. Let us commence with our arrangements for the New Year upon which we have entered. Let us review our fixtures for the comfort of the domestic animals upon whose thrift and rapid growth so much of the subsistence of the year depends. Let us see to it that every element of increased fertility—elements which may be dissipated or washed away—are carefully husbanded. Let us take care that pastures so ample and nutritious are provided that, come what may, from our cattle and swine and sheep both meat and clothing shall be afforded. Let us so largely increase the breadth of our grain crops that even drought will leave a sufficiency for us, for our stock, and for our servants. And afterwards, by skillful cultivation and heavy manuring, let us more than compensate for the diminished area of our cotton crop, receiving from a few acres that which previously we had wrung reluctantly from many acres. . . .

The Confederate States can never be a commercial people to any serious extent. Our form of labor forbids it. . . . So long as Negroes constitute our laboring population we cannot think of commerce as carried on in our own ships. . . .

Neither can we be extensively a manufacturing people. Our labor again determines this point. It is settled by experience that our Negroes cannot make available operatives in factories. They ought not to be so employed if they could make good operatives. It is a perversion of the institution whenever our Negroes are employed in any other way than in the house or on the plantation. We do not approve of even Negro mechanics beyond plantation mechanics. Negroes should never be brought into habitual contact with white men, beyond those to whom they owe obedience. It is at the hazard of themselves and of society when this occurs. The collection of Negroes in cities, sometimes nearly one hundred living in one yard and hiring out their time—their assemblage in workshops, their unguarded association with irresponsible and vicious white men, are evils worthy the notice of our legislators. . . .

We are to be not a commercial or a manufacturing but an agricultural people. Never was intention more evident than in the obvious purpose of Divine Providence in placing the white and black races in juxtaposition at the South. Never were means more perfectly suited to an end. In agriculture, so far as the human agents are concerned, there are two desiderata. The one patient, willing, vigorous, constant, and economical labor. This the Negro supplies. Unfitted for the ship or the factory he is in his element in the field. The other requisite is an intelligent direction of his labor. This direction the educated planter gives. As a class, with the exception of the English country gentlemen, no other country affords agriculturists of equal intelligence with the great body of Southern planters. This combination of mind and muscle gives an immense advantage. Add to it the possession of a soil in some instances very rich, generally and originally of fair fertility, a climate admirably adapted to agriculture and products of great value and universal necessity, and we are brought to the conclusion that good sense requires that we should become an agricultural people. We are so now. But it is one thing to be and another to know what we are.[1]

Then, in the very deep South, the New Orleans Picayune *commented in May:*

The effect throughout the Confederate States, so far, of the Lincoln coercive policy has been in the very highest degree beneficial to the permanent interests of our people. The threat of starving us into submission elicited universal derision within our bounds. It created a determination to free the South from dependence on the North for breadstuffs and provisions. . . .

Never before in the South has such a breadth of land been devoted to the growth of cereals as in the present year, and never before was there such general promise of abundant crops as now. The yield of wheat and corn, in fact of all the grain crops, accounts from all parts of the Southern states testify, will be enormous—in fact, equal to the home consumption this year in many places where it never grew before, and to an extent heretofore unknown in the sunny South. . . .

The South is not only capable of producing all the breadstuffs required for home consumption, but also all the beef, pork, and bacon as well. This is well known, and the spirit abroad among our people indicates that it will soon be made manifest to the world. . . .

Let every planter who has an available patch of land plant corn immediately.[2]

The home gardener also was doing his part and was learning to adjust to new conditions. Kate Stone lived with her brothers and widowed mother on their Louisiana plantation, across the Mississippi River from Vicksburg. She was extremely patriotic and devoted to "the Cause." She had a sense of humor which sometimes sparkled through her soberest thoughts, and although she considered herself "ugly," probably was overly modest. Physically, she was tall and slender. Temperamentally, she was shy and inclined to quietness. She was an avid and critical reader, Shakespeare and Sir Walter Scott being her favorite authors. She started a diary with the outbreak of war, when she was twenty-one. On May 27 she wrote:

Mamma has been busy all day sewing on Jimmy's shirts and going through the vegetable and flower garden, all in a flourishing state. So many flowers, though our garden is but a new one yet. We must save all sorts of seeds as we will get no more from the North. Mamma is having quantities of peas, potatoes, and all things eatable planted, as our only chance for anything from this time until the close of war will be to raise it ourselves. Strict economy is to be the order of the day.

It is probable that meat will be very high, and by advice of Mr. Fellowes Mamma will try to raise enough to do the place. She has put Jeffrey to devoting his whole time to the hogs and cattle. We have not a great quantity of either just now, but they will soon grow.[3]

The success of the beleaguered South in converting its agriculture from cotton to diversification would continue to rest upon the labor of its slaves. Much depended, therefore, on effective control over them while master or overseer was off to war. It was widely believed in the North that wartime conditions in the South would engender slave revolts. Blackwood's Edinburgh Magazine, *a brilliant Tory periodical friendly to the Confederacy but, like all the English, hostile to slavery, had a correspondent in Alabama in the autumn of 1861, who observed:*

Amongst the dangers which we had heard at New York threatened the South, a revolt of the slave population was said to be the most imminent. Let us take, then, a peep at a cotton field and see what likelihood there is of such a contingency.

On the bank of the Alabama River, which winds its yellow course through dense woods of oak, ash, maple, and pine, thickened with tangled copse of varied evergreens, lie some of the most fertile plantations of the state. One of these we had the advantage of visiting. Its owner received us with all that hospitality and unaffected BONHOMMIE which invariably distinguish a Southern gentleman. Having mounted a couple of hacks we started off through a large pine-wood and soon arrived at a "clearing" of about 200 acres in extent, on most of which was growing an average cotton crop. This was a fair sample of the rest of the plantation, which consisted altogether of 7,000 acres. Riding into the middle of the field we found ourselves surrounded by about forty slaves, men, women, and children, engaged in "picking." They were all well dressed and seemed happy and cheerful. Wishing to know what time of day it was I asked Mr. —— the hour, whereupon one of the darkies by my side took out a gold watch and informed me.

"Do your laborers generally wear gold watches, sir?" I inquired.

"A great many of them have. Why, sir, my Negroes all have their cotton-plots and gardens, and most of them little orchards."

We found from their own testimony that they are fed well, chiefly upon pork, corn, potatoes, and rice, carefully attended to when sick, and on Sundays dress better than their masters.

Many of them had six or seven hundred dollars of their own, which they either lend to the banks or hide in the ground. In the hot weather they begin work at six in the morning and go on till ten; they then go home till about three, and when the sun declines return to their work till six or seven. In the cool weather they begin soon after daylight and rest for two or three hours in the middle of the day.

We next visited the "Station," a street of cottages in a pine-wood, where Mr. ——'s "Family" reside. These we found clean and comfortable. Two of the men were sick and had been visited that morning by a doctor; in the meantime they were looked after by the nurses of the establishment, of whom there were three to take care of the children and invalids.

On the whole it can fearlessly be said, if this is a true type of the mode in which slaves are treated in the South that their physical condition is as good if not better than that of any laboring population in the world. The masters ridicule the idea of disloyalty. They live amongst them in the most perfect confidence and never bestow a serious thought upon what they consider such an impossibility as a "Negro insurrection." Having visited other plantations in Alabama, South Carolina, and Georgia, we cannot resist the belief that the great mass of the slaves in the South must be pronounced to be well cared for and contented; and although there are necessarily a thousand things connected with "the institution" of which no Englishman can approve, it is undoubtedly true that, not-withstanding the strenuous efforts of abolitionists, the Negroes bear the yoke cheerfully, and heartily join their fortunes to those of their masters in the great struggle in which they are now engaged.[4]

The battle for food, though somewhat successful, was not easily won. In the winter of 1861-2 the Southern Cultivator *was pleading with farmers.*

Let "King Cotton" stand aside for awhile until his worthier brother, Corn, receives our attention! With the crop of cotton already on hand and the prospects before us we think our readers would do wisely to plant a DOUBLE CROP of corn and a HALF CROP of cotton—putting the latter only on their most suitable cotton lands. Prepare for the corn crop NOW—leave no waste spot that will pro-duce a single stalk—put in every hill possible! PLOW DEEP —manure heavily, and plant as EARLY as you safely can. Plant more than you ever did before! If you have plenty of corn, you need want for nothing—it will make you MEAT as well as BREAD, and it will bring you money, also.[5]

A few months later patriotic Warren County, Georgia, farmers resolved:

That the time has arrived when the whole energies of our people should be directed in that channel best cal-culated to sustain the government in its efforts to achieve a national existence and independence.

Resolved, That no true and enlightened patriot will plant a full crop of cotton; and we earnestly recommend that no more be planted than is necessary to preserve seed, and for spinning purposes.

Resolved, That we will devote our best energies to the raising of grain, and will alike condemn its waste, or what is worse, its distillation into intoxicating liquors.

Resolved, That we heartily endorse the late proclamation of Gov. [Joseph E.] Brown on the subject of distillation and do hereby constitute ourselves into a vigilance com-mittee for the purpose of reporting to the proper officers information of the existence of any distilleries in the county, and that we will heartily co-operate in all proper efforts to suppress so great an evil.[6]

Concerted efforts began to show results. By January 1863 President Davis was able to proclaim:

The energies of a whole nation devoted to the single object of success in this war have accomplished marvels, and many of our trials have, by a beneficent Providence, been converted into blessings. The magnitude of the perils which we encountered have developed the true qualities and illustrated the heroic character of our people, thus gaining for the Confederacy from its birth a just appreciation from the other nations of the earth. . . . Our fields no longer whitened by cotton that cannot be exported, are devoted to the production of cereals and the growth of stock formerly purchased with the proceeds of cotton.[7]

But three months later rumors circulated that because of military reverses the North would agree to separation, and that the war would be over within a few months. Many farmers, acting on the rumor, began once more the planting of tobacco and cotton at the expense of food. Urged on by the press, the Confederate Congress passed a resolution.

Whereas, a strong impression prevails through the country that the war now being waged against the people of the Confederate States may terminate during the present year; and whereas this impression is leading many patriotic citizens to engage largely in the production of cotton and tobacco, which they would not otherwise do; and whereas, in the opinion of Congress, it is of the utmost importance, not only with a view to the proper subsistence of our armies but for the interest and welfare of all the people that the agricultural labor of the country should be employed chiefly in the production of a supply of food to meet every contingency; Therefore,

RESOLVED BY THE CONGRESS OF THE CONFEDERATE STATES OF AMERICA, That it is the deliberate judgment of Congress that . . . the amplest supply of provisions for armies and people should be the first object of all agriculturists; wherefore it is earnestly recommended that the people, instead of planting cotton and tobacco shall direct their agricultural labor mainly to the production of such crops as will insure a sufficiency of food for all classes and for every emergency, thereby with true patriotism subordinating the hope of gain to the certain good of the country.

Sec. 2. That the President is hereby requested to issue a proclamation to the people of these states urging upon them the necessity of guarding against the great perils of a short crop of provisions and setting forth such reasons therefor as his judgment may dictate.[8]

As public opinion and governmental urging produced sufficient food, ironically no one was more appreciative than red-bearded Union General William T. Sherman. To Lincoln's Secretary of War, Edwin M. Stanton, he wrote in the autumn of 1864:

Convey to Jeff. Davis my personal and official thanks for abolishing cotton and substituting corn and sweet potatoes in the South. These facilitate our military plans much, for food and forage are abundant.[9]

Generations of devotion to agriculture cost the embattled South severe shortages in other fields, those fields of manufacturing vital to a war. In 1860 the states that formed the Confederacy produced less than ten per cent of the manufactures of the country. That year they produced only 76,000 tons of the more than 2,500,000 tons of iron ore mined in the United States, and they rolled less than a sixteenth of the 400,000 tons processed in the mills of the country. Cotton mills in the Southern states were valued at $9,000,000 as compared to $90,000,000 in the rest of the country. Only one and one-third millions of dollars had been invested in Southern woolen mills as against more than thirty-five millions in the entire country.

Leather products in the South in 1860 were valued a
$4,000,000. Those in the remainder of the country a
$59,000,000.

These were staggering realities that confronted the man
whose task it was to arm and equip the Southern armies
the Secretary of War. Walker vacated the office in the
autumn of 1861 and was succeeded by Judah P. Benjamin
Benjamin struggled through the fall and winter months
trying to prepare the armies for the spring campaign
Then, in March 1862, he wrote President Davis:

The establishments for the manufacture of powder and
percussion-caps are sufficient for the wants of the army
but the chief material for the manufacture of powder
to wit, saltpeter, is not sufficiently abundant. The estab
lishments for the manufacture of arms are woefully de
ficient, and cannot furnish more than one-tenth part o
the necessary supply of small-arms. I know of no legisla
tion which could aid the Department in procuring a
supply of small-arms. Nearly every mechanic in the Con
federacy competent to manufacture small-arms is believed
to be engaged in the work. The manufacture of small
arms is a slow and tedious process, and the accumulation
of the supplies necessary for such an army as we now
require is the result of the labor and expenditure of long
series of years. . . .

The difficulty is not in the want of legislation. Law
cannot suddenly convert farmers into gunsmiths. Our
people are not artisans, except to a very limited degree
In the very armory here at Richmond the production
could be greatly increased if skilled labor could be pro
cured. In the absence of home manufactures no recourse
remains but importation, and with our commerce sub
stantially at an end with foreign nations the means o
importation are limited. I am unable to perceive in what
way we can procure arms by the passage of laws.[10]

But efforts were afoot to correct this imbalance. Fifteen
years before secession, James D. B. De Bow had migrated

from Charleston to New Orleans and had begun the publication of his famous Review. *De Bow was of picturesque, perhaps even of forbidding appearance. His heavy mustache and beard helped hide a sallow complexion and a lantern jaw; and his shaggy, unkempt hair drew attention from his unusually large nose. Within a few years his name was known beyond the borders of the South, and President Franklin Pierce appointed him Director of the Census. De Bow was an ardent disciple of Calhoun, who had befriended him, and was a strong defender of slavery and of State rights. The* Review, *which he continued to publish through most of the war, was primarily an economic journal, but concerned itself also with political and cultural questions. It was always influential in the South, and its jingoistic editorials probably played a part in bringing on secession and war.*

Long an advocate of industrialization in the South, De Bow enthusiastically recorded, in the fall of 1862, the growth of manufacturing in Virginia and the Carolinas.

CUTLERY.—Sabers, saber-bayonets, and other implements of war are now being manufactured for the Confederate government, and the manufacture of various kinds of edge tools in connection with the above will be carried on largely as soon as works, now in process of erection, are completed. Other establishments for the manufacture of various kinds of machinery are growing toward completion, and all the results of war.

CHARLOTTE.—One establishment for the manufacture of linseed or flaxseed oil, with a capacity to turn out five hundred gallons per day, will go into operation by the first of January next. One for the manufacture of cottonseed oil on a small scale, will turn out about fifty gallons per day; [and] will commence manufacturing in a couple of weeks. One hat manufactory for making soft hats, [its] machinery nearly all ready, will commence in about thirty days, with capacity to make one hundred and fifty hats per day —run by steam. One powder mill, The North Carolina

Powder Manufacturing Company, will manufacture one thousand pounds per day, with capacity to double the quantity. The state has loaned this company ten thousand dollars. But they are not bound to supply her with powder. Will commence operating by the sixteenth of January next. . . .

GREENSBORO'.—Messrs. Mendenhall, Jones & Gardner, of this place, are now engaged in the manufacturing of guns for the State of North Carolina. This establishment is just getting under way, and it is the intention of the proprietors to manufacture largely so soon as they can get their machinery in operation. In addition to this establishment, the Messrs. Garretts have commenced the manufacture of sewing-machines, pistols, guns, etc. We have also a hat establishment, lately gone into operation, working several hands, with a good prospect for patronage. Besides these, other smaller establishments have sprung up in various parts of the country for making guns, saddles, shoes, barrels, drums, sashes, etc., all of which promise to be remunerative to those engaged in the enterprise and to render us independent of the North.

LYNCHBURG.—The following branches of business have been commenced since the commencement of the existing war:

One envelope factory has been established—one for the manufacture of blacking and one for the making of lucifer matches. The manufacture of caps and hats is also being carried on quite extensively. Other factories will be established in a few days. In the neighborhood several tanneries have been established, and the tanning of leather is being carried on quite extensively.

ABINGDON.—Sixteen miles from this place the saltworks are located where they are manufacturing about two thousand bushels salt per day (twenty-four hours), and are putting up furnaces to increase the amount.

Across the Tennessee line and about fifteen miles south of us they have several iron forges with the greatest abundance of the best ore, and one furnace where they make a large amount of castings and pig iron.

G. E. Saltzgiver—Hat maker. Established several years ago. Has discontinued the hat making business because he wants materials that are not manufactured in North America. Has changed his business within the last few months into making caps of all kinds for men and boys. Materials made in the Confederate States. Has seven hands employed. . . .

WILMINGTON.—ALCOHOL is manufactured to a limited extent—former supplies received from the North—present produce results from the war.

ASHES.—The manufacture of potash in connection with salt-boiling is increasing—none ever made here before the war. . . .

SPARTANBURG.—The firm of John Bomar & Co., now own what was formerly called the Bivingsville Cotton Manufacturing Establishment of about one thousand five hundred spindles, twenty-six looms, wool-carding machine, with all the necessary preparations; besides, a good machine shop, well fitted up with turning lathes (five in number), cog cutter, plainer, upright drill, etc.; also, grist and flouring mills, blacksmith shops, sawmill, cupalo furnace, cotton gin, wheat threasher, a good grain farm, on about one thousand four hundred acres of land, well improved in good buildings and operator's houses—all forming a very pretty little village of about one hundred and fifty inhabitants. . . .

LAURENS.—All the old manufactures which may be gathered from the last census have recurred and have been infused with additional life and are now working to the extent of their means, more particularly the manufacture of shoe-leather; and the ladies of the country, generally, are making a great quantity of most excellent cloth of various descriptions for men's wear, children, Negroes, and even for their own wear, which are now taking the place of fine DELAINES AND SILKS. . . .

CHESTER C. H.—EVERY HOUSEHOLD has become a manufacturing establishment; the hum of the spinning-wheel may be heard in every hamlet, and the rattle of the loom sings the song of better times to our glorious South. Old and young, rich and poor of our females, are daily discarding the baser fabrics of Yankeedom and are bending their whole energies to keep us supplied with warm clothing, raised and made by their own industry.[11]

A few months after this cheering report from De Bow, Jefferson Davis announced:

The injuries resulting from the interruption of foreign commerce have received compensation by the development of our internal resources. Cannon crown our fortresses that were cast from the products of mines opened and furnaces built during the war. Our mountain caves yield much of the niter for the manufacture of powder, and promise increase of product. From our own foundries and laboratories, from our own armories and workshops, we derive in a great measure the warlike material, the ordnance and ordnance stores which are expended so profusely in the numerous and desperate engagements that rapidly succeed each other. Cotton and woolen fabrics, shoes and harness, wagons and gun carriages are produced in daily increasing quantities by the factories springing into existence.[12]

But all shortages could not be supplied by domestic manufacturers. A year later James A. Seddon, who had replaced Benjamin in the War Office, wrote President Davis:

The Quartermaster and Commissary Generals, in the administration of their respective departments, have had during the past year extraordinary difficulties and embarrassments to encounter. The manufacturing operations of the former, as in the other bureaus, have indeed been conducted on a large scale with more economy of material and with greater skill and energy than at past periods and have made more nearly the supplies for the army from internal resources; but still for some essential articles, such as shoes, blankets, and woolen cloths, partial dependence on importations could not be avoided. In these articles it can scarcely be expected that domestic production can be increased, for, under the wasting consumption of war, the production of the raw materials is more likely to be diminished than increased.[13]

It was a war in which railroads must be used to move materiél and to transport and supply troops, and here, too, the Confederacy found itself at a marked disadvantage. Its railroads were poorly co-ordinated. Gauges varied from section to section, so that freight had to be handled again and again in transit. Only one line, which forked at Chattanooga, connected the Mississippi Valley with the Atlantic seaboard. When this line was cut in 1862, a roundabout system had to be improvised. Everywhere the stress of war transport was greater than the rail system could accommodate. By the spring of 1863 the heavy traffic was taking its toll. In April J. B. Jones recorded:

The railroad presidents have met in this city and ascertained that to keep the tracks in order for military purposes 49,500 tons of rails must be manufactured per annum, and that the Tredegar Works here and the works at Atlanta cannot produce more than 20,000 tons per annum even if engaged exclusively in that work. They say that neither individual nor incorporated companies will suffice. The government must manufacture iron or the roads must fail! [14]

In November 1863 Secretary Seddon wrote:

The administration of the Department in all its extensive operations has been greatly impeded by the deficiency of transportation, especially on railroads. Shut off from the sea and with command of very few of its rivers, the Confederacy is dependent almost wholly on the railroads for communication and transportation. The roads were not constructed with reference to such extensive needs, and even in time of peace, with all facilities of supplies and repairs, would have been inadequate to such duties. How much less in time of war, with every drawback of deficient labor, insufficient stock, defective machinery, and scant supplies, and with exposure often to seizures or spoilations by the enemy, could they be expected to meet such unexpected requirements. It must be a matter of surprise and gratification that they have sustained themselves so well and have afforded to the government and the people the measure of accommodation they have. It is but a just tribute to them to say that in the main they have been managed in a patriotic spirit and have rarely failed to meet the requirements of the government with alacrity and zeal.

But while the dispositions of the railroad companies have been good their means have gradually been becoming less. The government has already given to many some aid but will have hereafter to render fuller and more constant assistance. Some of the minor roads will have to be sacrificed to keep up the tracks of the leading lines. Iron will have to be provided and rolled for machinery and the construction and repair of locomotives and rolling-stock. Skilled mechanics, to some extent, will have to be furnished from the army, and for some of the more delicate machinery needed by them importations from abroad may have to be attempted. With these aids it is hoped they may not only be maintained but improved in their means of transportation.

The lowest point of depression has probably passed. For the first year or more, under the delusive expectation of the early termination of the war, the companies relied almost wholly on their existing stock and made few efforts at supply or reparation. They scarcely husbanded their resources which, under the exhausting demands made on them, became greatly diminished. Of late, with more experience, a wiser prescience guides their management, and besides practicing economy of means they are sedulously engaged in endeavoring to increase their stock and to provide for the contingencies of future service or loss. In their best estate they will not be able to furnish adequate facilities of transportation for both the government and the people.[15]

These industrial and railroad shortages made such a manufactory as the great Tredegar Iron Works of Richmond indispensable. It employed over two thousand men and could manufacture everything from cannon to locomotives. T. C. De Leon tells of its operations.

Gamble's Hill, a pretty steep slope, cuts the river west of the bridge. Rising above its curves, from the Capitol viewpoint, are the slate-roofed Tredegar Works, their tall chimneys puffing endless black smoke against the sunshine, which reflects it, a livid green, upon the white foam of the rapids. So potent a factor in the aggressive power of the Confederacy was this foundry that it overtopped the regular government agencies. When the war began this was the only rolling-mill of great capacity of which the South could boast; the only one, indeed, capable of casting heavy guns. Almost the first decisive act of Virginia was to prevent, by seizure, the delivery to United States officers of some guns cast for them by the Tredegar Works; and from that day there were no more earnest and energetic workers for the cause of Southern independence than the firm of Jos. R. Anderson & Co. It was said at this time that the firm was in financial straits. But it thrived so well on government patronage—spite of sundry boards to consider if army and navy work was not paid for at ruinously low rates—that it greatly increased in size, added to its utility by importations of costly machinery through the blockade, stood loss of one-third of its buildings by fire, used a ship of its own for importation, and at the close of the struggle was in better condition than at the commencement. The senior partner was for a time in the field at head of his brigade; but affairs were so well managed in the interval by the Messrs.

Tanner—father and son who were partners with General Anderson—that his absence was not appreciable in the work.

It was at the Tredegar Works that the famous "Brooke gun"—a rifled 7-inch—was cast, tested, and perfected. Here the plates for the ironclads in almost all Southern waters were rolled or made ready for use. Here heavy ordnance for the forts was cast together with shells and shot; and here the torpedoes—sometimes so effective and usually so useless—were contrived and made. Indeed, the Tredegar Works so greatly aided the Confederacy that the lengthening of the war may be, in large measure, attributed to their capacity and to the able zeal with which they were managed.

So great and effective an agent could not fail to receive from the Richmond government every aid in obtainance of supplies, labor, and transportation. "The Works" had mines, mills, and pork-packeries in various sections of the South; thus obtaining coal and metals as well as food—at reduced rates, within reach of their wages—for an army of employees. So great was the necessary number of these —whites, skilled in labor—that even the closest conscription left the junior of the firm a full battalion of infantry. This, drilled and equipped from his own shops, Major Tanner led in person when raids or other straits made their soldiering paramount to other occupation. And— even when greatest scarcity of provisions came—the agents of the Works proceeded with those of the commissary of the Confederacy, PARI PASSU.

An odd incident, coming to mind just here, will point the general estimate of the importance of the Tredegar Works. A special train was crossing the bridge en route for Petersburg at a time when transportation was rare. A huge Negro, blacker than the spot upon his face, sat placidly on the platform of the rear car.

"What are you doing here?" was asked by the officer in charge.

"Rid'n' t' Petesbug," was the placid reply.

"Have you paid your fare?"

"Don' got nun t' pay, boss. Rides onner pass, I does!"

"Work for the government?"—this rather impatiently.

Ebo rolled his eyes, with expression of deep disgust, as he responded grandly:

"No—SAH! Fur t'uther consarn!" [16]

It was as much to protect the Tredegar Iron Works as to defend the nation's capital that Lee fought his troops almost to the last gasp in the lines around Petersburg and Richmond in the final nine months of the war. The loss of this great factory at any time would have been a blow that the Confederacy would have been unable to bear.

III: CHURCHES AND SCHOOLS

Of all the religious sects in the South, the two largest were the Methodist and Baptist. Both had separated from their Northern brethren in the 1840's over the question of slavery. By 1861 clergy and press of both churches, speaking as with one voice, defended slavery and secession, and the coming of war only intensified their regional loyalty and patriotism. Early that year the South Western Baptist *proclaimed:*

We have exhausted every effort for peace which duty and honor demand, but peace offerings are spurned, our commissioners sent home from Washington with the insulting declaration that they cannot be received, and now the roar of artillery on our Southern borders announces the purblind policy of an abolitionized government bent on the ruin of our country as well as its own. Let it come! In the name of God we will set up our banners: and by the blessing of Him who ruleth in the armies of Heaven the sword will never be sheathed until the last invader shall be driven from our shores. The battle of New Orleans [in the War of 1812], fought by Southern soldiers, commanded by Southern officers, may suggest to these hirelings of Mr. Lincoln what Southern men can do when their wives and children are behind them and an invading foe is before them. Let no man's heart fail him for fear. The spirit of our people is aroused, and hundreds of thousands stand ready to fly to the standard of our Southern Confederacy to maintain its integrity or perish in the attempt. "Let us play the man for our people, and for the cities of our God, and the Lord do what seemeth him good." Let prayer be made without ceasing unto God, and the result is not doubtful.[1]

The Episcopal Church, on the other hand, had weathered the storm of controversy over slavery prior to 1861 without division, but after the formation of the Confederacy its Southern members were embarrassed by Northern ties. Accordingly, a meeting of bishops and other clerical and lay delegates in Montgomery in July 1861 resolved:

1. That the secession of the States of Virginia, North Carolina, South Carolina, Georgia, Florida, Alabama, Mississippi, Louisiana, Texas, Arkansas, and Tennessee from the United States, and the formation by them of a new government called the Confederate States of America render it necessary and expedient that the dioceses within those states should form among themselves an independent organization.

2. That as preliminary to the organization declared necessary in the foregoing resolution, a committee of three bishops, three presbyters, and three laymen be appointed by the Convention to prepare and report to an adjourned meeting of this Convention, to be held at Columbia, South Carolina, on the third Wednesday in October next, a Constitution and Canons, under which such an organization may be effected.

A few months later the Columbia Convention adopted a constitution for the new organization.

ARTICLE I. This church . . . shall be known as the "Protestant Episcopal Church in the Confederate States of America. . . ."

ARTICLE III. The House of Bishops shall be composed of all the bishops of this Church having jurisdiction within the Confederate States or the territories thereof. . . .

ARTICLE VII. A new Diocese, formed in any of the Confederate States or in any territory thereof not now represented, may at any time hereafter be admitted to union with and representation in the General Council of this Church. . . .

ARTICLE IX. No person . . . shall be ordained either deacon or priest, until he shall have subscribed the following declaration, viz:

I do believe the Holy Scriptures of the Old and New Testament to be the Word of God, and to contain all things necessary to salvation; and I do solemnly engage to conform to the Doctrines and Worship of the Protestant Episcopal Church in the Confederate States of America.

No person ordained by a foreign bishop shall be permitted to officiate as a minister of this Church until he shall have complied with the Canon or Canons in such case provided.

At the same time the convention authorized Bishops William Meade, James H. Otey, and Stephen Elliott to issue a statement on faith and doctrine.

We propose no change in the doctrine, discipline, and worship of the Church in organization which has existed among us for eighty years past, [and] we think that no alteration should be made in our forms and offices, further than shall be found indispensable in consequence of the political changes which force them upon us.[2]

When war came Southern Presbyterians were equally eager to sever their Northern connections. A general assembly, meeting in Augusta, Georgia, in December 1861, organized the Presbyterian Church in the Confederate States of America. At the same time the Assembly issued an address "to all the churches of Jesus Christ throughout the earth."

Dearly Beloved Brethren: It is probably known to you that the presbyteries and synods in the Confederate States, which were formerly in connection with the General Assembly of the Presbyterian Church in the United States of America, have renounced the jurisdiction of that body, and dissolved the ties which bound them ecclesiastically with their brethren of the North. This act of separation left them without any formal union among themselves. But as they were one in faith and order, and still adhered to their old standards, measures were promptly adopted for giving expression to their unity. . . . Commissioners duly appointed from all the presbyteries of these Confederate States met accordingly in the city of Augusta on the 4th day of December . . . 1861, and then and there proceeded to constitute the General Assembly of the Presbyterian Church in the Confederate States of America. The Constitution of the Presbyterian Church in the United States, that is to say, the Westminster Confession of Faith, the Larger and Shorter Catechisms, the Form of Government, the Book of Discipline, and the Directory for Worship were unanimously and solemnly declared to be the Constitution of the Church in the Confederate States, with no other change than the substitution of "Confederate" for "United" wherever the country is mentioned in the standards. The church, therefore, in these seceded states presents now the spectacle of a separate, independent, and complete organization, under the style and title of the Presbyterian Church in the Confederate States of America.

Part of the Presbyterian statement explained the position of the Church in regard to slavery.

In the first place, we would have it distinctly understood that, in our ecclesiastical capacity, we are neither the friends nor the foes of slavery. . . . The policy of its existence or nonexistence is a question which exclusively belongs to the state. We have no right, as a church, to enjoin it as a duty or to condemn it as a sin. Our business is with the duties which spring from the relation; the duties of the master on the one hand, and of their slaves on the other. These duties we are to proclaim and to enforce with spiritual sanctions. The social, civil, political problems connected with this great subject transcend our sphere, as God has not entrusted to his Church the organization of society, the construction of governments, nor the allotment of individuals to their various stations. The Church has as much right to preach to the monarchies of Europe and the despotism of Asia the doctrines of republican equality as to preach to the governments of the South the extirpation of slavery. This position is impregnable unless it can be shown that slavery is a sin. Upon every other hypothesis it is so clearly a question for the State. . . . Is slavery, then, a sin?

In answering this question, as a church, let it be distinctly borne in mind that the only rule of judgment is the written word of God. The Church knows nothing of the intuitions of reason or the deductions of philosophy except those reproduced in the Sacred Canon. She has a positive constitution in the Holy Scriptures, and has no right to utter a single syllable upon any subject except as the Lord puts words in her mouth. She is founded, in other words, upon express REVELATION. Her creed is an authoritative testimony of God, and not a speculation, and what she proclaims she must PROCLAIM with infallible certitude of faith, and not with the hesitating assent of an opinion. . . .

Now . . . if men had drawn their conclusions upon the subject only from the Bible, it would no more have entered into any human head to denounce slavery as a sin than to denounce monarchy, aristocracy, or poverty. The truth is, men have listened to what they falsely considered as primitive intuitions . . . and then have gone to the Bible to confirm the crotchets of their vain philosophy. They have gone there determined to find a particular result, and the consequence is that they leave with having made, instead of having interpreted, Scripture. Slavery is no new thing. It has not only existed for ages in the world, but it has existed, under every dispensation of the covenant of grace in the Church of God. Indeed, the first organization of the Church as a visible society, separate and distinct from the unbelieving world, was inaugurated in the family of a slaveholder. . . . Slavery again reappears under the Law. God sanctions it in the first table of the Decalogue, and Moses treats it as an institution to be regulated, not abolished; legitimated and not condemned. We come down to the age of the New Testament, and we find it again in the churches founded by the Apostles under the plenary inspiration of the Holy Ghost. These facts are utterly amazing, if slavery is the enormous sin which its enemies represent it to be. It will not do to say that the Scriptures have treated it only in a general, incidental way, without any clear implication as to its moral character. Moses surely made it the subject of express and positive legislation, and the Apostles are equally explicit in inculcating the duties which spring from both sides of the relation. They treat slaves as bound to obey and inculcate obedience as an office of religion—a thing wholly self-contradictory if the authority exercised over them were unlawful and iniquitous.

But what puts this subject in a still clearer light is the manner in which it is sought to extort from the Scriptures a contrary testimony. The notion of direct and implicit condemnation is given up. The attempt is to show that the genius and spirit of Christianity are opposed to it—that its great cardinal principles of virtue are utterly against it. Much stress is laid upon the Golden Rule and upon the general denunciation of tyranny and oppression. To all this we reply that no principle is clearer than that a case positively excepted cannot be included under a general rule. Let us concede, for a moment, that the laws of love and the condemnation of tyranny and oppression seem logically to involve . . . the condemnation of slavery; yet, if slavery is afterwards expressly mentioned and treated as a lawful relation, it obviously follows, unless Scripture is to be interpreted as inconsistent with itself, that slavery is, by necessary implication, excepted. . . . The law of love has always been the law of God. It was enunciated by Moses almost as clearly as it was enunciated by Jesus Christ. Yet, notwithstanding this law, Moses and the Apostles alike sanctioned the relation of slavery. The conclusion is inevitable either that the law is not opposed to it or that slavery is an excepted case. . . . The master may, indeed, abuse his power, but he oppresses not simply as a master but as a wicked master.

But . . . the law of love . . . implies nothing as to the existence of various ranks and gradations in society. The interpretation which makes it repudiate slavery would make it equally repudiate all social, civil, and political inequalities. . . . It condemns slavery, therefore, only upon the supposition that slavery is a sinful relation. . . .

We cannot prosecute the argument in detail, but we have said enough, we think, to vindicate the position of the Southern Church. We have assumed no new attitude. We stand exactly where the Church of God has always stood—from Abraham to Moses, from Moses to Christ, from Christ to the Reformers, and from the Reformers to ourselves. We stand upon the foundation of the Prophets and Apostles, Jesus Christ Himself being the chief cornerstone.[3]

The Roman Catholic Church, although its hierarchal establishment emanated from Rome, was long accustomed to adjusting to an infinite variety of political and social systems. But its members, clerical and lay, were as Southern as their Protestant neighbors.

Southerners were a religious and churchgoing people. Whatever their denomination, theirs was a personal God who was concerned with their every want. Long convinced by their theologians that slavery was an institution sanctioned by Scripture, they prayed that their enemies might be confounded and that victory might come to them through Divine Providence. The Confederate government and state and municipal governments seized upon this religious sentiment to bolster the morale of the people. Presi-

dent Davis by proclamation set apart more than a dozen days during the war for fasting and prayer. By the fall of 1861 at least two such days had already been proclaimed. Some uniformity marked the observance by that time. On November 15 one common prayer was read in all churches in all denominations of the Confederate States. Synagogues also heard the prayer, but with the name of Christ omitted.

Almighty God, the Sovereign Disposer of events, it hath pleased Thee to protect and defend the Confederate States hitherto in their conflict with their enemies and be unto them a shield.

With grateful thanks we recognize Thy hand, and acknowledge that not unto us, but unto Thee, belongeth the victory; and in humble dependence upon Thy Almighty strength, and trusting in the justness of our cause, we appeal to Thee that it may please Thee to set at naught the efforts of all our enemies, and put them to confusion and shame.

O, Almighty God, we pray Thee that it may please Thee to grant us Thy blessing upon our arms, and give us victory over all our enemies, wherever they may be.

Preserve our homes and altars from pollution, and secure to us the restoration of peace and prosperity; all of which we ask in the name of Jesus Christ, our Blessed Lord and Savior, to whom with Thee, the Father and the Holy Spirit, we will give all the praise and glory in time and throughout all eternity. Amen and Amen.[4]

Less formal but no less sincere was the prayer of J. A. Randall, an overseer on Magnolia Plantation in Plaquemines Parish, Louisiana, a few miles below New Orleans. On Thursday, June 13, 1861, he entered in his journal:

This Day is set a part By presedent Jefferson Davis for fasting and praying owing to the Deplorable condition ower southern country is In My Prayer Sincerely to God is that every Black Republican in the Hole combined whorl either man woman o chile that is opposed to negro slavery as it existed in the Southern confederacy shal be trubled with pestilents and calamitys of all Kinds and Drag out the Balance of their existance in Misray and Degradation with scarsely food and rayment enughf to keep sole and Body to gather and o God I pray the to Direct a bullet or a bayonet to pirce The Hart of every northern soldier that invades southern soile and after the Body has rendered up its traterish sole gave it a trators reward a Birth In the Lake of Fires and Brimstone my honest convicksion is that every man wome and chile that has gave aide to the abolishionist are fit subjects for Hell I all so ask the to aide the southern Confederacy in maintaining ower rites and establishing the confederate Government Believing this case the prares from the wicked will prevaileth much Amen.[5]

Services on these fast days were sometimes attended by both blacks and whites. An old Negro gave a prayer before such a mixed audience.

Mars Lord, be pleased to blow wid dy bref an' sink de ships of de wicked enemy. Our boys, good marster, will drive 'em from de lan' but thou alone can reach de gunboats.[6]

With religion playing such an integral part in the lives of Southern people, it is not surprising that Southern clergymen were men of considerable leadership in their communities, and sometimes their influence was nation-wide. Many of the clergy were leaders in the secession movement and practically all were ardent supporters of the Confederacy. James H. Thornwell of South Carolina and Benjamin Palmer of New Orleans were only the most spectacular of a large number of Presbyterian clergymen whose sermons and writings buoyed up the morale of the people throughout the war. Thornwell was known as the "Calhoun of the Church" and Palmer's sermon in New Orleans on Thanksgiving Day 1860 was printed in pamphlet form and distributed by the thousands. After the fall of New Orleans in April 1862, Palmer journeyed through-

out the Confederacy exhorting both soldiers and civilians.

Another prominent Presbyterian minister was Thomas Smyth of Charleston. In June 1861 he indicted the Lincoln government:

See how these Christians hate one another, and how Republicans, by a sectional minority, take the government out of the hands of a million majority and put it into the hands of a military despotism; which sets aside the Supreme Court; tramples on the Constitution; ignores, and even opposes Congress; against all constitutional authority sets up [General Winfield] Scott as a military dictator; calls for seventy-five thousand and accepts two hundred and fifty thousand troops; proclaims war; creates a self-chosen military board to supersede state authorities; declares martial law; sets at defiance the fundamental right of HABEAS CORPUS and the decrees of courts, even of the Supreme Court; abolishes trial by jury; not only raises armies but orders their number and term of service, and compels them to take a test oath of allegiance; builds, purchases, and hires ships of war; mans, equips, and gives them secret and peremptory orders; blockades ports of states still declared to be in the Union; divides such states into military districts; takes military possession of Maryland against the declarations of her authorities; shoots down her citizens, forcibly seizes her arms, dwellings, and property; imprisons her citizens without charge or trial; establishes a hostile camp commanding Baltimore and opens the batteries of Fort McHenry on the city; takes military possession of St. Louis and shoots down men, women, and children in her streets; foments and aids civil war in Virginia, Kentucky, Texas, and Missouri; invades Virginia and takes military possession of Hampton and Alexandria where it brutally murders a peaceful citizen defending his own house, family, and property against an infamous soldiery who were permitted to rob and pillage an unarmed and unresisting population and to outrage helpless women; has destroyed public property in ships, buildings, and forts, to an amount of some twenty millions of dollars, and involved the country, even in the period of a few months, in a loss of not less than one thousand millions of dollars; which has justified the cowardly assassination of a resident citizen of Washington at the door of his own house, to which he had been summoned for the cold-blooded purpose of murder; hung, without trial, a merchant of Hampton, Virginia, for shooting an officer who took forcible possession of his store and goods and struck him in the face with his drawn sword; stripped a gentleman of the same town stark naked, and in that condition marched him as a prisoner to Fortress Monroe; destroyed crops and houses and other property in a single county and in a single week to the extent of five hundred thousand dollars; commanded the retention of all fugitive slaves; attempted, through a slave cook, to poison the food of the soldiery; plots the assassination of President Davis; violated all the confidential sanctities of the telegraph and post office; established a reign of terror, by a system of espionage and threats, over men and women, over the press and free speech, and against all law, human and divine; is now proceeding, unless God prevent, to carry devastation throughout the South until it is brought into prostrate subjection; who privateers, while proclaiming it to be piracy and worthy of death; and who employs mercenary foreign hirelings to invade, ravage, and destroy unarmed and unsuspecting towns of a neutral state, shooting its inhabitants and barbarously trampling and kicking to death an infirm old man eighty years of age.[7]

Not only did Southern preachers defend the Confederacy from the pulpit but many of them also became chaplains in the army. Others, notably Bishop Leonidas Polk and William N. Pendleton, became active officers. One minister gave a gun to a soldier with the advice "if you get in a tight place and have to use it, ask God's blessing if you have time, but be sure and not let your enemy get the start of you. You can say amen after you shoot."

William Porcher Miles, chairman of the military committee in the Confederate House of Representatives, stated near the end of the war: "The Clergy have done more for the success of our cause than any other class. They have kept up the spirits of our people, have led in every philanthropic movement. . . . Not even the bayonets have done more."

So highly did the Union government regard the influence of the Southern clergy on their people that the Federal army decided on a counterstroke. In the fall of 1863 Adjutant General E. D. Townsend sent an order to all generals commanding departments in the South.

You are hereby directed to place at the disposal of Rev. Bishop Ames all houses of worship belonging to the Methodist Episcopal Church South in which a loyal minister, who has been appointed by a loyal bishop of said church, does not now officiate.

It is a matter of great importance to the government, in its efforts to restore tranquility to the community and peace to the nation, that Christian ministers should, by example and precept, support and foster the loyal sentiment of the people.

Bishop Ames enjoys the entire confidence of this Department, and no doubt is entertained that all ministers who may be appointed by him will be entirely loyal. You are expected to give him all the aid, countenance, and support practicable.[8]

A similar letter was sent to all generals concerning other denominations in their departments.

The war was an occasion for self-examination by some Southern religious groups. The Baptist Association of Georgia in a meeting in 1864 resolved:

That it is the firm belief and conviction of this body that the institution of marriage was ordained by Almighty

God for the benefit of the whole human race without respect to color; that it ought to be maintained in is original purity among all classes of people and in all countries and in all ages until the end of time; and that, consequently, the law of Georgia, in its failure to recognize and protect this relation between our slaves, is essentially defective and ought to be amended.[9]

The churches suffered in the war by the disruption of congregations and the scattering of their preachers. Nor did they escape the wrath of invading armies. Church buildings were desecrated and sometimes destroyed. James J. Marks, a chaplain in the Army of the Potomac, visited historic Pohick Church in the Virginia Northern Neck in the spring of 1862.

I have spoken of Pohick Church as one of the most remarkable relics of the days of Washington. This church stands to the left of the Richmond road and twelve miles west of Alexandria. The situation is beautiful on the green hill above Pohick Creek. It was built by various distinguished families who formerly lived in this neighborhood, such as the Lees, the Masons, McCartys, Washingtons, Fairfaxes, and Lewises. Of these families but few survive; and these feeble remnants, like the fragments of a noble vessel broken on the rocks, have in them little to remind us of the greatness of the past. Our troops took possession of this church, and the walls were blackened with a thousand names. The seats were cut to pieces and borne away as memorials of the church of Washington. The old square pews remained at this time, and the pew of Washington, nearly untouched, because probably not known as such by the soldiers.[10]

Pohick seems to have suffered only from casual acts of vandalism. A more premeditated act of destruction was described by Stephen F. Fleharty of the 102nd. Illinois. Fleharty was with Sherman in South Carolina in January 1865. He wrote:

We abandoned the camp at Hardee Farm on the 17th of Jan., and marched ten miles to Hardeeville, a little town on the Charleston and Savannah railroad. . . .

Again the work of destroying buildings commenced. Among others, a large beautiful church was attacked. Men of various regiments were engaged in the work. First the pulpit and seats were torn out, then the siding and the blinds were ripped off. Many axes were at work. The corner posts were cut, the building tottered, the beautiful spire, up among the green trees, leaned for a time several degrees out of the perpendicular, vibrating to and fro. A tree that stood in the way was cut. By the use of long poles the men increased the vibratory motion of the building, and soon, with a screeching groan the spire sunk down amidst the timbers which gave way beneath, and as the structure became a pile of rubbish, some of the most wicked of the raiders yelled out: "There goes your d——d old gospel shop."

Next day scarcely a vestige of the church was visible.

It was barbarous, yet it verified the words of the Bible: —"FOR THEY HAVE SOWN THE WIND AND THEY SHALL REAP THE WHIRLWIND."[11]

The churches provided Bibles and religious tracts for the army. Before the war the South had depended on Northern and European publishers for its Bibles. The war interrupted regular channels of this trade, but hundreds of thousands of Bibles were contributed to the Confederacy by English Bible societies and were run through the blockade. These were eagerly sought by the soldiers, more than one of whom claimed to have been miraculously saved by having an enemy bullet spend itself against a Bible carried in a breast pocket.

The churches were concerned also with relief to dependents of soldiers. In almost every city of the Confederacy relief societies were formed and church congregations were in the forefront of them everywhere.

The war had a blighting effect on education. In 1860 education in the South was backward, even by standards of the time. There were some excellent schools at the secondary or "academy" level; frequently these were denominational, and often the parish rector was the instructor. But these, as well as grammar schools, were too few, and the number of illiterates ran high in the South, in 1860 roughly thirty per cent.

In higher education the record looked better. Although the Southern states contained only one-third of the population of the country they contained half of the colleges with enrollment about equal to that of Northern institutions. At an earlier period many of the Southern universities had attained eminence, but several decades before secession they had slipped into a conservatism that retarded intellectual progress. J. D. B. De Bow, while primarily an economist, was interested in all things Southern; and at the outset of the Confederacy he took a look at Southern colleges and universities.

While much has been gained by the withdrawal of Southern youth from the colleges of the North, still more good might be accomplished by raising those of the South to the position of universities in the proper acceptation of that term. Many of the latter are already universities in name, but in name only—being really inferior, in many respects, to the best high schools of which England can boast. Perhaps the only exception to this remark is afforded in the University of Virginia; and its success has shown that the lack of institutions of learning of the highest order in the South has not been owing to a want of ability to sustain them. We have had, within the last few years, some cheering prospects in other quarters which we sincerely hope may not be blighted by the existing war; for, with the establishment of Southern universities of equal grade with those of Europe we may anticipate the dawn of a new era in Southern literature. . . .

The states comprising the Southern Confederacy are supplied with a vast number of institutions established by private beneficence and designed for the education of young women. While it cannot be denied that these institutions have effected a great amount of good, it is also true they have not accomplished all that their benevolent founders intended, nor have they (except in a few cases) established that high grade of scholarship with literary attainment which ought to characterize Southern women. . . .

The great and prevailing vice in our system, both of male and female education, has been and is now, to a great extent, YANKEEISM. . . . It is not a matter of wonder that Southern men surrendered commerce and manufactures into the hands of the North; for, as citizens, obedient to the laws of the Federal Union, they were compelled to pay their money, in the shape of bounties to sustain Northern shipping, and of duties to uphold Northern manufacturers. But there was no law to bind us to take Northern teachers and their books. THIS yoke of bondage was not imposed but voluntarily assumed. Yet, not altogether voluntarily, for there was a public sentiment which, if not universal, yet had sufficient power to drive away intelligent Southern men from the profession of teaching, and thus necessitate the employment of Yankees. There has been a disposition at the South to rank teaching among the MENIAL employments, and hence fit for the Yankees only. Thus, from these two causes, viz: a belief in Northern superiority on the part of some, and a belief on the part of others that teaching was socially degrading, the whole Southern country, until within a few years past, has been overrun by Yankee teachers of every grade, from the professor down to the common-school teacher. They necessarily brought with them their habits, modes of thought, their prejudices and errors— their books and their systems of education. . . . Even now, though the social stigma upon the profession of teacher has been almost removed; though the belief in the absolute superiority of everything of Northern origin has been shaken; though the wandering Yankees have all returned home, yet they have left traces of their presence. Our schools have been based upon Northern models. . . .

Passing by some minor objections, the grand characteristic of the system is SUPERFICIALITY. The appeal may be confidently made to every intelligent teacher, who has had under his charge pupils who have been members of institutes of high-sounding names and lofty pretensions, for confirmation of the truth of the above statement. In general, the system may be described as one for SHOW and not for use. The great object of education, viz: the training and developing all the powers of the mind into active and vigorous exercise, is quite ignored. The knowledge imparted is a mere smattering; the accomplishments mere tinsel gloss.[12]

There were tax-supported schools in cities, but more than ninety per cent of the people lived in rural areas where schools were either unknown or else woefully inadequate. There, quite frequently, only those able to afford private tutors had an opportunity for regular and formal education. But these tutors had come, generally, from the North, until the war interfered. Concerned about the education of her young brothers, Kate Stone wrote in the fall of 1861:

Oct. 17: No war news and no teacher. It is late for the boys to be out of school. . . .

Oct. 21: Mamma wrote to engage Mr. Wilkinson from Virginia as teacher. None of us will ever like another teacher as well as Mr. Newton. . . .

Nov. 29: We are looking for the teacher every day. He was to leave Virginia on the fourteenth and should have been here some days ago. The boys are very impatient over the delay. They realize the importance of this year's study. . . .

Nov. 30: Mr. Wilkinson, the teacher, at last arrived this morning, and Dr. Buckner, Aunt Laura, and dear little Beverly arrived this evening. . . .

Mr. Wilkinson is quite a young man, graduated in June at Columbia College, D. C. Very tall and ungainly, topped by a high stovepipe hat and riding on a little mule with short stirrups, he was a figure of fun when he rode up. He betrays a weakness for jewelry and fancy vests and has decidedly a verdant look. He is exceedingly polite, rises and remains standing when a lady enters or leaves a room, a Virginia custom, I hear. . . .

Dec. 2: School opened today, Mr. Wilkinson's first attempt. . . .

Dec. 7: Mr. Wilkinson has tried teaching this one week and is utterly incapable of teaching any but the two youngest children. Mamma has had an explanation with him, and he will stay here until he gets other employment, or if he fails in that Mamma has asked him to stay until spring. Mamma wrote at once for another teacher and Mr. Wilkinson will do the best he can for the boys until the other teacher arrives. He is wonderfully ignorant to have graduated anywhere. When Mamma spoke to him, he confessed that he could not teach the boys. He said he thought he was coming to an out-of-the-way, illiterate place and would have no trouble teaching anybody he might be thrown with. But he said he realized the first day that he had made a mistake, that Brother Coley was already far in advance of him, that the other boys knew as much as he did, and that he did not know what to do. He thanked Mamma very heartily for her kindness as he had no money to return. His home will be here until Mamma can find a place for him to teach little children. There may be an opening near here. For several days he was very sad, but now that there has been an explanation, he has brightened up and is quite cheerful. He has the most grotesque way of nodding his head up and down, up and down, all the time he is talking, or eating, or even reading. Does it unconsciously and looks like a toy Mandarin. . . .

Dec. 22: Hurrah! Mr. Wilkinson has secured a situation at Mr. Matt Johnson's at a salary of $100 per month to teach Mrs. M. Johnson's little brothers. I think they live at Wilton near Goodrich. Certainly it seems "a fool for luck" is verified in his case. He is so silly and so green, altogether hateful. Can only interest him by talking about girls. He pretends to be desperate about Anna Dobbs and has seen her only twice. He asked Brother Coley did not the teachers down here always marry rich girls? That was enough for the boys and Robert and Joe. They have been telling many marvelous tales of the great wealth of the girls, how especially susceptible they are to teachers from a distance and so admire their manners and style, and running many "rigs" on him. He has not sense to see it. He will leave us a few days after Christmas.[13]

Most Southern schoolbooks had been published in the North and the war caused a critical shortage of them. A "Richmond Lady" wrote in the fall of 1862:

The stock on hand when the war commenced soon became exhausted, and there were no new ones to supply the constant demand. Very few came to us through the blockade. Books were the last consideration in that eccentric trade. . . . Schoolbooks which had long before been cast aside as obsolete and banished from the shelves of the library and hidden away to molder in dark closets were brought to light and placed in the hands of children, from which to add to the stock of ideas in the process of youthful development.[14]

That fall, the State Education Association of North Carolina called a general convention of the teachers of the Confederate States to consider the best means for supplying textbooks for schools and colleges and for uniting their efforts for the advancement of education in the Confederacy. The convention met at Columbia, South Carolina,

the following spring. A correspondent of the Richmond
Dispatch *reported:*

Some sixty members are in attendance representing
Virginia, the Carolinas, Georgia, Alabama, and Louisiana.
They organized a permanent body to meet annually, and
to be known as The Educational Association of the Confederate States of North America, and to consist of such
teachers and other persons identified with the educational
interests of the country as may be elected. . . . Letters
were read from President Davis, Governor [Zebulon]
Vance [of North Carolina], and various professors and
teachers of the South . . . making sundry suggestions on
the general subjects to engage the Convention.

Today has been pretty much occupied in hearing from
the different states as to textbooks, either prepared or in
course of preparation. . . . It seems that spelling-books,
readers, arithmetics, grammars, and Latin books, are being
produced in abundance. North Carolina, especially, has
already gotten out quite a variety of primary books, which
have been published in very neat style in Greensboro. . . .

Strong resolutions were adopted favoring the preference
of primary textbooks prepared and published in the South.
In the course of the discussion . . . many suggestions
were made as to modes of teaching. . . .

A committee was appointed to issue an address to the
public on the objects of the Association; and another . . .
to consider and report at the next meeting of the body a
course of study for male and female colleges.[15]

*The new Confederate texts frequently attempted to
counteract Northern propaganda, and some were aggres-
sively warlike in tone. L. Johnson, professor of mathe-
matics at Trinity College, Archdale, North Carolina, published in 1864 an* Elementary Arithmetic Designed for
Beginners; Embracing the First Principles of the Science.
*Ten thousand of this edition were published, but almost
all were destroyed by Sherman's army. One of its exam-*

ples wanted to know "If one Confederate soldier can whip 7 Yankees, how many soldiers can whip 49 Yankees?" A reader, published in Greensboro, was said to consist chiefly "of selections from the writings of authors of the highest literary attainments in the Confederate States." A geography text published by Branson and Farrar of Raleigh, in 1863, stated that the United States was

Once the most prosperous country in the world. . . . In the meantime both English and American ships went to Africa and brought away many of those poor heathen Negroes and sold them for slaves. Some people said it was wrong and asked the King of England to stop it. He replied that "he knew it was wrong; but that slave trade brought much money into his treasury, and it should continue." But both countries afterwards did pass laws to stop this trade. In a few years, the Northern states finding their climate too cold for the Negro to be profitable, sold them to the people living farther south. Then the Northern states passed laws to forbid any person owning slaves in their borders.

Then the Northern people began to preach, to lecture, and to write about the sin of slavery. The money for which they had sold their slaves was now partly spent in trying to persuade the Southern states to send their slaves back to Africa. And when the territories were settled they were not willing for any of them to become slaveholding. . . .

In the year 1860 the Abolitionists became strong enough to elect one of their men for President. . . . So the Southern states seceded. . . .

This country [the United States] possesses many ships, has fine cities and towns, many railroads, steamboats, canals, manufactures, etc. The people are ingenious and enterprising, and are noted for their tact in "driving a bargain." They are refined and intelligent on all subjects but that of Negro slavery; on this they are mad.

The same text says of the Southern Confederacy:

This is a great country! The Yankees thought to starve us out when they sent their ships to guard our seaport towns. But we have learned to make many things; to do without others. . . .

The Southern people are noted for being high-minded and courteous.

Questions and answers which were to serve as a review portion of the text emphasized trust in the Almighty.

Q. What kind of men should we elect to govern our country?

A. Good and wise men.

Q. Why?

A. "When the righteous are in authority, the people rejoice, but when the wicked beareth rule the people mourn."

Q. Where do you learn this?

A. From the Bible.

Q. Will God curse a nation because of wicked rulers?

A. He says He will.

In 1864 a new edition of the geography text included the following:

Q. Has the Confederate States any commerce?

A. A fine inland commerce, and bids fair, sometime, to have a grand commerce on the high seas.

Q. What is the present drawback to our trade?

A. An unlawful blockade by the miserable and hellish Yankee nation.[16]

The "Richmond Lady" observed:

As the war went on a marked change was made in the educational interests of the South. For a certain number of pupils the teachers of schools were exempt from military duty. To their credit be it recorded that few, comparatively, availed themselves of this exemption, and the care of instructing the youth devolved, with other added responsibilities, upon the women of the country. Only boys under the conscript age were found in the schools; all older were made necessary in the field or in some department of government service, unless physical inability prevented them from falling under the requirements of the law. Many of our colleges for males suspended operation, and at the most important period in the course of their education our youths were instructed in the sterner lessons of military service.

Female schools were supported as best they could be where there was a lamentable scarcity of books and where the expenses of education were so great that only the most wealthy could afford to give their daughters the advantages of a liberal course. Such were the difficulties that hedged the way to mental cultivation that it seemed, in many instances, almost a matter of impossibility to pursue any regular plan of education for girls.

The operations of the Richmond Female College were suspended, or rather the building was given up for hospital purposes, and the excellent institution of Mr. Le-Febvre was entirely broken up; but the Southern Female Institute, a first-grade seminary under the supervision of Mr. Lee Powell, the fine school of Miss Pegram, St. Joseph's Academy, and other institutions under the patronage of the Catholic Church, were sustained. Though the encouragement to these schools was thoroughly liberal, so heavy were the expenses that it was almost impossible to keep them in successful operation.[17]

Some institutions managed to survive the first year of the war, but conscription laws in 1862 and later deprived them of students. Perhaps one of the greatest tragedies to befall the South in all its history was the grinding of its "seed corn" during the Civil War.

Most Southern critics frankly admitted that the South had always been backward in literary production. But by 1860 Henry Timrod, Paul Hamilton Hayne, and John R. Thompson had established themselves as poets of distinction, and they all wrote verse of good quality during the war. Timrod's "Ethnogenesis," his "Carolina," and "A Cry to Arms" are among his best work. Thompson's "Dirge for Ashby," and James R. Randall's "Maryland, My Maryland" were perhaps more popular, if not as good poetry. William Gilmore Simms, the Southerner of greatest literary stature in 1860, was strangely silent and unproductive during the war.

One natural reflection of the times was the number of war themes used. Dirges for the dead, histories of battles, and adventures at blockade-running were common topics. Romance was little indulged, although there was some pirating of Dickens, Eliot, Hugo, and other European authors. Probably the most popular novel written by a Southerner during the war was Macaria: or Altars of Sacrifice, *by Augusta Jane Evans of Mobile. Another popular work was Sally Rochester Ford's* Raids and Romance of Morgan and His Men.

While a literary revival was hardly to be expected during the war, yet considerable writing was done, and some of it had merit. In 1861 the New Orleans Delta *was looking into the future when it said:*

A nation cannot live upon bread alone. The moral and intellectual must assist the material or the whole fabric will fall. They are equally necessary to pedestal and capital, to basement and dome. It is they that impart the vital instinct which guides the roots to sources of nourishment; and it is they that cause the tree to shoot skyward, spread its lusty branches, robe itself in verdure, and crown its head with flowers and fruits. The destiny of the South will be but a crude and unfinished attempt, and unmeaning, inconsequential projection into time and space, unless along with her political independence she achieves her independence in thought and education and in all those forms of mental improvement and entertainment which by a liberal construction of the word are included in literature.

The development of the South up to this time has been almost purely economical and political. Her statesmanship has been almost entirely unsupported by literature. Certainly such literature as she was able to claim for her own, intrinsically rich and vigorous as much of it may have been, was woefully inadequate to cope with the literature arrayed against her. The pens and the presses, the books, the periodicals and journals, the pulpits, the lecture desks, and the schoolrooms of the Northern states, of England, of France, of Germany, all, for the most part, openly or insidiously hostile to her institutions, her rights, her interests, her aspirations, placed her at a fearful disadvantage in the controversy she was compelled to maintain before the tribunal of public opinion. She had no friend on the bench; she was arraigned before a court whose mind was poisoned against her cause. The witnesses who came forward were nearly to a man her enemies. Her advocates could scarcely get a hearing. Their voice was drowned in a storm of denunciation and in a furious and unceasing clamor for her conviction and execution.

Thus the South was struggling for life against overwhelming odds. She was verging upon the penumbra of her fate—she was passing into the jaws of death when her escape from a Union which claimed her as a culprit and prisoner; and the war which followed changed the field of conflict and armed her anew for the assertion of her right to live, to grow and prosper, materially and socially, politically, intellectually, aesthetically. She now stands upon the threshold of a mysterious and wonderful future. . . . But she must not pause in hesitation; she must not cast one regretful look upon the doomed cities of the plain, under peril of being petrified upon the spot, to remain a melancholy monument of national suicide.

For the South to neglect to employ every instrumentality appertaining to the production of a vigorous, healthy, native, loyal, and beneficent literature; for her to depend almost exclusively upon foreign sources for her reading, and outside of local politics, for her thinking, would be to manifest a fatal hesitation—to throw away a magnificent future—to doom herself to dwell amid the defilements and abominations of a detested past and, famishing in arid plains, to feed upon apples of ashes.[1]

There was hope for the future in what the Delta *said. Three years later, F. H. Alfriend, editor of the* Southern Literary Messenger, *surveyed the production of Confederate authors:*

In the opinion of the world at large we should be guilty of not a little arrogance in making any pretension to a national literature, notwithstanding the evidence of intellectual activity which the war has evoked and the number of publications which it has called into being. That would be an exceedingly superficial view of the matter which could suppose the mere temporary efflorescence of the popular mind a certain indication of well-grounded [talent] promising a permanent and luxuriant growth of healthful and enduring fruits. Nor will the achievement of our independence alone constitute a great millenium of

literary regeneration. Just as in the establishment of our
political and commercial interests upon a wise and safe
basis, we shall need a careful circumspection, we shall
have still greater occasion to employ all our energies and
all our sagacity in the embarkation of the delicate interests of literature upon the uncertain tide of the future.
Having no history except the tragic present . . . a long
time will elapse before we have our [David] Humes and
[William] Robertsons, [François Pierre Guillaume] Gui-
zots and [Edward] Gibbons to trace our national progress;
the inspiration will not be wanting to create poets. Indeed,
in [James Barron] Hope, Thompson, Timrod, Hayne, and
others we have them already; but centuries perhaps will
elapse before we can distinguish between our "Schools"
of the "Transition" and the "Lake," between our Chaucers
and Spensers, Miltons and Cowpers, Burns', Byrons, and
Wordsworths. Having virtually no history and, PAR CON-
SEQUENCE, comparatively few of those great landmarks of
thought and reflection in the shape of grand events teaching the significance of historic order in the majestic march
of centuries, we shall necessarily find the earlier exhibitions of Southern genius imitative of others rather than
creative of a type of our own. . . .

Like all people much given to talking, Southerners, as
a people, are little given to reading. Our education, like
that of an old Greek, is derived chiefly from conversation
and verbal discussion; and though from this cause our
opinions and perceptions are always ready and generally
clever in subtlety, they are too often characterized by the
sophistry of superficiality. We can never become profound in either thought or education until this superficial
habit of education shall be supplied by some more dur-
able form of instruction. Indeed, not until we shall become
more of a reading and less of a talking people, which
latter result cannot be consummated until such reading
is placed in the hands of the people as will arrest their
interested attention. The mass of men cannot be trans-

formed in an instant into philosophers and savants, and until the dream of Utopia is realized, when all men shall occupy one common footing of blissful equality, some concession must be made to degrees of intellectual advancement as well as to degrees in cultivation of taste. Let our literary men remember this; otherwise those who embrace the profession of letters will do little more than save themselves from starvation while the people look to others for the entertainment which they cannot find at home.

There is nothing whatever in the prospective condition of the Confederacy, either political, commercial, or social, which forbids the sanguine expectation of a permanent advancement of the literary profession. All the theories which can be urged, such as the incompatibility of the predominance of agricultural interests and an advanced state of letters, the indifference of the Southern mind to its literary interests, and the numerous other suggestions of insuperable obstacles to the growth of literature, should be but so many additional incentives to exertion with those who have the matter in hand. What fact of physiology or suggestion of common sense can furnish a tangible reason why a planter of Virginia or South Carolina should be more disinclined to reading than a shoemaker of Massachusetts or a coal digger of Pennsylvania, provided acceptable matter is offered him? We who are most interested in this matter have only to obey the suggestions of practical wisdom, to disregard the wild theories based upon anything else than practical experience and common sense, which will be urged upon us for adoption; to consult the popular taste; if necessary to make proper concessions to it, and thus to control it gradually along the successive stages of improvement.[2]

At about the same time William M. Burwell, literary editor of De Bow's Review, was summarizing the literary production of the war years.

There can be little question that the intellect of the country is searched for now in the army, and this will ex-plain why it happens that so little is being done for its literature. In this titanic struggle which is going on, the genial pursuit of letters is at an end, and for nearly three years little has appeared which is worthy either of the genius or attainments of our people. The glorious struggle has scarcely inspired one song which will live beyond the generation that now burns with martial ardor and rushes to the deadly field.

Books we have had—not a few. Works upon the army, works upon the navy, treatises interesting to the medical staff, translations and digests, some attempts at history, occasional schoolbooks, and now and then a work of romance. We are not doing injustice to these. Many are of great value, some of literary merit, and a few which deserve more than passing comment. Still, the truth with which we set out can not be gainsaid, and the development of Southern literature remains for the future.

Why is it that those who are in the civil walks find no utterances now? Are there not grand themes enough to arouse them to exertion? Can Simms be content with silence and not give, as of yore, his stirring and classic romances? Upon the great questions of international law will not the chaste and cultivated [William Henry] Trescot speak? Has [George] Fitzhugh no profound treatise upon social politics? Where are Hayne, Thompson, Randall, [Alexander B.] Meek, and [Augustin Julian] Requier, and a host of others of whom these but occur to us at the moment? Some of them do indeed speak occasionally in the lighter effusions of the press; but this is not what is wanted. They must rise to elaborate effort. The country requires more than this at their hands.

"Why stand ye all the day idle?" [3]

Book publishing in the Confederacy about kept pace with book writing—the quantity was impressive, but the quality left much to be desired. There had been little publishing of books in the South before the war, and after hostilities broke out Southern printing houses were called upon for services for which they were unprepared. They answered the call with indifferent success. More than a hundred titles were published in the Confederacy, about half of them works of fiction, and another third volumes of poetry. With the wretched paper printers were forced to use, together with the dearth of skilled workers, it is not to be wondered at if the press work was less than excellent. West and Johnston of Richmond was the leading publishing house in the Confederacy. Others of note were: Ayres and Wade, and Randolph and English in Richmond; Sigmund H. Goetzel in Mobile; Branson and Farrar in Raleigh; and Burke, Boykin and Company of Augusta, Georgia.

But literary publications were not the only concern of cultural leaders. Samuel Davis, a frequent contributor to the Southern Literary Messenger, *had concrete suggestions to make.*

If we are to be a cultivated and, at the same time, a warlike people, then the arts become the most appropriate and efficient auxiliaries of science in accomplishing this twofold purpose. Nor need they want for inspiration. The present grand and striking manifestations of human power and feeling have already furnished abundant themes deserving the highest embellishments of poetic genius; for poetry in its fullest sense is "the music of man's whole manner of being," and its beautiful creations will have for the future citizen of the republic a far more intelligible significance, a far more direct and penetrating influence upon his feelings, than all the forces that argument and eloquence can ever command. . . .

We set out with the intention of recommending the establishment at the South of an institution devoted to the encouragement of the arts, founded on a popular basis but administered by individuals whose taste and judgment qualify them for such an office. . . . Without intending to offer any original or fully developed plan, we think an institution combining the following general features would probably answer the object to be attained.

Firstly, an association of individuals formed for the purpose of encouraging and supporting the arts by pecuniary means to be derived from voluntary contributions, and employed in purchasing such artistic productions as have been affirmed and recommended by competent judges: such productions to be distributed among the members of the association or retained collectively as a common stock. . . .

Secondly, the formation of societies of artists within their respective departments, with a view to inspire that ESPRIT DE CORPS which dignifies the common purpose, develops a duplicated zeal and activity in its prosecution and, in general, renders all combined exertion so infinitely superior to isolated individual effort. . . .

Thirdly, stated public exhibitions of art-productions in order to popularize the influence of taste and stimulate the artist to his best exertions. . . .

Fourthly, the award of premiums to be paid from the treasury of the association independently of the price of the article to be purchased, as a gratuitous tribute to the genius of the author. We present these ideas only as an imperfect outline which may be filled up or entirely replaced by some other and better plan. . . .

It is not expected that the considerations suggested by our subject will be viewed as at all practicable at the present time; but when we shall have succeeded, under the divine favor, in emancipating ourselves from the degraded and degrading despotism that is now seeking to force the chains upon us; when we shall have the proud consciousness that, through our own unaided efforts, we have rescued our liberties from the grasp of the usurper and enshrined them on the inviolable and indestructible temple of our Southern nationality, then may our people, confident that the strength and valor which preserved them once can preserve them through all time, commence the grand movement that shall carry them to the most conspicuous height of moral and intellectual dignity.[4]

While Alfriend, Burwell, and other literary devotees were striving, with indifferent success, to stimulate belles-lettres, and men like Davis, other arts, one artistic institution that seemed to flourish was the theater. Not that the quality of dramatic productions was universally acclaimed. But even mediocre performances seem to have played before packed houses. One critic observed, midway through the war, that "there is a certain class of our people who would go to the theater, no matter who acted or what was played, and unfortunately, perhaps from this very cause, we have scarcely anything but bad acting. Still all the Southern managers are growing rich."

And this seemed to be true in all parts of the Confederacy. In December 1862, Theodore Hamilton and Ella Wren gave repeat performances in Columbia, South Carolina, of a play entitled Black Eyed Susan. *At the same time a Montgomery, Alabama, theater manager was* "reaping a golden harvest" *from a tragedy called* Ingomar *starring Ida Vernon.*

Many of the companies went on tour and had successful stands throughout the principal cities. Richmond was, however, the theatrical center, and some of the leading stars remained there most of the war. The most celebrated house was the Richmond New Theatre, completed in February 1863, after fire had destroyed the old building the year before. Money had not been spared in the construction, and the new building was expensive and elaborate. Weeks of fanfare preceded the grand opening, and the initial performance was eagerly awaited. Certain citizens, however, looked with a jaundiced eye on such frivolity in the midst of sorrow and travail. Such a one was the Reverend John Lansing Burrows who, in a sermon at the First Baptist Church, declared:

Tomorrow night the New Richmond Theatre is to be

opened. I deem it fitting, in addition to the notices so liberally given through the daily press, to give this public notice from the pulpit. With surprising energy and regardless of cost in these pinching times of war, a splendid building with most costly decorations has been reared from the ashes of the old. Builders, artists, workmen, have devoted themselves with an enterprise and industry that would be praiseworthy, if, in any sense, their work were useful in these pressing times of war. Enough able-bodied men have escaped from the conscription, have, perhaps, purchased the right to keep away from the camp and the battle in order to accomplish this magnificent work, for a consideration. The work is completed; the decorations are finished, and tomorrow night the New Richmond Theatre is to be opened.

A strong corps of actors, male and female, have been secured, and, in addition to them, "twenty GENTLEMEN for the chorus and the ballet." No cripples from the battlefields are these—they can sing and dance; they can mimic fighting on the stage. For the serious work of repelling a real enemy they have neither taste nor heart. But they can sing while the country groans and dance while the cars are bringing, in sad funeral procession, the dead to their very doors, and the dismal ambulance bears the sick and the wounded under the very glare of their lights and within the sound of their music. They keep themselves out of the war for the noble duty of amusing the populace. Should they not, in these times, be especially encouraged, particularly by those whose own brave sons are in the camp or in the hospital, or whose mangled bodies are moldering in uncoffined graves? Does it not seem a peculiarly happy time for theatrical amusements? Shall we all go and laugh and clap to the music and the dance while the grasp of relentless foes is tightening upon the throats of our sons, and the armed heels of trampling hosts are bruising the bosom of our beloved mother land? What fitter time for opening a theater in the capital of our bleeding country, unless it could have been on the evening of the battle of Malvern Hill or of Fredericksburg? But enterprise and industry could not secure the completion of the building in time for those bloody days, or we should, doubtless, have had the theater open every night while the battle raged by day around the very suburbs of Richmond. "A strong stock company," and "twenty gentlemen for the chorus and the ballet," besides artists, musicians, etc., etc. Men enough, perhaps, to form an effective artillery company deny themselves the patriotic desire to aid in defending the country against assailing foes in order that they may devote themselves, fellow citizens, to your amusement. . . .

The New Richmond Theatre is a public assignation house where any vile man may be introduced to an infamous woman by paying the price of a ticket. [The third tier] is a part of the building especially appropriated to harlots where your sons may meet them and by their enticements be drawn into the very depths of debasement and vice. It is expressly designed by the architect, fitted up and decorated that it may be used for these infamous purposes. . . .

We are to have inaugurated tomorrow night in this capital of our new Confederacy one of these nefarious establishments which have been the disgrace of European and Northern cities, to be conducted on precisely the same principles and for the same ends.

Away then with the impudent and preposterous plea that the theater, as it is, is a school of morals. It is what it always has been, a school of immorality and vice. I could as readily conceive of a church in Hell as a theater in Heaven.[5]

Despite such hostility, opening night was a gala event. The critic of The Southern Illustrated News *wrote:*

According to announcement the new Richmond Theatre was opened on Monday night last. Glowing descriptions of the magnificence of the building and the lengthy an-

nouncements in all the Richmond papers of the opening,
by the manager, had raised public expectation to its very
highest pitch. The old man who had not crossed the por-
tals of a hall of amusement since his hair had become
tinged with gray—the young cavalier who had read, seen,
or heard of nothing but "wars and rumors of wars" since
the vandal horde had invaded our land—the gay-hearted
maiden with sweet and ruby lips—the politician or man
of office with careworn look, as if great matters of state
still weighed heavily upon his heart—all might have been
seen about seven o'clock last Monday night quietly wend-
ing their way to the new and gorgeous temple of Thespis.
Through the courtesy of the manager we, in company with
several other members of the press, were UNDESERVEDLY
shown through a private entrance to a box (thus saving
ourselves the necessity of elbowing through the crowd).

At half-past seven a full head of gas is turned on—the
interior of the building is brilliantly illuminated—the dress
circle is lined with a bevy of handsome and bright faces
—some with that beautiful rosy tinge upon the cheeks and
the lips which nature alone gives, while others appear
fresh from the artist's hand, the superfluous ROUGE not yet
brushed away—the soldier with his immense circular-saw
spurs jingling like so many sleigh bells—the gay gambler
with his flash apparel and magnificent diamonds dazzling
the eye as the soft lambent light falls upon them, while
he saunters to and fro with a NONCHALANT air, and seemingly wondering if the whole audience is not gazing ad-
miringly upon him. . . . At quarter to eight the door in
the orchestra box opens—the members of the orchestra
singly appear and take their respective seats—Prof. Loeb-
man nods his head and the members join in one grand
"concord of sweet sounds."

The strains of the music had scarcely died away when
Mr. [Walter] Keeble entered from the door under the
private box and delivered the . . . INAUGURAL POEM by
Henry Timrod. . . .

The reading of the poem was followed by the singing of the "Marsellaise" by Mr. Chas. Morton, aided by a full chorus. . . .

Then came the play—Shakespeare's AS YOU LIKE IT, but not as WE LIKE IT. The principal female character, that of "Rosilind," was sustained by Miss Kate Estelle in a manner which did the lady no credit. . . .

The "Celia" of Miss Wren was a better performance, though this lady was, throughout the entire play, guilty of the very bad practice of playing to the audience. . . .

One great fault of this lady's was the OUTRE manner in which she dressed the character.

The Shepherdess dress was very bad. We candidly ask the lady if she ever saw, heard, or read of a shepherdess wearing diamonds, and that in a forest, too. . . .

The wrestling scene in the play was done up too much in the style of the duel scene in the Corsican Brothers— much the same movements and tergiversations were gone through. As a whole the performance passed off with entire satisfaction to the large audience. . . .

Thus was our new Richmond Theatre dedicated. We trust it will ever continue a place of amusement where all may be able to enjoy themselves in a rational manner without the fear of having the blush brought to their cheeks by the imprudence of jack-plain actors who have no ambition.[6]

As the Illustrated News *critic suggests, audiences sometimes were quite disorderly, and on occasion curtains had to be rung down and the play interrupted while inebriated and noisy patrons were ejected by the management. One critic, upon the opening of the New Theatre, was pleased to note the lack of "rowdyism" in the house. Clapping of hands, he said, was the loudest manifestation of noise. Another critic, after attending a performance at the Varieties, a second-rate theater in Richmond, noted:*

It is a pleasure to attend the Varieties now—formerly it was otherwise. The audiences are very orderly, and [are a]

class of persons who attend for the love of the drama, and
not for the purpose of making up a mixture of rowdyism
and buffoonery in the pit, which was vastly more pleasing
to the old frequenters of the place than the play itself.
The absence from the boards of that bane of the acting of
the present day generally, to wit, "gagging," is very
creditable to the company at the Varieties. The costume
is, in most instances, well selected and in good taste.[7]

*Critics differed, of course, as to the quality of per-
formances and productions, and some reviewers were
brutally frank. The editor of* The Southern Illustrated
News, *after viewing a performance of the* Old House and
Bridge of Notre Dame *at the Richmond New Theatre in
the summer of 1863 wrote:*

[D'Orsay] Ogden, who personated both the COUNT and
the BOHEMIAN, did it in his usual style—with NONCHA-
LANCE and NERVOUSNESS. In all such pieces he invariably
makes a dead failure. He should, if he has any thought of
success as an actor, stick to light comedy. THORPE, as the
ROUE, was as usual, tame and unsuccessful. BATES and
GUION, as DESARMES and DEVREAUX, were very good, and
well received. Decidedly the best enacted character in
the piece was that of RENARD, by DUNCAN, who is indeed
a most promising young actor.

The female characters in the piece were of small importance, and badly impersonated. Miss WREN, as ZOE,
strutted the stage with as many tragic attitudes and in-
tonations of voice as if she were playing "Lady Macbeth."
Constant study would be of immense benefit to her, provided she wishes to become an actress. . . .

The greatest fault at this establishment appears to be in
the castings of the pieces. The manager [Ogden] never
fails to cast himself for all the best parts, especially those
that allow him to array himself "In gloss of satin and
glimmer of pearls."

To adorn his person gorgeously and strut upon the
stage like a pea-fowl with feathers spread seems to be the

height of his ambition. And this is done nightly in total disregard of all established rules. It seems to make no sort of difference in regard to the acknowledged rights of the actors, who are always engaged for a certain line of business—all must yield precedence to the King Bee of the establishment. If the new play from the French had been properly cast, and the part of the young COUNT LAVERGNE placed in the hands of a more competent actor than OGDEN, of whom there are several in the company, the piece would have made a decided hit, and doubtless had a good run. But, as it was, it was stripped of its fair proportions and fell "still-born."

The scenery of the theater would do credit to many better establishments, and the working of the intricate stage machinery reflects great credit upon the principal machinist. The building is pretty and admirably arranged, but the great desideratum is a directing head—one that will not attempt to usurp all the honors of all the various positions in the building.[8]

The attrition of war took its toll of actors, too; the Richmond Examiner *noted in January 1864:*

D'Ogden, the manager of the New Theatre, has gone South to look up stock for his boards, the best of the old troupe having stampeded. Miss Wren having fluttered away on her little wings, and Miss Estelle having lifted her skirts in indignation over the green room threshold, Miss Percey is leading woman. Her promotion, so far from being a recognition of her talent, is only an evidence of the desperate straits to which the management is reduced in the matter of supplying competent actors and actresses for leading parts. Harrison and Bates—two of the most useful and versatile of the old troupe—have gone on too, we believe.

On Saturday, D'Ogden announced the "fifty-fourth night" of the VIRGINIA CAVALIER. Now, this is downright "fibbing" on the part of the billwriter. The play has not been produced over thirteen or fourteen nights, if that many, we know to our positive knowledge. So, D'Ogden has added another grace to his many accomplishments— that of a perverter of truth and a "fibber." We wonder what accomplishment he will lay claim to next.[9]

But another critic, a few months later, noted:

According to announcement, Miss Ida Vernon made her first appearance at the Richmond Theatre on Monday night last as Lady Isobel in the new domestic play of EAST LYNNE. The house was densely crowded, and the audience greeted the young artiste, upon her appearance in the first scene, with the most enthusiastic applause. Miss Vernon never appeared to better advantage than on Monday night—her acting was graceful, easy, and above all, natural—indeed, the death scene was rendered in such a touching manner as to affect many ladies and gentlemen to tears—one lady gave vent to her feelings in such an audible manner that her escort had to request her to withdraw into the reception room for a few minutes in order to prevent disturbing the audience. We are even told that several of the actors wept. No greater compliment could possibly be paid an artiste. Great as Miss Vernon is in the expression of powerful emotion, she is still greater in those scenes which require the display of extreme tenderness and feminine pathos, as was evidenced by her rendition of Lady Isobel on Monday night. She was well supported by Messrs. Ogden [and] Charles, and Mrs. De Bar. The piece is up again for tonight.[10]

In music and the other fine arts, too, the South, although a generation behind the North, was showing activity. After the war, in surveying the artistic side of the Confederacy, T. C. De Leon wrote:

In art and her twin sister, music, the South displayed taste and progress truly remarkable in view of the absorbing nature of her duties. Like all inhabitants of semitropic climes, there had ever been shown by her people natural love and aptitude for melody. While this natural taste was wholly uncultivated—venting largely in plantation songs of the Negroes—in districts where the music-master was necessarily abroad, it had reached high development in several of the large cities. Few of these were large enough or wealthy enough to support good operas, which the wealth of the North frequently lured to itself; but it may be recalled that New Orleans was genuinely enjoying opera, as a necessary of life, long before New York deemed it essential to study bad translations of librettos, in warmly packed congregations of thousands.

Mobile, Charleston, Savannah, and other cities also had considerable latent music among their amateurs; happily not then brought to the surface by the fierce friction of poverty. And what was the musical talent of the Capital has elsewhere been hinted. When the tireless daughters of Richmond had worked in every other way for the soldiers themselves, they organized a system of concerts and dramatic evenings for benefit of their families. At these were shown evidence of individual excellence truly remarkable; while their average displayed taste and finish which skilled critics declared would compare favorably with any city in the country.

The bands of the Southern army—so long as they remained existent as separate organizations—were indisputably mediocre, when not atrociously bad. But it must be recalled that there was little time to practice, even in the beginning; literally no chance to obtain new music or instruments; and that the better class of men—who usually make the best musicians—always preferred the musket to the bugle. Nor was there either incentive to good music or appreciation of it among the masses of the fighters. The drum and fife were the best they had known "at musters"; and they were good enough still, to fight by. So, recalling the prowess achieved constantly in following them, it may be wondered what possible results might have come from inspiration of a marine band, a Grafulla, or a Gilmore.

Likewise, in all art matters the South was at least a

decade behind her Northern sisterhood. Climate, picturesque surrounding, and natural warmth of character had awakened artistic sense in many localities. But its development was scarcely appreciable, from lack of opportunity and of exemplar. The majority of Southern girls were reared at their own homes; and art culture—beyond mild atrocities in crayon or water-color or terrors bred of the nimble broider's needle—was a myth, indeed. A large number of young men—a majority, perhaps, of those who could afford it—received education at the North. Such of these as displayed peculiar aptitude for painting were usually sent abroad for perfecting; and returning, they almost invariably settled in Northern cities, where were found both superior opportunities and larger and better-paying class of patrons. But when the tug came, not a few of these errant youths returned, to share it with their native states; and some of them found time, even in the stirring days of war, to transfer to canvas some of its most suggestive scenes.

Of them, the majority were naturally about Richmond; not only as the great army center but as the center of everything else. Among the latter were two favorite pupils of [Emanuel] Leutze, William D. Washington and John A. Elder. Both Virginians by birth and rearing, they had the great advantage of Düsseldorf training, while they were thoroughly acquainted and sympathetic with their subjects. Some of Washington's figure-pieces were very successful; finding ready sale at prices which, had they continued, might have made him a Meissonnier in pocket as well as in local fame. His elaborate picture illustrating the "Burial of Latané"—a subject which also afforded MOTIF for Thompson's most classic poem—attracted wide attention and favorable verdict from good critics. Mr. Washington also made many and excellent studies of the bold, picturesque scenery of his western campaigning, along the Gauley and Kanawha.

Elder's pictures—while, perhaps, less careful in finish

than those of his brother student—were nothing inferior
as close character-studies of soldier-life. Their excellence
was ever emphasized by prompt sale; and "The Scout's
Prize" and the "Raider's Return"—both horse and land-
scape studies; as well as a ghastly but most effective picture of the "Crater Fight" at Petersburg, made the young
artist great reputation.

Washington's "Latané" had POST-BELLUM reproduction
by the graver, becoming popular and widely known, North
and South. The three of Elder's pictures, named here,
were purchased by a member of the British Parliament;
but unfortunately were destroyed in the fire of the DIES
IRAE. The two first were duplicated after the peace, and
they gained praise and successful sale in New York.

Mr. Guilliam, a French student, worked carefully and
industriously at his Richmond studio, producing portraits
of Lee, Jackson, and others which, having exaggerated
mannerisms of the French school, still possessed no little
merit. A remarkable life-size picture of General Lee which
produced much comment in Richmond was done by a
deaf-mute, Mr. Bruce. It was to have been bought by the
State of Virginia, possibly from sympathy with the subject
and the condition of the artist rather than because of
intrinsic merit as an art-work.

But perhaps the most strikingly original pictures the
war produced were those of John R. Key, a Maryland
lieutenant of engineers [and] one of those descendants of
"The Star Spangled Banner". . . . Young, ambitious, and
but little educated in art, Mr. Key made up that lack in
boldness of subject and treatment. His school was largely
his own, and he went for his subjects far out of the beaten
track, treating them afterward with marked boldness and
dash.

"Drewry's Bluff" was a boldly handled sketch of what
the Northern army persisted in calling "Fort Darling." It
showed the same venturesome originality in color-use, the
same breadth and fidelity that marked Mr. Key's later

pictures of Sumter, Charleston Harbor, and scenes on the James River.

These pictures named in common, with minor sketches from pencils less known at that time—among them that of William L. Sheppard, now famous as graphic delineator of Southern scenes—illustrate both the details of the unique war and the taste and heart of those who made it. Amid battles, sieges, and sorrows, the mimic world behind the Chinese wall revolved on axis of its own. War was the business of life to every man; but, on the short pauses of its active strife were shown both the taste and talent for the prettiest pursuits of peace. And the apparently unsurmountable difficulties through which these were essayed makes their even partial development more remarkable still.

The press, the literature, and the art of the Southern Confederacy—looked at in the light of her valor and endurance, shining from her hundred battlefields—emphasize strongly the inborn nature of her people. And while there were many whom the limits of this sketch leave unnamed, that sin of omission will not be registered against the author; for the men of the South—even in minor matters—did their work for the object and for the cause, not for self-illustration.[11]

V: INFLATION

Because it was an agricultural region and profits were reinvested in slaves and land—property in which there was no quick turnover—the South had always suffered from a shortage of hard money. This shortage created a problem that the Confederate government never solved— how to finance the war.

By seizure of Federal customs houses and branch mints, by sequestration of property of Northerners who were now aliens, by import duties, and by an early sale of bonds, the Treasury was able to accumulate $30,000,000 in gold. In addition, there was about $25,000,000 in specie in Southern banks, but about half of it was in New Orleans and most of the New Orleans gold was lost when that city fell in April 1862.

Neither the Confederate Congress nor the states ever faced up to the duty of imposing heavy war taxes. According to Robert Toombs, the Confederate government collected not a single cent of taxes during the entire first year of the war and postponed until a later period collection of those levied for the second year. A distinguished scholar of the period estimates that all taxes raised through the life of the Confederacy amounted only to about one per cent of its expenditures.

For the other ninety-nine per cent of its income the

government was forced to rely on bond issues and Treasury notes. In order to enable farmers and planters without money to purchase bonds, Congress, in May 1861, passed an act known as the Produce Loan. J. D. B. De Bow was appointed chief agent of the Treasury to market the bonds authorized by the act. Shortly thereafter he issued an appeal to Southern patriotism.

The duty which has been assigned us of organizing and regulating the details of matters connected with the COTTON AND OTHER PRODUCE LOAN is one that will require patient labor, and one in which we trust to perform an acceptable public service. In the resource which is here opened the Government, by the liberality and patriotism of its citizens, will find its arm made strong and supported in the giant struggle in which it is engaged. Already millions of dollars have been subscribed under a formula which follows, and the aggregate will be swelled several fold before the canvass is completed:

We, the subscribers agree to contribute to the defense of the Confederate States, the portion of our crops set down to our respective names; the same to be placed in warehouse or in our factors' hands, and sold on or before the first day of ———— next; and the net proceeds of sale we direct to be paid over to the Treasurer of the Confederate States, for Bonds for same amount bearing 8 per cent interest.

Planters of the South, the appeal is in an especial manner to you. In the great resources of our soil, blessed as it now is with prolific harvests, the ready means are afforded of sustaining the armies that have been or may hereafter be called into the field to maintain our liberties and possessions, menaced by an enemy who threatens no less than subjugation and extermination. Come forward and come promptly. Whilst half of our people are in arms the other half are competent by their resources to keep them in the field. Bring forth these resources, or such part of them as shall be beyond your pressing wants, and make an offering of them on the altar of your country. Thousands have already responded to the call, and the thought is not entertained for a moment that any one will hesitate. The vindications of our rights and the speedy termination of the war depend upon the unanimity and the prompt responses of the people to every call that shall be made upon them.[1]

This ingenious scheme to provide the necessities of war in a money-shy economy met with indifferent success. The act as amended provided for issuance of $100,000,000 worth of bonds. But only about $35,000,000 was eventually subscribed, almost a third of which for one reason or another was never collected.

Meanwhile, in order to obtain some ready cash the government had, in March, issued a million dollars in interest-bearing Treasury notes. But five months later the Congress committed the country to a program from which there was no turning back. At that time it passed

AN ACT to authorize the issue of Treasury notes and to provide a war tax for their redemption.

THE CONGRESS OF THE CONFEDERATE STATES OF AMERICA DO ENACT, That the Secretary of the Treasury be, and he is hereby, authorized, from time to time, as the public necessities may require, to issue Treasury notes payable to bearer at the expiration of six months after the ratification of a treaty of peace between the Confederate States and the United States, the said notes to be of any denomination not less than $5, and to be reissuable at pleasure until the same are payable; but the whole issue outstanding at one time, including the amount issued under former acts, shall not exceed $100,000,000. The said notes shall be receivable in payment of the war tax hereinafter provided and of all other public dues except the export duty on cotton, and shall also be received in payment of the subscriptions of the net proceeds of sales of raw produce and manufactured articles.

SEC. 2. That for the purpose of funding the said notes

and of making exchange for the proceeds of the sale of raw produce and manufactured articles or for the purchase of specie or military stores, the Secretary of the Treasury, with the assent of the President, is authorized to issue bonds, payable not more than twenty years after date, and bearing a rate of interest not exceeding 8 per cent per annum until they become payable . . . the said bonds not to exceed in the whole $100,000,000. . . . The said bonds shall not be issued in less sums than $100. . . .

SEC. 3. The holders of the said Treasury notes may at any time demand in exchange for them bonds of the Confederate States. . . .

SEC. 4. That for the special purpose of paying the principal and interest of the public debt and of supporting the Government, a war tax shall be assessed and levied of 50 cents upon each $100 in value of the following property in the Confederate States, namely: Real estate of all kinds; slaves; merchandise; bank stocks; railroad and other corporation stocks; money at interest or invested by individuals . . . except the bonds of the Confederate States of America, and cash on hand or on deposit in bank or elsewhere; cattle, horses, and mules; gold watches, gold and silver plate, pianos, and pleasure carriages. . . .

SEC. 5. That . . . each state shall constitute a tax division, over which shall be appointed one chief collector. . . .

SEC. 24. If any state shall, on or before the first day of April next, pay in the Treasury notes of the Confederate States or in specie the taxes assessed against the citizens of such state, less 10 per cent thereon, it shall be the duty of the Secretary of the Treasury to notify the same to the several tax collectors of such state, and thereupon their authority and duty under this act shall cease.[2]

The tax of one-half of one per cent levied by this act on all kinds of property, including land and slaves, was permissible under the Provisional Constitution, then in force. But under the permanent Constitution, which be-

came effective the next year, such a tax must be apportioned among the states according to a census which was to be taken within three years. As the census was never taken, this lucrative tax source was constitutionally unavailable after 1861. It should be noted, too, that the act permitted the states to assume the tax and receive a ten per cent credit for collection expenses. All but three of the states paid their quotas by borrowing instead of passing the tax on to their people.

The effect of this heavy borrowing without adequate taxation was sharp inflation and a withholding of products from market. Conditions were growing serious by the spring of 1862. At that time the Montgomery Advertiser *spoke of*

ENEMIES AT HOME.—There is scarcely an article to be found in the market either to eat or to wear, which has not been affected by the vile crew of speculators. Especially is this the case with the necessaries of life and in the articles most generally used for wearing apparel throughout the country. Cloth for soldiers' clothing has been sold for three or four times its cost to the merchant, and the poor men and women whose needs compelled them to make the purchase at any price have been looked upon as legitimate prey by the sharpers. There must be a limit to this. If the spirit of extortion and speculation in the South is not soon checked it will utterly blast and destroy everything in its course. If men will persist in turning a deaf ear to the appeals of patriotism and common honesty, they may not be able to close them to a suggestion from the civil or military authorities. . . . If the South should fail in her struggle for independence, it will not be because she has been conquered by our Northern enemies, but it will be through the selfishness, the accursed thirst for gain which has manifested itself and been allowed to develop until it has nearly overspread the land. . . . In the name of eternal justice, a just cause, and an outraged people, we ask that a stop be put to this swindling and robbery which has too long been carried on.[3]

But things grew steadily worse. Six months after the Advertiser's complaint against "speculators and extortioners" Governor Zebulon Vance of North Carolina told his legislature that "the demon of speculation and extortion seems to have seized upon nearly all sorts and conditions of men, and all the necessaries of life are fast getting beyond the reach of the poor." And Jefferson Davis agreed that speculation was creating a crisis. "It has," he said, "seemed to take possession of the whole country, and has seduced citizens of all classes from a determined prosecution of the war to a sordid effort to amass money." On January 20, 1863, J. B. Jones entered in his diary a list of groceries, comparing current and prewar prices. His chart showed that costs had risen more than tenfold in three years.

With prices rising mercilessly and Congress unable or unwilling to devise or levy sufficient taxes, the government had no recourse but to issue more currency. More currency led to ever more speculation in commodities and thus to still higher prices. By the beginning of 1863, alarm was general and T. S. Bocock, Speaker of the Confederate House of Representatives, wrote Secretary Memminger asking what Congress should do. In answer Memminger said:

In a former report it was shown that the circulation of the Confederate States before the war might be estimated at $100,000,000. In the existing state of things it is probable that a larger amount of currency is required. In time of peace money passes rapidly from hand to hand, and the same money in a single day will discharge many obligations. A large portion, too, of the operations of business are performed by bills of exchange and bank checks. In the present stagnation of commerce and intercourse larger amounts of ready money are kept on hand by each individual and the Confederate Treasury notes and call certificates are used as a substitute for bills and drafts as much as 50 per cent to the usual amounts of currency, and this would raise the sum total at which it might stand to $150,000,000. The difference between this sum and the actual circulation will show the redundancy. . . .

The issue of Treasury notes on the last day of December amounted to $290,149,692, exclusive of interest-bearing notes. By adding to this sum a sufficient amount to cover the state treasury notes and the bank notes in circulation we can arrive at the sum total of the currency; $20,000,-000 added to the Treasury notes would probably represent the whole. It is this aggregate which must be kept in view when we deal with the currency as a measure of values. It is the whole mass as it is accepted by the community in exchange for its various commodities which by its proportional relation to those commodities determines their prices. By a law as invariable as any law of physical nature these prices rise or fall with the actual volume of the whole currency. Neither skill nor power can vary the result. It is in fact a relation subsisting between two numbers, the one representing the total values of property and the other the total circulating medium. The nature of that medium cannot change it. It would exist with a currency of gold with as much certainty as with one of paper, if the gold were kept within the country by restraints equal to those which retain the paper. Assuming, then, that entire confidence exists in our currency, the mere fact that its actual volume has been increased threefold, would lead us to expect a corresponding increase in prices. Such increase, although eventually certain, does not usually appear at the same moment with the expansion. . . . Prices will reach the height adjusted by the scale of issues and they can only be restored to their usual condition by a return to the normal standard of currency. In other words, the only remedy for an inflated currency is a reduction of the circulating medium. . . .

To be effective the currency must be reduced at least

to $150,000,000, already shown to be its extreme limit, and this reduction must be so prompt as to take effect before prices can undergo further increase. . . . But it is essential to good faith that ample means should be provided by the government to secure and pay the principal and interest of the securities in which the holders are required to invest. This can only be effected by an ample and permanent tax. Such a tax is the cornerstone of the whole fabric. Without it the scheme has no foundation and can secure neither public confidence nor success.[4]

Meanwhile the press was clamoring for action that would save the situation. In March 1863 the Richmond Enquirer *said:*

We are the advocates of taxation because we believe it to be the only mode and means by which a nation can provide for its pecuniary necessities. It is the CHEAPEST, as well as the only, means of defraying the expenses of the war. Our people are paying daily in all their necessary wants higher and more onerous taxes because of the present redundant currency than is required for the expense of the war. Any system of taxation which will speedily reduce the currency to a specie base will be a measure of relief, and should be adopted by Congress. To ORIGINATE a tax bill is the duty of the House of Representatives, a duty wholly and shamefully neglected by that body; a dereliction of duty which cannot and shall not be forgotten. . . .

The people are demanding a tax bill, and the press of the country, without an exception, have urged the measure; and yet the House of Representatives hesitates and wastes in useless palaver the valuable time of the country, imposing by its delay daily an ever-recurring tax, onerous and ruinous to all business of the country, and yet returning not one dollar to the Treasury. This daily tax is paid by every man that spends a Confederate dollar, the real value of which is only about thirty cents. . . .

We understand that a tax bill of one per centum is

talked of; but whether the one per centum is upon actual capital, or upon profits, or both combined, we are unable to say. . . . One per centum will do upon some kinds of businesses, but is it not simply absurd upon many others? For instance—take the Crenshaw Woolen Factory and the Belvidere Manufacturing Company. These concerns were lately examined before a committee of the Virginia House of Delegates on Extortion and business facts of a startling character were brought to light.

President [William G.] Crenshaw deposed on oath that his company on a cash capital of $200,000 had declared and divided a dividend of $530,000 with $100,000 "subject for dividend, should the directors think it desirable."

President Whitfield, of the Paper Mill, deposed on oath that the "net profits for the years 1860, 1861, and 1862 combined amounted to $235,750" on an "actual capital of $41,000" and, he added, that "fully three-fourths of the dividend mentioned above was made in 1862." . . . A stockholder of the Belvidere Manufacturing Company informed us that since the war began, he had received dividends on $1,000 of shares, amounting to $6,450. . . .

Is there not ample room here for taxation? What is one per cent upon the actual capital of the Crenshaw Woolen Company?—$200,000 at one per cent is $2,000. On the paper mill $41,000 at one per cent is $410. What is one per cent on the profits of the Crenshaw Woolen Company? Only $6,000—which added to the $2,000 imposed upon the capital would amount to only $8,000. The tax of one per cent, on the capital of the paper mill would be $410; on the profit of the paper mill would be $2,357.50; in both combined $2,767.50. Is not such taxation worse than ridiculous on such profits?

It is concerns like these that should be made to bleed by taxation as they have made the public bleed through its necessities. It is nonsense to investigate the cost of manufacture where such profits are admitted. A tax bill upon a rising scale, that starts at one per centum on actual capital and profits under ten per centum of the capital and that rises with increasing ratio as the per centum of profits increase, should at once be adopted.

We have selected these two concerns because the evidence of their presidents before the Extortion Committee have furnished reliable data for example.

There are doubtless many other concerns throughout the country whose profits have been equally large.

There can be no dodging or shirking this question of taxation. Congress must meet it and must draw from soulless corporations the hoarded wealth of immense profits. The soldier that returns from the army and looks upon the charred ruins of a once prosperous and happy home and finds himself in poverty, will very naturally inquire how some pampered PARVENU had been able to purchase a fine estate or to own many houses and town lots.[5]

At about the same time the Augusta (Georgia), Chronicle and Sentinel commented:

Our Congress has been in session more than a year and has as yet passed no tax bill. It is the custom of our state legislature, of our city council, and of every government in the world to levy an annual tax; but our Congressmen entered upon their duties twelve months since and have done nothing towards supplying the Treasury. Engaged as we are in the most gigantic and the most expensive war the world has ever seen, in comparison with which the outlays of the English or the French in the Crimean campaign were insignificant, our public men at Richmond seem to think we can go on forever with promise to pay. New issues of Confederate notes are voted without difficulty or delay; but money bills or tax bills they seem to dread as if all were sure to lose their places if they called on the people for a single dollar. The Chairman of the Committee on Ways and Means introduced a bill last year and pressed it on the House with earnestness and ability, but it was lost; and the Confederate States are without any revenue except the duties received from a few vessels that run the blockade. Such a state of affairs is not only disgraceful, but ruinous. Our cause cannot succeed without money. Soldiers and money are the sinews of war, and the one is as indispensable as the other.[6]

In response to these and other urgent appeals Congress passed its first comprehensive tax bill in April 1863. It combined features of license, sales, and income taxes. There was an eight per cent ad valorem tax on all products of farm and forest. Licenses were placed on all occupations that could be classified. There was a special ten per cent tax on profits from sales of merchandise—this aimed at speculators—and there was a graduated income tax. The most ingenious feature of this bill, however, was aimed at circumventing the constitutional restriction on the taxing of slaves and land.

THE CONGRESS OF THE CONFEDERATE STATES OF AMERICA DO ENACT. . . .

Sec. 11. Each farmer and planter in the Confederate States, after reserving for his own use fifty bushels of sweet potatoes and fifty bushels of Irish potatoes, one hundred bushels of the corn or fifty bushels of the wheat produced in the present year, shall pay and deliver to the Confederate government, of the products of the present year, one-tenth of the wheat, corn, oats, rye, buckwheat or rice, sweet and Irish potatoes, and of the cured hay and fodder; also one-tenth of the sugar, molasses made of cane, cotton, wool and tobacco; the cotton ginned and packed in some secure manner, and tobacco shipped and packed in boxes, to be delivered by him on or before the first day of March in the next year. Each farmer or planter, after reserving twenty bushels of peas or beans, but not more than twenty bushels of both, for his own use, shall deliver to the Confederate government, for its use, one-tenth of the peas, beans and ground peas produced and gathered by him during the present year. . . . The said producer shall be required to deliver the wheat, corn, oats, rye, buckwheat, rice, peas, beans, cured hay and fodder, sugar, molasses of cane, wool and tobacco, this to be paid as a tithe in kind, in such form and ordinary marketable condition as may be usual in the section in which they are to be delivered, and the cotton in such manner as hereinbefore provided, within two months from the time they have been estimated as aforesaid, at some depot not more than eight miles from the place of production, and if not delivered by that time, in such order, he shall be liable to pay fifty per cent more than the estimated value of the portion aforesaid, to be collected by the tax-collector as hereinafter prescribed. . . .

Sec. 12. That every farmer, planter or grazier shall exhibit to the assessor, on or about the first of March, eighteen hundred and sixty-four, an account of all the hogs he may have slaughtered since the passage of this act and before that time. After the delivery of this estimate to the post quartermaster hereinafter mentioned by the assessor, the said farmer, planter, or grazier shall deliver an equivalent for one-tenth of the same in cured bacon, at the rate of sixty pounds of bacon to the one hundredweight of pork. That on the first of November next, and each year thereafter, an estimate shall be made, as hereinbefore provided, of the value of all meat cattle, horses, mules, not used in cultivation, and asses owned by each person in the Confederate States, and upon such value of the said owners shall be taxed one per cent, to be paid on or before the first day of January next ensuing.[7]

This was known as the tax-in-kind. The act was amended from time to time, but its basic structure was preserved throughout the life of the Confederacy. It was difficult to administer, was not uniformly enforced, and caused much bitterness among farmers. About $150,-000,000 worth of produce was collected under this act, but because of spoilage and transportation and other difficulties less than a third reached the armies.

To supply its needs the army had early begun to impress food and forage. This was done without legal sanc-

tion until March 1863, when Congress passed a complex law legalizing and regulating the procedure. But the problems facing those responsible for supplying Confederate armies were staggering. In November 1863, six months after passage of the impressment law, Secretary of War Seddon wrote President Davis:

The inflation of the currency and the insatiable thirst for gain and speculation induced by it have caused inordinate enhancement of the prices of all products, and a yet continuing advance, stimulated in part by the increasing volume of the currency and in part by the sordid calculation of large gains from hoarding by holders or speculators. To this has likewise contributed some distrust, not of the cause of the Confederacy, but of its future ability, however earnest its desire to preserve its credit and good faith, to redeem the large issues which such enhancements of price rendered inevitable. The consequences have been an almost universal repugnance on the part of producers and holders to sell at any price, except under compulsion.

This evil had begun to manifest itself before the close of the last Congress to such a degree that some legislative remedy was recognized to be indispensable. To buy at current prices was seen to be suicidal to the credit of the government, to swell its indebtedness, in a brief period, beyond its utmost capacities for redemption, and at the same time to raise by daily accessions the advancing scale of extravagant prices, until both the fears and interest of the holders would forbid sales at all.

Under these circumstances Congress devised and authorized a system of impressment of all property required "for the good of the service," or the accumulation of adequate supplies for the Army, at the same time recognizing that under the exceptional circumstances of the country and the disturbance of the ordinary laws of trade regulating supply and demand current prices constituted no criterion of just compensation required by the

Constitution to be allowed for the appropriation of private property to public uses. Congress provided for the ascertainment of such just compensation by reference, in the first instance, in part to local appraisers, and then to two commissioners to be appointed for each state, one by the Governor and the other by the President of the Confederacy. These officers, combining by their appointment the sanction of the state and Confederate authorities, were not only to entertain appeals from local appraisements, but from time to time to ascertain and prescribe fair rates of valuation to govern in impressments.

As there seems no other alternative this was, perhaps, as judicious an arrangement on this delicate and difficult subject as was practicable, and on it the government has been compelled to rely almost exclusively during the past year. This resource, operating with increasing stringency and strain, is at this time its only reliance. The evils attending it are, however, very great, and only less than the failure or deficiency of supplies which, so far, it has managed to avert. Impressment is evidently a harsh, unequal, and odious mode of supply. With the utmost forbearance and consideration even its occasional exercise is harassing and irritating; but when it has to prevail as a general practice, to be exercised inquisitorially and summarily in almost every private domain by a multitude of subordinate officers, it becomes beyond measure offensive and repugnant to the sense of justice and prevalent sentiment of our people. It has been, perhaps, the sorest test of their patriotism and self-sacrificing spirit afforded by the war, and no other people, it is believed, would have endured it without undue manifestations of discontent and resistance. It has caused much murmuring and dissatisfaction, but a knowledge of the necessities which alone justified it has caused the outcry to be directed rather to the mode and, as alleged, occasional excesses of its exercise than against the system itself. . . .

Yet it is found that all prices have only the more rapidly

advanced and are still advancing, and that neither are the markets of the city adequately supplied nor can consumers, by purchase at current rates, without the utmost difficulty supply themselves.

The truth is that the explanation, as the cause, is to be found outside of the impressment law or the action under it. The real difficulty is that the price advancing from day to day with an accelerated ratio and a steady depreciation of the currency, the holders, unless required by positive necessity, prefer to retain their supplies and will not sell for any temptation of present price.

The impressment law is, in fact, almost the only corrective of this feeling, which would else be well-nigh universal. It favors the supply of the market and of consumers. The apprehension that surplus products if retained may be impressed by the government at the rates prescribed by the state appraisers constitutes the strongest, as it is nearly the only, inducement to holders to sell at market rates. Setting aside feelings of humanity and patriotism, which to a creditable degree may induce sales, and testing the matter by the general motive of self-interest alone, this is a plain matter of calculation, who would sell unless forced by a present necessity for the money, when constant advance in the price of the product is sure, and the money, if received at once, is no less certain of its depreciation before the occasion of its future use? The difficulty, therefore, with the consumer, as with the government, is the redundancy of the currency and the consequent steady inflation of prices. This in its direct, and even more in its indirect, influences, not merely on the market and on the property of citizens but on their instincts of selfishness, on their sentiments, tastes, and aspirations, is a fearful evil, and more demoralizing to our people than the more dire calamities of war. . . . If the present system be continued, prices, already many hundred per cent above true values, must be indefinitely enhanced, the credit of the government must be wrecked utterly, and no alternative left for the continuance of our patriotic struggle and the preservation of our lives and liberties but grinding taxation and the systematized seizure, with present compensation, of all supplies needed for the employees as well as the armies of the Confederacy.[8]

At the same time Seddon was concerned about the welfare of the clerks in his department.

The inflation of the currency and inordinate prices of all supplies have caused to the Department a painful embarrassment from the inadequacy of the salaries and allowances to its clerks and employees to maintain them. Single men in such positions are barely able to subsist on their official compensation, and those with families, when without other means, have been obliged to yield their places, depend on the charity of friends, or suffer dire privations. Cases of such real suffering have resulted from this cause that it would be culpable remissness or unfeeling obduracy not to urge earnestly a more just provision for them. Their whole time and labor are given with a zeal, devotion, and industry rarely surpassed, to the toilsome and unostentatious duties of the bureaus and offices. Means, at least, of subsistence and lodging should be accorded without delay by the government to such faithful laborers.[9]

But there was something to be said for the farmers whose produce was taken. The "pressmen," as they were called, became the most hated of government officials. In December 1863 Governor John Milton of Florida received a letter from a farmer in Calhoun County.

After my best respects to you as my friend and chief justice of the state of Florida, I avail myself of this opportunity of writing to you a few lines to ascertain if it is the law for these "pressmen" to take the cows from the soldiers' families and leave them to starve. Colonel [J. P.] Coker has just left my house with a drove for Marianna of about 200 or 300 head. Some of my neighbors went after him and begged him to give them their milch cows, which he, Mr. Coker, refused to do, and took them on. And now, my dear Governor, I assure you on the honor of a gentleman, that to my knowledge there are soldiers' families in my neighborhood that the last head of cattle have been taken from them and drove off, and unless this pressing of cows is stopped speedily there won't be a cow left in Calhoun County. I know of several soldiers' families in this county that haven't had one grain of corn in the last three weeks, nor any likelihood of their getting any in the next three months; their few cows taken away and they left to starve; their husbands slain on the battlefield at Chattanooga. This is a true state of things in my county; I vouch for them as an honest man.

Now, if this is law I should be glad to know it, so I could know how to act by the law, for I have had a different notion of the law; and as a sound man I think this pressing of all the cattle will have a bad end, in my judgment, and I am not all that think so. I think if it could be stopped it would have a good effect on this part of the community. I should be obliged to you if you feel a freedom to write me on this subject soon, as I look upon procrastination as the great thief of time.

I remain, your obedient servant,
JOHN R. RICHARDS.[10]

But not all impressment agents were as zealous as those in Calhoun County, Florida. They generally fixed prices considerably under the market, which made their task the harder, as farmers used every stratagem to prevent seizure of their products. Then in July 1864 commissioners in Virginia suddenly announced a schedule of prices far in excess of those prevailing to stimulate the flow of goods. A Virginia farmer wrote the Secretary of War.

I feel impelled by a sense of duty to apprise you of the state of public sentiment in this section of the state with reference to the schedule of prices recently adopted and published by the commissioners. It has cast a gloom over this community, and done more to destroy the Confederate

currency than any circumstance which has transpired
since the commencement of the war. I have conversed
with many farmers on the subject, and have yet to meet
with the first man who does not express the most profound regret on account of this action of the commissioners. They all say it was entirely unlooked for and has
taken them completely by surprise. I am perfectly confident that the government could have gotten just as much
wheat in this county by offering $10 per bushel as by
offering $30.

Under a recent circular issued from your Department
making an appeal for grain the people of this county
will furnish liberally from their exhausted supplies, notwithstanding the enemy has recently visited us and
foraged all over the county. The fears of patriotic men
everywhere are aroused for the currency. They had
fondly hoped that under the recent legislation of Congress
the currency would soon be improved, but now they
regard this action of the commissioners as a declaration on
the part of the Government that the depreciation of the
currency cannot and will not be remedied, and plain men
cannot understand how the government is ever to redeem
its obligations and pay off a debt piled up at the rates
fixed by the commissioners. In other words, they look
upon repudiation as almost inevitable. It is in this view
of the subject that our farmers would prefer to have their
wheat taken at $10 per bushel than at $30.

Again, all the counties of this commonwealth have a
large number of soldiers' families to support, and in doing
so they find themselves compelled under this act of assembly to resort to impressment. They cannot impress at a
lower rate than the government, and how can they pay
the enormous debt which will be incurred by paying $30
per bushel for wheat, $24 for corn, and $25 for corn meal?
How are the nonproducers of the country to live when the
inevitable effect of this action must be to double the prices
of the necessaries of life in the markets? The seller will say

at once that if the government is giving $30 for wheat the market price will be $60, and many of them will hoard with the expectation of realizing that price.

I fully appreciate the difficulties which surround you. I know that the scarcity is great and that our noble army must be fed at all hazards, but have not the commissioners overrated the difficulties? Cannot the army be supplied without inflicting this serious blow upon the currency? Regarding the recent action of the commissioners as more fatal in its consequences than the defeat of our armies in the field, I have taken the liberty of calling your attention to this subject with the earnest hope that their action may be either reversed or essentially modified.

Very respectfully, etc.,

JOHN GOODE, JR.

P. S.—If you deem it inadvisable to change the schedule with reference to the community generally, ought it not to be changed so far as the detailed men are concerned? They were very glad to take the details in order to avoid military service when they supposed they would be required to furnish corn at $4 and wheat at $5 per bushel. So far from rendering service to the government, they will esteem it an inestimable privilege to be allowed to remain at home and furnish their products at those rates.[11]

Within two months the government had priced itself out of the market. Impressment was delegated to the Bureau of Subsistence in the War Department. In September 1864 Commissary-General L. B. Northrop received a letter from one of his subordinates.

I beg leave to call your attention to the fact that we are without fifteen days' supply of meat in this city for the subsistence of General Lee's army and other troops, employees, etc., dependent upon us; nor have we an accumulation in any of the states upon which to draw in the future. The collection of meat from all sources during the past thirty days would not subsist the Army of Northern

Virginia for one week, the operations of the department having been seriously interfered with from the want of adequate means with which to purchase, liquidate accrued indebtedness, and thus restore public confidence, so seriously impaired in many sections of the Confederacy from our past inability to comply with obligations and from the financial policy heretofore pursued.

The impressment act has signally failed in affording the relief that was anticipated, simply because payment is required to be made when the law is enforced, a clause which practically nullifies it, since our restricted means will not enable us to offer currency, and the mass of the people refuse to accept the 6 per cent certificates and nontaxable bonds, although our officers have been instructed to make every effort to induce their acceptance, believing it obligatory upon us to aid the Treasury in every practicable way. In all the states impressments are evaded by every means which ingenuity can suggest, and in some openly resisted. In North Carolina our receipts are insignificant, and in Georgia and Alabama we are unable to purchase corn for want of money, which necessitates the consumption of our limited stock of flour, so desirable to preserve for active campaigning. In Virginia the meat supply has been exhausted, but it is believed that considerable cattle and bacon are yet to be had in Georgia, Alabama, and Mississippi, provided the necessary funds are at our command.

Within thirty days the Army of Tennessee will have consumed the present supply of meat. Our officers in all of the states are fully alive to the interests of the department, but the difficulties which beset them are insurmountable, and must receive due consideration in connection with the present condition of the commissariat.

Very respectfully, your obedient servant,

S. B. FRENCH

Major and Commissary of Subsistence[12]

*As with all business operations of such gigantic nature,
corruption and fraud crept into the impressment service.
In the autumn of 1864 the Secretary of War admonished
a general in the field.*

Richmond, Va., September 27, 1864.
Lieut. Gen. R. Taylor,

Commanding, Meridian, Miss.:

GENERAL: . . .

A second source of abuse is the manner in which private
property has been taken, upon the pretense that it is for
the public use. The power to take private property for
public use is conferred by Congress in the acts concerning
impressments. It is a power to be exercised only in cases
of necessity and according to law.

The general commanding a department can direct an
impressment of property for public use, and this Department has conferred the same power upon the chiefs of the
bureaus of supply by the authority of the law. In either
case the power should be executed under specific orders,
and by officers accountable for the property taken.

In the state of Mississippi, officers of every grade and
of every arm have gone through the state without special
orders, without money, gathering up property where they
could find it, refusing payment, neglecting to ascertain or
adjust the price, leaving insufficient evidence of their acts,
and in most of the cases rendering to none of the departments of supply, nor to the department commanders, any
account of these acts or authority for their acts.

The most scandalous outrages have been practiced upon
the citizens of that state by the lawless conduct of subaltern officers. A special source of grievance is the formation of cavalry bands by the impressment of horses for
the purpose. The general orders of the Department prohibit this. The Department anticipates from your action
a correction of these abuses.[13]

Before the end of the war Confederate currency had practically ceased to be a medium of exchange, and bartering of commodities became general. In December 1864 a South Carolina doctor made an interesting proposal to one of his patients, a lady from one of the most distinguished of the South Carolina rice-planting families.

MY DEAR MRS. ALLSTON, In view of the enhanced price of everything, the Medical Society of this, as well as of many other districts throughout the state, resolved two years ago to double their charges. During the last year the very large advance in the price of horses and of grain necessary to sustain them, found the medical men entirely unable to live at the rates agreed upon, and they again met as a society and resolved to regulate their charges according to the price of grain and forage leaving it to each individual to do the best he could in arranging with his patients for the means of living. In Williamsburg the medical charges are five times the old rates. So in Charleston, and most of the other cities. I am exceedingly reluctant to adopt any rates, that, with some, might prove almost prohibitory. I am too well aware that all classes are suffering severely the privations incident to this cruel war, and that in sickness the distress and affliction is tenfold compared with what we have to endure in ordinary health. After mature deliberation, therefore, I have concluded to continue the OLD RATES of charging for all PAST AND FUTURE services to those who will furnish to me grain or forage AT OLD PRICES. In a large number of cases this proposition has been readily accepted as fair and just, and the easiest way to arrive at a rate of charge satisfactory to all parties. Especially does it seem just and equitable to the agriculturists.

I am willing to receive corn, rice, peas, potatoes, fodder, pork, mutton, lard, butter, eggs, in fact, any and everything that will enable my family to live and feed my horses. Few are aware of my embarrassment, and I would not allude to them, but in justification of the course I have concluded to adopt I have not made one grain for market since 1861. My Negroes removed to Clarendon, so far from being self-supporting in the simple item of BREAD have cost me thousands per year. The last spring with a view to remedy this condition I risked the removal of a portion of them back to the rice fields. The result has been entirely unsatisfactory. The birds have been so destructive that I have not made my provisions, taking all the rice into account in addition to the upland crop. I must purchase provisions to carry me through the next year, and if I have to pay eight and ten times the old prices it seems to me not unreasonable that my bills should be multiplied accordingly. As before stated I am disinclined to this. I prefer being SUPPORTED by contributions of grain etc., and if there are any who think this unreasonable or unjust, they have only to bear in mind that the government is so monopolizing that private individuals are almost debarred the privilege of purchasing even for their families, though in some instances they may be willing to pay three or four times the government schedule rates.

The fact is, at old prices, one year's entire practice will scarce pay for one horse and sulkey at their present valuation. I merely wish to live. My profession has positively not been able to supply horses, vehicles, and harness necessary to carry it on, and the expense of feeding my horses has been for two years past, entirely beyond my receipts.

The proposition to attend at old rates, for grain or provisions of any kind at old prices is general and will be tendered to all who wish my services for the future, or are willing to settle bills of this year in this way. I beg therefore that you will do me the favor to say at once if my proposition is accepted by you, as I must have provisions for the next year, and wish to secure them at once. I shall be very happy to include Col. Ben Allston's interest with yours if you feel authorized to act for him.[14]

By this time there was more than $1,000,000,000 in currency in circulation; the needs of the country could properly have been served by perhaps one-fifth of that amount. Repudiation of one-third of the currency in the preceding spring resulted only in further reducing the confidence of the people. Soon the money was worth little more than the paper on which it was printed.

*To the people of the South the Civil War was considerably
more than high prices, shortages, and reports of loved
ones lost in distant battle. They knew what it was to be
invaded and occupied by an enemy army and what it was
to conform to the will of conquerors. The aggressive
Union armies, although repulsed time and again, returned
relentlessly and with ever-increasing vigor. Many border
areas of the Confederacy—northern and western Virginia
and large portions of the Mississippi Valley—were seized
and held by the enemy from the first year of the war.
Hardy County, Virginia, was such a place, and in September 1861 Jacob Van Meter and others wrote President
Davis:*

The undersigned, citizens of Hardy County, Va., desire
to call your attention to the exposed and suffering condition of our county. We have been invaded for the past few
months by Northern thieves; our houses have been forcibly entered and robbed; our horses, cattle, and sheep in
large numbers driven off; our citizens arrested, carried off
and confined only because they are loyal citizens of
Virginia and the Southern Confederacy. . . .

Our county unfortunately is divided, the western portion being disloyal. The Union men, as they call themselves, have called upon Lincoln for protection. He, in

answer to their call, has sent amongst us a set of base
characters who not only protect the Union men but, under
their guidance, are committing acts unheard of in any
country claiming civilization. We have been wholly un-
protected and unable to protect ourselves. Our enemies
have met with no resistance. We do not complain, as it is
perhaps impossible to give protection to all who are
suffering like depradations; but we would suggest whether
the interest of the Confederacy, apart from the large
private interest involved, does not require the protection
of our beef, our pork, and our corn for the use of the
Southern army. . . . There is perhaps no valley in America of the same extent that produces more fat cattle and
hogs than the valley of the South Branch. Were we protected in the possession of our property we should be able
to supply the army with several thousand cattle and hogs,
and at the season of the year when the supply from other
sources fails; but if no protection should be given us and
the present state of things suffered to go on, we may well
despair not only of feeding the army but of feeding ourselves. . . .

We placed ourselves under the protection of the Confederate States with a full knowledge of our exposed
situation, being a border county, yet relying upon the
ability and willingness of our more Southern brethren,
who are less exposed, to defend us.

We now would most earnestly call upon you . . . for
relief and continued protection, if not inconsistent with
more important interests.[1]

*A year later, New Orleans had fallen and was in the
grip of the notorious Ben Butler. A Massachusetts politician turned soldier, Butler's career in the Crescent City
was turbulent and his conduct questionable, to say the
least. He started off with the barbaric execution of William
B. Mumford, and climaxed his regime with his infamous
"woman order," in which he ordered his troops to treat
as a "woman of the town plying her avocation," any fe-*

*male who was contemptuous or insulting toward Federal
soldiers. Alexander Walker was a citizen who incurred the
wrath of Butler and was arrested. In September 1862 he
wrote President Davis from prison:*

SIR: A close prisoner on this desolate island [Ship
Island, Mississippi] with some fifty others of my fellow
citizens, I have thought it my duty at every risk to communicate to you some, at least, of the incidents of the
administration of the brutal tyrant who has been sent by
the United States government to oppress, rob, assault,
and trample upon our people in every manner, which the
most fiendish ingenuity and most wanton cruelty could
devise, and in gross violation of all the laws and usages of
the most remorseless wars between civilized and even
savage nations and tribes. . . .

A description of the causes and circumstances of the imprisonment of our citizens who are now held on this island
will afford some of the mildest illustrations of Butler's bru-
tality. There are about sixty prisoners here, all of whom are
closely confined in portable houses and furnished with the
most wretched and unwholesome condemned soldiers' rations. Some are kept at hard labor on the fort; several, in
addition to labor, are compelled to wear a ball and chain
which is never removed. Among these is Mr. Shepherd, a
respectable, elderly, and weakly citizen, who is charged
with secreting certain papers belonging to the naval
officer of the Confederate States, which the latter left in
his charge when he departed from New Orleans. Mr.
Shepherd had the proof that the officer who had deposited
these documents afterwards returned and took them and
that they had been carried into the Confederate States.
This testimony Butler would not receive and declared that
if it existed it would make no difference in his case.

Doctor Moore, a dealer in drugs, is also at hard labor
with ball and chain, on the charge of having sent a few
ounces of quinine into the Confederate States. . . . Alder-
man Beggs, on the charge of denouncing those who, having

taken the oath to the Confederate States, afterwards swore allegiance to the United States, and Mr. Keller, a vender of books, stationery, and scientific apparatus, on the charge of permitting a clerk to placard the word "Chicka-hominy" on a skeleton which was suspended in his show window for sale for the use of students of anatomy, are condemned also to close imprisonment and hard labor for two years. . . .

A like condemnation and punishment were imposed upon Judge John W. Andrews, a most respectable citizen, recently a member of the judiciary of the state, of the legislature, and of the city council, and a prominent merchant. This gentleman is advanced in years and in very delicate health. There is little hope that his health can long sustain his present burdens and hardships. The circumstances of Mrs. Phillips' imprisonment are probably known to you. As, however, I desire this to be an authentic and studiously accurate statement of the facts I will here relate them.

In the raid of the U. S. troops near Warrenton, Miss., a young officer named De Kay was mortally wounded. He died in New Orleans and an attempt was made by the Federal authorities to get up a pompous funeral ceremony and procession in honor of so "gallant and heroic a young officer," who had fallen in an expedition which had no other purpose or object but the pillage of defenseless farms and villages. The efforts to excite the sympathies of our people on this occasion proved a ridiculous failure, and the funeral ceremony had no aspect of solemnity or even propriety, a long line of carriages composing the cortege designed for the Union citizens being all empty.

As this procession passed the residence of P. Phillips, Esq., Mrs. Phillips, standing on the balcony with several lady friends, was observed by some Federal officer to smile, so it was charged. She was immediately arrested and taken before Butler who, in the most brutal and insolent manner, sought to terrify the heroic lady. In this he did not succeed. Whilst denying that her gaiety had any reference whatever to the funeral ceremony, Mrs. Phillips refused to make any apologies or concessions to the vulgar tyrant. Thereupon she was condemned to close imprisonment in a filthy guardroom, thence to be transported to Ship Island, where she was to be held in close confinement for two years with no other fare but soldiers' rations, no intercourse or correspondence with any person, except through General Butler.

This sentence was published in the newspapers, accompanied by words of the grossest insult and most vulgar ribaldry, in which Mrs. Phillips was denounced as "not a common but an uncommon bad woman," referring to his proclamation, denounced by Lord Palmerston and the whole civilized world as "so infamous," in which his soldiers are authorized to treat "as common women plying their profession" all who may manifest any contempt or discourtesy toward them. To add further insult, in the order condemning Mr. Keller it was made part of his sentence to permit him to hold converse and intercourse with Mrs. Phillips, to which condition this honest man was induced to protest from the belief that his fellow prisoner was a notorious courtesan of the city who bore the name Phillips.

This protest was published in the paper with Butler's order granting the request of Keller, so as to convey to the world the idea that a poor vender of periodicals declined association with a lady of the highest respectability, the wife of a distinguished lawyer and ex-member of Congress. I can bear personal testimony to the rigorous execution of the sentence against Mrs. Phillips, having been imprisoned for weeks in a building adjoining to that which she was never allowed to leave. Such was the treatment of a delicate lady of the highest refinement, the mother of nine children. . . .

So much for the prisoners at Ship Island, with the facts of whose cases I am personally acquainted. I refrain from any reference to my own case, hard as my doom is, closely confined on this island with all my property appropriated by the enemy and my family placed under strict espionage and subject to many annoyances, insults, and discomforts. With all its trials and hardships the condition of the prisoners here is quite easy and endurable compared with that of those who are confined in the damp and unwholesome casemates of Forts Jackson and Saint Phillip, on the Mississippi, and in Fort Pickens, on Santa Rosa Island. Among the latter is the mayor of the city, who has been imprisoned for four months for the offense of writing a letter to Butler protesting against his order relative to the treatment of the ladies of the city and declaring his inability to maintain the peace of the city if the Federal soldiers were thus authorized to insult and outrage our women at their own pleasure and will. The secretary of the mayor, who wrote the letter signed by the mayor, was included in the same committal and imprisonment. Several members of the council for like or smaller offenses suffer the same punishment. . . . There are, too, many prisoners who are confined on the information of political and personal enemies as dangerous characters for offenses alleged to have been committed by them months and years before Butler's arival in the city.

Doctor McPhevroa, an elderly and most respectable citizen, was condemned to the casemates of Fort Jackson for speaking in a circle of his friends of Butler's proclamation, No. 28, that relative to the ladies of New Orleans, as "infamous," the very epithet which Lord Palmerston in the House of Commons declared as the only appropriate one. Dr. Warren Stone, the distinguished surgeon and philanthropist, was consigned to a like punishment for refusing to recognize an individual who had been announced as president of a Union association and yet who, a few months before, had made in public a most violent speech against the Yankess and had advised our people to cut the throats of all invaders.

Several ladies of the highest social position have been imprisoned for the expression of sympathy with the Confederates and the wearing of ribbons of certain colors. Mrs. Dubois, an elderly lady long engaged in the business of teaching our children, was imprisoned on the charge of not being able to account for certain keys and books belonging to the schools which were never in her possession. . . . There are many other cases of equal atrocity and hardships of citizens of the highest respectability, who upon the most frivolous charges have been dragged from their homes by a brutal soldiery and immured in cells or the casemates of forts and condemned to hard labor. I have not the time nor the exact information to state these cases fully. The prisons of New Orleans are crowded with citizens whose highest offense consists in the expressions of opinions and hopes of the success of the Confederate cause. Not a few are confined for repeating reports of Confederate victories or for having in their possession newspapers containing such reports. . . .

Besides these instances there are a great many citizens who have only escaped imprisonment by the payment of large fines, and in many cases by corrupting Federal officers of influence. To enumerate the cases of confiscation by order of Butler, and in many cases even by the order of his subordinates, would exceed the bounds I have affixed to this report. I have, however, kept a record of these cases and will communicate them at some other time. Suffice it to say that nearly all the large and commodious houses of our citizens, especially those of absentees and officers in our army and government, have been thus appropriated. Officers of no higher grade than lieutenants occupy houses which have cost our citizens $30,000; and where furniture has been removed, and when deficient any articles which the appropriators may deem necessary to their comfort, are purchased at the expense of the owners of the property. The wives and families of our citizens are frequently ejected from their houses to make way for coarse Federal officers and the

Negro women whom they appropriate as their wives and concubines. Ships have been loaded with costly articles of furniture stolen—they say confiscated—from our citizens and transmitted North to the families of Federal officers. . . . A vast amount of silver has been appropriated in like manner.

The example was set by Butler in appropriating the house of General [David E.] Twiggs's minor heir and furnishing it in a most lavish and luxurious style at the expense of the estate, and in transmitting the plate and swords of the deceased veteran to Lowell; the seizure and removal to the North of the statue of Washington by Powers and of the state library from the capitol at Baton Rouge, have been extensively followed by Butler's subordinates. Nor have I here space to expose the extortions of Butler through the agency of his brother, an abandoned gambler and speculator, who has compelled our citizens by all kinds of threats to sell their property to him at rates fixed by him . . . who has acted as broker to obtain remissions of penalties and the restoration of fugitive slaves, in many cases on condition of the payment of half their value and on pledges of half the growing crops. . . .

I content myself with this mere epitome of Butler's crimes. . . . It would not be becoming in me to solicit or suggest that some steps be taken by the President and government of the Confederate States to correct and to avenge these wrongs done our people. . . . I cannot but say, however, that a feeling prevails among our people that they have been forgotten or abandoned by the government for which they suffer.[2]

Up the river at Vicksburg, six months later, a Union army was besieging that stronghold, and the country around became occupied territory. Union soldiers were a disturbing influence in the relations of master and slave. In the Louisiana country across the river, the Emancipation Proclamation was being implemented, and fear of slave uprisings or desertions was causing many owners to

*flee. Sometimes carrying their slaves with them, these
refugees made their way into the interior and even to
Texas. Kate Stone had noted a changed attitude on the
part of her mother's slaves, as well as those of her neighbors. In the spring of 1863 she recorded in her diary:*

On Thursday, March 26, hearing that Mr. Hardison had
returned from Monroe, Sister and I walked up in the
afternoon to hear what news he had brought. As we approached the house it struck me that something was
wrong. As we were going through the garden, George
Richards came out and told us a party of Yankees and
armed Negroes had just left, carrying with them every
Negro on the place, most of Mrs. Hardison's and the children's clothes, and all the provisions they could manage.
They were led by Charles, Mr. Hardison's most trusted
servant, and they were all vowing vengeance against Mr.
Hardison. They said they would shoot him on sight for
moving two of his Negroes a few days before. Mr. Hardison had fortunately seen them coming and, knowing he
would be arrested or perhaps killed as a conscript officer,
had escaped to the woods.

We walked in and found Mrs. Hardison and the children all much excited and very angry, with flaming cheeks
and flashing eyes. The Negroes had been very impertinent.
The first armed Negroes they had ever seen. Just as we
were seated someone called out the Yankees were coming
again. It was too late to run. All we could do was to shut
ourselves up together in one room, hoping they would
not come in. George Richards was on the gallery. In a
minute we heard the gate open and shut, rough hoarse
voices, a volley of oaths, and then a cry: "Shoot him,
curse him! Shoot him! Get out of the way so I can get
him."

Looking out of the window, we saw three fiendish-look-
ing, black Negroes standing around George Richards, two
with their guns leveled and almost touching his breast.
He was deathly pale but did not move. We thought he

would be killed instantly, and I shut my eyes that I might not see it. But after a few words from George, which we could not hear, and another volley of curses, they lowered their guns and rushed into the house "to look for guns," they said, but only to rob and terrorize us. The Negroes were completely armed and there was no white man with them. We heard them ranging all through the house, cursing and laughing, and breaking things open.

Directly one came bursting into our room, a big black wretch, with the most insolent swagger, talking all the time in a most insulting manner. He went through all the drawers and wardrobe taking anything he fancied, all the time with a cocked pistol in his hand. Cursing and making the most awful threats against Mr. Hardison if they ever caught him, he lounged up to the bed where the baby was sleeping. Raising the bar, he started to take the child, saying as he waved the pistol, "I ought to kill him. He may grow up to be a jarilla. Kill him." Mrs. Hardison sprang to his side, snatched the baby up, and shrieked: "Don't kill my baby. Don't kill him." The Negro turned away with a laugh and came over where I was sitting with Little Sister crouched close to me holding my hand. He came right up to us standing on the hem of my dress while he looked me slowly over, gesticulating and snapping his pistol. He stood there about a minute, I suppose. It seemed to me an age. I felt like I would die should he touch me. I did not look up or move, and Little Sister was as still as if petrified. In an instant more he turned away with a most diabolical laugh, gathered up his plunder, and went out. I was never so frightened in my life. Mrs. Hardison said we were both as white as marble, and she was sure I would faint. What a wave of thankfulness swept over us when he went out and slammed the door. In the meanwhile, the other Negroes were rummaging the house, ransacking it from top to bottom, destroying all the provisions they could not carry away, and sprinkling a white powder into the cisterns and over everything they left. We never knew whether it was poison or not.

The Negroes called and stormed and cursed through the house, calling each other "Captain" and "Lieutenant" until it nearly froze the blood in our veins, and every minute we expected them to break into our room again. I was completely unnerved. I did not think I could feel so frightened.

Mrs. Alexander went into her room hoping to prevent their robbing her bed, when one of them pointed his pistol at her and said: "I told you once before, old woman, to keep out of here and stop your jaw." Mr. McPherson and George were all the time on the gallery with Negroes guarding them with leveled guns.

After carrying on this way about two hours they lit matches, stuck them about the hall, and then leisurely took themselves off, loaded down with booty. We rushed around, put out all the matches, gathered up the few little articles left, and started at once for home. Since the Negroes declared as they moved off that they were coming back in a little while and burn every house on the place, I took the baby, and Mrs. Hardison, Mrs. Alexander, and the children with George and Mr. McPherson gathered up everything of any value left, and we hurried home, reaching there spent with excitement. Mrs. Hardison was almost crazy.

As we passed through our quarters there were numbers of strange Negro men standing around. They had gathered from the neighboring places. They did not say anything, but they looked at us and grinned, and that terrified us more and more. It held such a promise of evil. Jimmy went out at once to where Mr. Hardison was in hiding to tell him his family were with us. Jimmy just escaped being shot by Mr. Hardison, who, in the dusk, took him for a Yankee. Mr. and Mrs. Hardison and the small children went off as soon as possible, not thinking it safe to remain so near home. During the night a party came to the yard looking for them, but on the house servants' assuring them that the Hardisons were gone, they did not come to the house.

We made preparations that night to move at daybreak, but something deterred us. Mamma thought she would go out and get letters of protection, but later abandoned the idea. It was then too late for us to get off, and we spent a night and day of terror. The next evening the Negroes from all the inhabited places around commenced flocking to Mr. Hardison's, and they completely sacked the place in broad daylight, passing our gate loaded down with plunder until twelve at night. That more than anything else frightened Mamma and determined her to leave, though at the sacrifice of everything we owned.

We made arrangements to get Dr. Carson's skiffs and sent Webster around collecting saddles and bridles. On account of the water we could go only on horseback to take the skiffs. With much difficulty we got everything ready for the start at midnight. Aunt Laura was the only one who did not want to go. She begged Mamma to let her and Beverly stay, saying that she would get old Mr. Valentine to stay with her, but of course Mamma could not allow that. The boys brought in everything we had buried out, except Aunt Laura's silver. That had to be left packed in a barrel and buried in the yard. The boys had done it one very dark night, when they hoped all the Negroes were in their cabins, as it was raining. All the servants behaved well enough, except Webster, but you could see it was only because they knew we would soon be gone. We were only on sufferance.

Two days longer and we think they would all have gone to the Yankees, most probably robbing and insulting us before they left. About eleven, the boys went off with their guns to have the horses saddled and brought up. After a good deal of trouble they came. The boys carried their guns all the time. Without them I think we

would never have gotten off. Webster tried every artifice
to get hold of one of them, but the boys never relaxed
their watch. The night was cloudy and dark with occasional claps of thunder, but we had to go then or never.
We knew the news would be carried to camp, and the
Yankees had forbidden citizens to leave their places. Aunt
Laura, protesting all the time she could not ride, was at
last after much coaxing and fixing mounted on poor Little
Jack Fisher, the family pony, old and gentle, with Annie
perched behind her. I took Beverly in my lap. All the
others mounted, and with the baggage cart with Uncle
Bob driving and Jimmy guarding it in the extreme rear,
the procession moved off.

It was too dark to see the road, but Johnny led off and
each one followed the shadow in front. At first Aunt Laura
was loud in exclamation and complaint, until someone
suggested that she would bring the Negroes down on us.
That acted as a quietus, and thereafter she groaned only
in spirit. Several times as the clouds lifted and it grew
lighter, I saw her pony struggling in a mud hole and Aunt
Laura reeling in the saddle, but not a scream disturbed
the stillness of the night. As we opened gates and rode
through place after place in perfect silence, not a light
was visible anywhere. After passing Out Post, the road
was so bad and it was so dark that we were forced to wait
for daylight. We dismounted in the middle of the road,
and to Aunt Laura's surprise and amazement Mamma lay
her head down in Johnny's lap and went sound to sleep.
Riding in the dark had made her sick, and she was worn
out with excitement and loss of sleep.

As soon as it was light enough to see, the sleepers were
awakened, and we mounted and went on over the very
worst road it was possible for ladies to travel—just a long
bog from one end to the other. The morning air was
pleasantly cool, and as the red light crept up the sky we
heard all kinds of wildwoods sounds—squirrels chattering
in the trees, birds waking with a song, the calls of the

wild ducks and turkeys, and three or four deer bounding into the woods just before us.

When we reached within a mile of our place of debarkation [SIC], the road became impassable, and we struck off into the woods. The cart had to be left there and the baggage carried on by mules. After much trouble, getting lost and riding through water up to our saddle skirts—I actually swam a bayou with Beverly in my arms—we succeeded in getting all of our party and a little of our baggage to the landing place below Mrs. Stevens's. We sent Webster back to the cart for the baggage, and no sooner was he out of sight than he mounted a horse and set off for home. He told Charles that he knew he was not going to Bayou Macon with Miss Manda and that Charles had better come on with him. Thus by his treachery we lost everything we brought away with us, for when we heard it it was already too late to send back for the things. We knew the Yankees would certainly be where we were by eight o'clock, and it was nearly that hour. We knew that we must get off at once if at all, for when the Yankees came they would turn us back. They never allow anyone to leave if they can help it. . . .

We left our clothes in care of Uncle Bob who has been as faithful as any white man could be. He is Mamma's driver on the plantation. And we piled ourselves and our scanty luggage into two rocking, leaky dugouts and pushed off, Jimmy paddling one and Coffee, one of Dr. Carson's hands, the other. The sight of a body of horsemen in the distance coming our way lent strength to their arms, and as fast as they could ply the paddles we glided through the water. The men came on down the road, and we saw they were Yankee soldiers. But the water was so deep that they could not ride fast and we kept ahead. At last, after nearly a mile of this race, the boats shot out into deep water, and we were safe from pursuit. Then what a shout rang out for Jeff Davis and the Confederacy.[3]

From July 4, 1863, Vicksburg became an occupied city with General James McPherson as governor of the district. An entirely different kind of man from Butler, he nevertheless had difficulties with the citizens, particularly the ladies. In December he issued an order.

The following-named persons—Miss Kate Barnett, Miss Ella Barnett, Miss Laura Latham, Miss Ellen Martin, Mrs. Moore—having acted disrespectfully toward the President and Government of the United States, and having insulted the officers, soldiers, and loyal citizens of the United States who had assembled at the Episcopal Church in Vicksburg on Christmas Day for divine service by abruptly leaving said church at that point in the services where the officiating minister prays for the welfare of the President of the United States and all others in authority, are hereby banished, and will leave the Federal lines within forty-eight hours, under penalty of imprisonment.

Hereafter, all persons, male or female, who by word, deed, or implication do insult or show disrespect to the President, Government, or flag of the United States, or to any officer or soldier of the United States, upon matters of a national character, shall be fined, banished, or imprisoned, according to the grossness of the offense.[4]

By the spring of 1864 Union armies were driving into all sections of the Confederacy, and there were comparatively few Southerners who did not know what it meant to be in the path of a conquering enemy. Those who fled fared little better than those who remained in their homes. The great majority of fugitives went to towns where they thought there were possibilities of shelter and employment. Richmond became a "city of refuge." Thousands sought its shelter, and its normal population of about 40,000 swelled to perhaps three times that number. The Richmond Whig *was concerned for these refugees. In April the following appeared in its pages:*

Even in times of peace the spring months are months of scarcity. Now they are months of distress. We have passed the ordeal of winter with comparative ease, but today the pinch is on us, and each succeeding day we will be pinched more. What are the rich doing to alleviate the sufferings of the poor? Are the country people sending all they can spare to town, or are they hoarding . . . ?

No city in the Confederacy has had more refugees than Richmond, yet we have yet to learn that any special favor has been shown them by merchants and others. . . .

Many of the refugees in Richmond—perhaps the majority of them—are people of the highest social standing who have been driven from luxurious homes and are now toiling like slaves in obscure rooms and offices in the city. Many of them are suffering for the necessaries of life— suffering severely. But they suffer in silence. If it were not for the government we verily believe some of them would starve. As it is, many of them live mainly on bread and water. . . .

But refugees are not the ONLY sufferers. Anyone who will take the trouble to walk by the office of the Young Men's Christian Association will there see a crowd of women with baskets and anxious faces. . . . Some of these women bear no traces of privation, but others are haggard and worn beyond mistake. Want and overwork have made their faces pale and their eyes lusterless. They need help, and the Association, exhausted in funds and supplies, have been forced to appoint agents to visit the citizens of Richmond and solicit contributions.

But all the poor women are not found in front of the doors of the public benevolent institutions. Many of them shrink from this open acknowledgement of their poverty, but they will be found in the counting rooms and offices of charitable gentlemen. And as the spring wears on a notable increase of well-born ladies will be observed at the city provision stores. They must come to this if our men of wealth open not their hands and our farmers bring not forth their hoarded corn and meat.

The time has come when we must bestir ourselves in active charities.[5]

Many city dwellers generously opened their doors to their less fortunate countrymen; but buildings, whether homes or hotels, had limited capacities. House-hunting— actually room-hunting—became progressively disheartening.

Mrs. Abel Upshur, the wealthy widow of John Tyler's Secretary of State, had to seek aid in finding a room to accommodate her sister, her little grandson, and herself, because the price of the third-floor room she was occupying was being raised beyond her means. Her search was unavailing. Another refugee who had known better days was Judith Brockenbrough McGuire. Born in Richmond fifty years before, she was the daughter of a distinguished Virginia jurist, and as a girl she had played in her uncle's home, a mansion now the Confederate White House. She had married a minister who was principal of the Episcopal High School at Alexandria when the war came. With her two sons in the army, Mrs. McGuire, her husband, and their daughters repaired to Richmond. Intensely patriotic and eager to sacrifice, she had been living in the capital three years when she recorded in her diary:

10th. [September 1864] We must give up our rooms by the last of this month, and the question now arises about our future abode. We are searching hither and thither. We had thought for a week past that our arrangements were most delightfully made and that we had procured, together with Dr. M. and Colonel G., six rooms in a house on Franklin Street. The arrangements had been made and the proprietor gone from town. The M.'s and ourselves were to take four rooms on the third story; the back parlor on the first floor was to be used by all parties; and Colonel G. would take the large front basement room as his chamber and, at his request, as our dining-room, as we could not be allowed to use the upper chambers as eating-rooms. Our large screen was to be transferred to the Colonel's bedstead and washing apparatus, and the rest of the room furnished in dining-room style. These rooms are all furnished and carpeted. Nothing could have suited us better, and we have been for some days anticipating our comfortable winter-quarters. The M.'s have left town with the blissful assurance of a nice home; to add to it all, the family of the proprietor is all that we could desire as friends and companions.

Last night I met with a friend who asked me where we had obtained rooms. I described them with great alacrity and pleasure. She looked surprised and said: "Are you not mistaken? Those rooms are already occupied."

"Impossible," said I, "we have engaged them."

She shook her head, saying: "There was some mistake; they have been occupied for some days by a family who say that they have rented them."

None but persons situated exactly in the same way can imagine our disappointment. The Colonel looked aghast; Mr. —— pronounced it a mistake; the girls were indignant, and I went a little farther and pronounced it bad treatment.

This morning I went up before breakfast to hear the truth of the story—the family is still absent, but the servants confirmed the statement by saying that a family had been in the rooms that we looked at for a week; and that a gentleman, a third party, had been up the day before to claim the rooms, and said that the party occupying them had no right to them, and must be turned out. The servant added that this third gentleman had sent up a dray with flour which was now in the house and had put his coal in the coal-cellar. All this seems passing strange. Thus have we but three weeks before us in which to provide ourselves with an almost impossible shelter. The Colonel has written to Mr. —— for an explanation, and the M.'s have been apprised of their dashed hopes. I often think how little the possessors of the luxurious homes of Richmond know of the difficulties with which refugees are surrounded, and how little we ever appreciated the secure home-feeling which we had enjoyed before the war began.

We have this evening been out again in pursuit of quarters. The advertisements of "rooms to let" were sprinkled over the morning papers so that one could scarcely believe that there would be any difficulty in our being supplied. A small house that would accommodate our whole party, five or six rooms in a large house, or two rooms for ourselves, if it were impossible to do better, would answer our purpose—anything for a comfortable home. The first advertisement alluded to basement rooms—damp, and redolent of rheumatism. The next was more attractive—good rooms, well furnished, and up BUT TWO flights of stairs; but the price was enormous, far beyond the means of any of the party, and so evidently an extortion designed to take all that could be extracted from the necessity of others, that we turned from our hard-featured proprietor with disgust. The rooms of the third advertisement had been already rented, and the fourth seemed more like answering our purpose than any we had seen. There were only two rooms, and though small and rather dark, yet persons whose shelter was likely to be the "blue vault of heaven" could not be very particular. The price, too, was exorbitant, but with a little more self-denial it might be paid. The next inquiry was about kitchen, servant's room, and coal-house; but we got no further than the answer about the kitchen. The lady said there was no kitchen that we could possibly use; her stove was small, and she required it all; we must either be supplied from a restaurant, or do our own cooking in one of the rooms. As neither plan was to be thought of, we ended the parlay.

A PART OF A KITCHEN is indispensable, though perhaps the most annoying thing to which refugees are subjected. The mistress is generally polite enough, but save me from the self-sufficient cook. "I would like to oblige you, madam, but you can't have loaf-bread tomorrow morning because my mistress has ordered loaf-bread and rolls, and our stove is small"; or, "No, madam, you can't 'bile a ham nor nothing else today because it is our washing-day"; or, "No, ma'am, you can't have biscuits for tea because the stove is cold, and I've got no time to heat it." So that we must either submit or go to the mistress for redress, and probably find none, and thus run the risk of offending both mistress and maid, both of whom have us very much in their power.

As I walked home from this unsuccessful effort it was nearly dark; the gas was being lighted in hall, parlor, and chamber. I looked in as I passed, and saw cheerful countenances collecting around center-tables, or sitting here and there on handsome porticoes or marble steps, to enjoy the cool evening breeze—countenances of those whose families I had known from infancy, and who were still numbered among my friends and acquaintances. I felt sad, and asked myself if those persons could realize the wants of others would they not cheerfully rent some of their extra rooms? Rooms once opened on grand occasions, and now, as such occasions are few and far between, not opened at all for weeks and months together. Would they not cheerfully remove some of their showy and fragile furniture for a time, and allow those who had once been accustomed to as large rooms of their own, to occupy and take care of them? The RENT would perhaps be no object with them, but their kindness might be twice blessed—the refugees would be made comfortable and happy, and the money might be applied to the wants of the soldiers or the city poor. And yet a third blessing might be added—the luxury of doing good. Ah, they would then find that the "quality of mercy is not strained," but that it would indeed, like "gentle dew from heaven" fall into their very souls, and diffuse a happiness of which they know not. These thoughts filled my mind until I reached the present home of a refugee friend from Wash ington. It was very late, but I thought I would run in and see if she could throw any light upon our difficulties. I was sorry to find that she was in a similar situation, her husband having that day been notified that their rooms would be required on the first of October. We compared notes of our room-hunting experiences, and soon found ourselves laughing heartily over occurrences and conversations which were both provoking and ridiculous. I then wended my way home, amid brilliantly lighted houses and badly lighted streets.[6]

Another Virginia lady of distinguished family was Sara Agnes Pryor, wife of Colonel Roger Pryor, who followed her husband in the early years of the war. When he was promoted to brigadier for gallantry and found himself without a command, he did a remarkable thing. He resigned and enlisted as a private in Fitzhugh Lee's cavalry, where he served until he was captured late in the war. During the Seven Days Mrs. Pryor was in Richmond where she worked as a volunteer nurse. From the fall of 1863 she lived in Petersburg with her small children and was there when Grant laid siege in the summer of 1864. In the autumn of that year she wrote:

As soon as the enemy brought up their siege guns of heavy artillery, they opened on the city with shell without the slightest notice, or without giving opportunity for the removal of noncombatants, the sick, the wounded, or the women and children. The fire was at first directed toward the Old Market, presumably because of the railroad depot situated there, about which soldiers might be supposed to collect. But the guns soon enlarged their operations, sweeping all the streets in the business part of the city, and then invading the residential region. The steeples of the churches seemed to afford targets for their fire, all of them coming in finally for a share of the compliment.

To persons unfamiliar with the infernal noise made by the screaming, ricocheting, and bursting of shells, it is impossible to describe the terror and demoralization which ensued. Some families who could not leave the besieged city dug holes in the ground five or six feet deep, covered with heavy timbers, banked over with earth, the entrance facing opposite the batteries from which the shells were fired. They made these bomb-proofs safe, at least, and thither the family repaired when heavy shelling commenced. General Lee seemed to recognize that no part of the city was safe, for he immediately ordered the removal of all the hospitals, under the care of Petersburg's esteemed physician, Dr. John Herbert Claiborne. There were three thousand sick and wounded, many of them too ill to be moved. A long, never-ending line of wagons, carts, everything that could run on wheels, passed my door, until there were no more to pass. We soon learned the peculiar, deep boom of the one great gun which bore directly upon us. The boys named it "Long Tom." Sometimes for several weeks "Long Tom" rested or slept—and would then make up for lost time. And yet we yielded to no panic. The children seemed to understand that it would be cowardly to complain. One little girl cried out with fright at an explosion; but her aunt, Mrs. Gibson, took her in her arms, and said: "My dear, you cannot make it harder for other people! If you feel very much afraid come to me, and I will clasp you close, but you mustn't cry."

Charles Campbell, the historian, lived near us, at the Anderson Seminary. He cleared out the large coal-cellar, which was fortunately dry, spread rugs on the floor, and furnished it with lounges and chairs. There we took refuge when the firing was unbearable. Some of our neighbors piled bags of sand around their houses, and thus made them bomb-proof.

The Rev. Dr. Hoge, who had come South from the Brick Church, New York, of which he had been pastor, was lying ill and dying a few miles from Petersburg, and my friend Mrs. Bland invited me to accompany her to visit him. She had borrowed an ambulance from General Bushrod Johnson.

We made our call upon our sick friend, and were on our return when we were suddenly startled by heavy firing. . . . We were glad to arrive at my door.

It was closed. There was not a soul in the house. One of the chimneys had been knocked down, and the bricks lay in a heap on the grass. I thought of Mr. Campbell's bomb-proof cellar; there we found my children, and there we remained until the paroxysmal shelling ceased.

One night, after a long, hot day, we were so tired we slept soundly. I was awakened by Eliza Page, standing trembling beside me. She pulled me out of bed and hurriedly turned to throw blankets around the children. The furies were let loose! The house was literally shaking with the concussion from the heavy guns. We were in the street on our way to our bomb-proof cellar when a shell burst not more than fifty feet before us. Fire and fragments rose like a fountain in the air and fell in a shower around us. Not one of my little family was hurt.

Another time a shell fell in our own yard and buried itself in the earth. My baby was not far away, in her nurse's arms. The little creature was fascinated by the shells. The first word she ever uttered was an attempt to imitate them. "Yonder comes that bird with the broken wing," the servants would say. The shells made a fluttering sound as they traversed the air, descending with a frightful hiss to explode or be buried in the earth. When they exploded in mid-air by day, a puff of smoke, white as an angel's wing, would drift away, and the particles would patter down like hail. At night the track of the shell and its explosion were precisely similar in sound, although not in degree, to the Fourth of July rockets, except that they were fired not upward but in a slanting direction. I never felt afraid of them! I was brought up to believe in predestination. Courage, after all, is much a matter of nerves. My neighbors, Mr. and Mrs. Gibson and Mrs. Meade, agreed with me, and we calmly elected to remain in town. There was no place of safety accessible to us. Mr. Branch removed his family, and, as far as I knew, none other of my friends remained throughout the summer.

Not far from the door ran a sunken street, with a hill, through which it was cut rising each side of it. Into this hill the Negroes burrowed, hollowing out a small space where they sat all day on mats, knitting, and selling small cakes made of sorghum and flour, and little round meat pies. I might have been tempted to invest in the latter except for a slight circumstance. I saw a dead mule lying on the common, and out of its side had been cut a very neat, square chunk of flesh! With all our starvation we never ate rats, mice, or mule-meat. We managed to exist on peas, bread, and sorghum. We could buy a little milk, and we mixed it with a drink made from roasted and ground corn. The latter in the grain was scarce. Mr. Campbell's children picked up the grains wherever the army horses fed.[7]

As Grant drew his lines tight around Richmond, the inhabitants were less concerned about bombardment than with securing food and shelter. In the early years of the war, boarding houses had sprung up everywhere, but soon food scarcity and high prices drove proprietors from this business. In the spring of 1863 no fewer than fourteen of the largest boarding houses in Richmond closed their doors to table boarders, and soon the "European plan" was in vogue both in boarding houses and in hotels. Under these circumstances light-housekeeping became the almost universal living style, and families of three or more cooked, ate, slept, and performed all other domestic chores in one room. An unidentified young lady, who was living at the Arlington Hotel in the last months of the war, wrote:

Though the last act of our heroic tragedy was already beginning, I was so far from suspecting it that I joined mother at the Arlington, prepared to make a joke of hardships and wring every possible drop of pleasure out of a

winter in Richmond, varied, as I fondly imagined, by
frequent if brief visits from Dan.

The Arlington was kept on something like the European plan, not from choice of landlady or guests but from
grim necessity. Feeding a houseful of people was too
arduous and uncertain an undertaking in those days for
a woman to assume. Mrs. Fry, before our arrival in July,
had informed her boarders that they could continue to
rent their rooms from her, but that they must provide their
own meals. We paid her twenty-five dollars a month for
our room—the price of a house in good times and in good
money. During my absence in Mansfield, Hicksford, and
other places, Mother, to reduce expenses, had rented half
of her room and bed to Delia McArthur, of Petersburg. I
now rented a little bed from Mrs. Fry for myself and set
it up in the same room.

We had become so poor and had so little to cook that
we did most of our cooking ourselves over the grate, each
woman often cooking her own little rations. There was an
old Negress living in the back yard who cooked for any
or all of us when we had something that could not be
prepared by ourselves over the grate. Sometimes we got
hold of a roast, or we would buy two quarts of flour, a
little dab of lard, and a few pinches of salt and treat ourselves to a loaf of bread which the old Negress cooked
for us, charging ten dollars for the baking. But as a rule,
the grate was all sufficient. We boiled rice or dried apples
or beans or peas in our stewpan, and we had a frying-pan
if there was anything to fry.

Across the hall from us Miss Mary Pagett, of Petersburg, had a room to herself. She worked in one of the departments, and in order that she might have her meals in
time she went into partnership with us. Every morning she
would put in with our rations whatever she happened to
have for that day, and Mother would cook it and have it
ready when she came. Downstairs under our rooms, Mr.
and Mrs. Sampson, their daughters, Nan and Beth, and

their son, Don, all of Petersburg and old neighbors and friends of ours, lived, slept, cooked, and ate in two rooms, a big and a little one. They lived as we did, cooking over their grates.

Sometimes we all put what we had together and ate in company. When any of us secured at any time some eatable out of the common, if it was enough to go around we invited the others into breakfast, dinner, or tea, as the case might be. It must be understood that from the meal called "tea," the beverage from which the meal is named was nearly always omitted. Our fare was never very sumptuous—often it was painfully scanty. Sometimes we would all get so hungry that we would put together all the money we could rake and scrape and buy a bit of roast or something else substantial and have a feast.

We all bought coal in common. Mother's, mine, and Delia's portion of the coal was a ton, and we had to keep it in our room—there was no other place to store it. We had a box in our room which held a ton, and the coal was brought upstairs and dumped into that box. I can see those darkies now, puffing and blowing, as they brought that coal up those many steps. And how we had to scuffle around to pay them! For some jobs we paid in trade—only we had very little to trade off. How that room held all of its contents I can't make out. Dan sent me provisions by the quantity when he could get any and get them through to me. He would send a bag of potatoes or peas, and he never sent less than a firkin of butter—delicious butter from Orange County. The bags of peas, rice, and potatoes were disposed around the room, and around the hearth were arranged our pots, pans, kettles, and cooking utensils generally. When we bought wood that was put under the beds. In addition to all our useful and ornamental articles, we had our three selves and our trunks; such clothing as we possessed had to be hung up for better keeping—and this was a time when it behooved us to cherish clothes tenderly. Then there was our laundry-ing, which was done in that room by ourselves. . . .

We devised many small ways for making a little money. We knit gloves and socks and sold them, and Miss Beth Sampson had some old pieces of ante-bellum silk that she made into neckties and sold for what she could get. For the rest, when we had no money we went without those things which it took money to buy. With money a bit of meat now and then, a taste of sorghum, and even the rare luxury of a cup of tea sweetened with sugar, was possible. Without money, we had to depend upon the bags of peas, dried apples, or rice. . . .

One day we agreed to have a feast. The Sampsons were to bring their contributions, Miss Mary and Delia Mc-Arthur to put in theirs as usual, and Mother and I to contribute our share, of course. Each of us had the privilege of inviting a friend to tea. Our room was chosen as the common supper room because it had fewer things in it and was less crowded than the Sampsons'. The Sampsons, in addition to their coal-box, wood-pile, bags and barrels of provisions, had one more bed than we had, and also a piano. We had our tea-party and, guests and all, we had a merry time.

I never remember having more fun in my life than at the Arlington. . . . For hungry and shabby as we were, crowded into our one room with bags of rice and peas, firkins of butter, a ton of coal, a small wood-pile, cooking utensils, and all of our personal property, we were not in despair. Our faith in Lee and his ragged, freezing, starving army amounted to a superstition. We cooked our rice and peas and dried apples, and hoped and prayed.[8]

VII: "STITCH, STITCH, STITCH"

Women in the South were, as a general rule, as militantly secessionist as their fathers, brothers, and husbands. Chivalrous Southern writers may have overstated the patriotic part they played in the war; nevertheless, it is probably true that, in the early months particularly, their fervor sent many a reluctant volunteer into army camps.

As the men left the farms and plantations, women took over the management and, in some cases, the hard physical toil in the fields. And there was work to be done in the cities, too. In the summer of 1861 a Richmond woman wrote:

There was now work for everyone to do. The effects of the blockade of our ports was very early felt. The numberless and nameless articles for which we depended upon foreign markets were either to be dispensed with or to be manufactured from our own industry and ingenuity. With a zeal as commendable as that which answered the call to arms in the South, and especially in Virginia, the people set themselves to work to meet the demands made by the exigencies of the times.

Troops continued to pour into Richmond. Regiment after regiment came without the necessary uniform or equipment to send them to the field. Our ladies engaged to prepare them properly for the work upon which they were committed to enter.

Sewing societies were multiplied, and those who had formerly devoted themselves to gaiety and fashionable amusement found their only real pleasure in obedience to the demands made upon their time and talents, in providing proper habiliments for the soldier. The quondam belle of the ballroom, the accomplished woman of society, the devotee of ease, luxury, and idle enjoyment found herself transformed into the busy sempstress. The click of the sewing-machine was the music which most interested them, and the "stitch, stich, stich," from morning till night, as the ladies plied the needle and thread, was their chief employment. They very soon became adepts in the manufacture of the different articles which compose the rough and simple wardrobe of the soldier. To these, necessary for him, they took delight in adding various other articles which taste or friendship might suggest. There were very few of the soldiers who were not furnished with a neat threadcase, supplied with everything necessary to repair his clothing when absent from a friendly pair of hands which would do it for him; a visor to shield his face from the too fierce heat of the summer sun or to protect him from the cold of winter; a warm scarf and a havelock.

The sewing operations were varied by the scraping and carding of lint, the rolling of bandages, and the manufacture of cartridges, and many things unnecessary to mention, but which were the work of the women. The poor of the city were supplied with such employment as secured to them a plentiful support. While the demand was great for clothing for the troops, the ladies of the higher and independent classes of society would undertake nothing which might deprive those who depended upon such employment for a livelihood, nor did they choose only the lighter work for themselves while they permitted the heavier and more difficult to go to the poor; but disregarding position, they employed themselves cheerfully upon anything necessary to be done. Heavy tents of cumbrous sail-cloth, overcoats, jackets, and pantaloons of stiff, heavy material, from the sewing on which they were frequently found with stiff, swollen, bleeding fingers, were nevertheless perseveringly undertaken. . . .

During the existence of the war, coffee was a luxury in which only the most wealthy could constantly indulge; and when used at all, it was commonly adulterated with other things which passed for the genuine article, but was often so nauseous that it was next to impossible to force it upon the stomach. Rye, wheat, corn, sweet potatoes, beans, ground-nuts, chestnuts, chicory, ochre, sorghum-seed, and other grains and seeds, roasted and ground, were all brought into use as substitutes for the bean of Araby; but after every experiment to make coffee of what was not coffee, we were driven to decide that there was nothing coffee but coffee, and if disposed to indulge in extravagance at all, the people showed it only by occasional and costly indulgence in the luxurious beverage.

Tea, sugar, wines, and all imported liquors, increased rapidly in expense as the supply grew scarce, but not in the same ratio as coffee, which had been in universal use at the South—the low price at which it had been purchased, and its stimulating and pleasant effects making it agreeable, necessary, and possible for even the poorest to indulge in its use.

The leaves of the currant, blackberry, willow, sage, and other vegetables, were dried and used as substitutes for tea by those who could not or did not feel justified in encouraging the exorbitant demands of successful blockade-runners and dealers in the article. When sugar grew scarce and so expensive that many were compelled to abandon its use altogether, there were substituted honey, and the syrup from sorghum, or the Chinese sugar cane, for all ordinary culinary purposes. The cultivation of the latter has become a very important consideration with the agriculturists of the more northern of the South-

ern states, being peculiarly adapted to the soil and climate
and furnishing a cheap and excellent substitute for the
syrup of the sugar cane of the Gulf States and the West
Indies.[1]

Blackwood's *"roving reporter" visited Charleston in the
autumn of 1861:*

At Charleston we had an opportunity of visiting one
of those societies which are organized throughout the
whole South for supplying the army with clothes. The
central depot is situated in the middle of the town. In
the basement floor we found large packages marked for
different regiments then at the seat of war. Upstairs several ladies were engaged in arranging in "lots" different
kinds of uniform, and measuring out cloth, flannel, linen,
cotton, to be made up by the hands of the fairest in the
land.

We learnt from those who have the superintendence of
this vast establishment that about a thousand ladies are
daily employed at their sewing machines making different
articles of military attire. The work of the week which
had then just elapsed consisted of 200 coats, 300 pairs of
trousers, 300 shirts, besides worsted gloves for the winter,
stockings, old linen, and many fancy articles which were
sold for the benefit of the society's funds.

These establishments save the government enormous
sums of money, and appear to be increasing in numbers
and efficiency every day.

The army, being composed in a great measure of volunteers, possesses the hearty sympathy and affection of the
whole population; and as most families have more than
one of its members at the war, the comfort of the soldier
is not only universally considered a subject of patriotic
interest, but also one which excites the anxiety and stimu-
lates the energy of every household.[2]

*And a thousand miles away, out in the Louisiana bayou
country, Kate Stone observed:*

All the boys are out on the river and we expect them

to bring Anna Dobbs back with them to stay a few days. It seems odd to be expecting company and no flour or any "boughten" delicacy to regale them on, but we have been on a strict "war footing" for some time—cornbread and home-raised meal, milk and butter, tea once a day, and coffee never. A year ago we would have considered it impossible to get on for a day without the things that we have been doing without for months. Fortunately we have sugar and molasses, and after all, it is not such hard living. Common cornbread admits of many variations in the hands of a good cook—eggbread (we have lots of eggs), muffins, cakes, and so on. Fat meat will be unmitigated fat meat, but one need not eat it. And there are chickens, occasional partridges, and other birds, and often venison, vegetables of all kinds minus potatoes; and last but not least, knowing there is no help for it makes one content. There is hardly a family in the parish using flour constantly. All kept some for awhile for company and for the sick, but it is about exhausted now.

Clothes have become a secondary consideration. Fashion is an obsolete word and just to be decently clad is all we expect. The change in dress, habits, and customs is nowhere more striking than in the towns. A year ago a gentleman never thought of carrying a bundle, even a small one, through the streets. Broadcloth was DE RIGEUR. Ceremony and fashion ruled in the land. Presto-change. Now the highest in rank may be seen doing any kind of work that their hands find to do. The men have become "hewers of wood and drawers of water" and pack bundles of all sorts and sizes. It may be a pile of blankets, a stack of buckets, or a dozen bundles. One gentleman I saw walking down the street in Jackson, and a splendid-looking fellow he was, had a piece of fish in one hand, a cavalry saddle on his back, bridle, blankets, newspapers, and a small parcel in the other hand; and over his shoulder swung an immense pair of cavalry boots. And nobody thought he looked odd. Their willingness to fetch and carry is only limited by their strength. . . . Broadcloth is worn only by the drones and fireside braves. Dyed linsey is now the fashionable material for coats and pants. Vests are done away with, colored flannel, merino, or silk overshirts taking the place. A gentleman thinks nothing of calling on half a dozen young ladies dressed in home-dyed Negro cloth and blue checked shirt. If there is a button or stripe to show that he is one of the country's defenders, he is sure of warmest welcome. Another stops to talk to a bevy of ladies. He is laden down with a package of socks and tin plates that he is carrying out to camp, and he shifts the bundles from side to side as he grows interested and his arms get tired. In proportion as we have been a race of haughty, indolent, and waited-on people, so now are we ready to do away with all forms and work and wait on ourselves.[3]

Not only did soldiers get hungry and cold, but they suffered wounds and had to be nursed. Here, too, the women did their part. Hundreds volunteered for full-time duty in army hospitals, and hundreds of others did part-time duty when battle came their way. Constance Cary was one of them. Beautiful, gay, vivacious, talented, she must have been one of the most charming girls in all the Confederacy. She, her mother, and her aunt were refugees in Richmond throughout the war, having fled from their plantation near Alexandria when Union troops occupied that region in the spring of 1861. The Carys took a house on Franklin Street, where they were neighbors of General Lee's family, and their home soon became the center of a lively group, where amateur theatricals and tableaux vivants were planned and rehearsed. Constance was to win the heart of President Davis's handsome young private secretary, Burton Harrison, and they were married before the end of the war. But she was not yet seventeen when the battle of Seven Pines was fought just outside Richmond in the spring of 1862. Years later she recalled the stirring scene:

And now we come to the 31st of May, 1862, when the eyes of the whole continent turned to Richmond. On that day Johnston assaulted the Federals who had been advanced to Seven Pines. In face of recent reverses we in Richmond had begun to feel like the prisoner of the Inquisition in Poe's story, cast into a dungeon of slowly contracting walls. With the sound of guns, therefore, in the direction of Seven Pines, every heart leaped as if deliverance were at hand. And yet there was no joy in the wild pulsation, since those to whom we looked for succor were our own flesh and blood, barring the way to a foe of superior numbers, abundantly provided, as we were not, with all the equipments of modern warfare, and backed by a mighty nation as determined as ourselves to win. Hardly a family in the town whose father, son, or brother was not part and parcel of the defending army.

When, on the afternoon of the 31st, it became known that the engagement had begun, the women of Richmond were still going about their daily vocations quietly, giving no sign of the inward anguish of apprehension. There was enough to do now in preparation for the wounded: yet, as events proved, all that was done was not enough by half. Night brought a lull in the cannonading. People lay down dressed upon beds, but not to sleep, while the weary soldiers slept upon their arms.

Early next morning the whole town was on the street. Ambulances, litters, carts, every vehicle that the city could produce, went and came with a ghastly burden; those who could walk limped painfully home, in some cases so black with gunpowder they passed unrecognized. Women with pallid faces flitted bareheaded through the streets searching for their dead or wounded. The churches were thrown open, many people visiting them for a sad communion-service or brief time of prayer; the lecture-rooms of various places of worship were crowded with ladies volunteering to sew, as fast as fingers could fly, the rough beds called for by surgeons. Men too old or infirm to fight went on horseback or afoot to meet the returning ambulances, and in some cases served as escort to their own dying sons.

By afternoon of the day following the battle, the streets were one vast hospital. To find shelter for the sufferers a number of unused buildings were thrown open. I remember, especially, the St. Charles Hotel, a gloomy place where two young girls went to look for a member of their family, reported wounded. We had tramped in vain over pavements burning with the intensity of the sun, from one scene of horror to another, until our feet and brains alike seemed about to serve us no further. The cool of those vast dreary rooms of the St. Charles was refreshing; but such a spectacle! Men in every stage of mutilation lying on the bare boards, with perhaps a haversack or an army blanket beneath their heads—some dying, all suffering keenly, while waiting their turn to be attended to. To be there empty-handed and impotent nearly broke our hearts. We passed from one to the other, making such slight additions to their comfort as were possible, while looking in every upturned face in dread to find the object of our search. This sorrow, I may add, was spared, the youth arriving at home later with a slight flesh-wound.

The condition of things at this and other improvised hospitals was improved next day by the offerings from many churches of pew-cushions, which, sewn together, served as comfortable beds; and for the remainder of the war their owners thanked God upon bare benches for every "misery missed" that was "mercy gained." To supply food for the hospitals the contents of larders all over town were emptied into baskets; while cellars long sealed and cobwebbed, belonging to the Old Virginia gentry who knew good Port and Madeira, were opened by Ithuriel's spear of universal sympathy.

There was not much going to bed that night, either; and I remember spending the greater part of it leaning from my window to seek the cool night air, while wondering as to the fate of those near to me. There was a summons to my mother about midnight. Two soldiers came to tell her of the wounding of one close of kin; but she was already on duty elsewhere, tireless and watchful as ever. Up to that time the younger girls had been regarded as superfluities in hospital service; but on Monday two of us found a couple of rooms where fifteen wounded men lay upon pallets around the floor, and, on offering our services to the surgeons in charge, were proud to have them accepted and to be installed as responsible nurses under direction of an older and more experienced woman.

The constant activity our work entailed was a relief from the strained excitement of life after the battle of Seven Pines. When the first flurry of distress was over, the residents of those pretty houses standing back in gardens full of roses set their cooks to work, or, better still, went themselves into the kitchen to compound delicious messes for the wounded after the appetizing old Virginia recipes. Flitting about the streets in the direction of the hospitals were smiling, white-jacketed Negroes, carrying silver trays with dishes of fine porcelain under napkins of thick white damask, containing soups, creams, jellies, thin biscuit, eggs À LA CRÈME, boiled chicken, etc., surmounted by clusters of freshly gathered flowers. A year later we had pause to pine after these culinary glories when it came to measuring out, with sinking hearts, the meager portions of milk and food we could afford to give our charges.

As an instance, however, that quality in food was not always appreciated by the patients, my mother urged upon one of her sufferers (a gaunt and soft voiced Carolinian from the "piney woods district") a delicately served trifle from some neighboring kitchen.

"Jez ez you say, old miss," was the weary answer: "I ain't a-contradictin' you. It mout be good for me, but my stomick's kinder sot agin it. There ain't but one thing I'm sorter yarnin' arter, an' that's a dish o' greens en bacon fat, with a few malarses poured onto it." [4]

Another volunteer worker was Sarah Page Andrews, who lived in the lower Shenandoah Valley across the Potomac River from Sharpsburg, Maryland. When war came her clergyman husband went to St. Louis, for reasons which are not clear, and her newly married son went to work in one of the government bureaus in Richmond. Mrs. Andrews and her daughters remained at home and were there in the autumn of 1862, when Lee invaded Maryland. On September 18, she wrote to her son:

I am writing at the parlor window and have in sight ambulances filled with wounded, who fill every house in this place. We have the chamber and little room occupied by three dangerously wounded—Colonel Liddell from Columbia, South Carolina—a young man sixteen years old from South Carolina on General Evan's staff—his name I can't remember, and I do not know the other. [General] Rooney Lee is at Mr. E. I. Lee's, wounded.

The most desperate battle of the war is going on in Maryland—before this reaches you it will be decided. We are of course sanguine as to the result, but the slaughter is fearful. Anne and Lila do not write because with all their efforts they can make, the poor soldiers cannot be attended to properly and supplied with garments. . . . At French Hill . . . numbers [of stragglers] loiter about the premises, and Ellen says they are cooking for them all day. We keep two pots on the fire all the time with tomato soup, which is dealt out to the sick and, indeed, all who apply. The number is immense who have no place but the street.

Lila, Fanny, and Rose, and Virginia Bedinger, and all the girls in a measure down to little Minnie Bedinger, cook all the time. They have opened the warehouses and swept them and filled them with the sick and wounded—dressed their wounds with their own hands. I saw Fanny just now dressing a man's foot, at the style—it is wonderful what they accomplish. Anne is making shirts for them and helping me to attend to those here. Cornbread and soup is dealing out all the time to those who come to the doors and windows to beg for it. Ellen is at home doing all she can with her Mamma and Jennie and Nan. Jennie says she is very sorry for the wounded, but not for the stragglers. . . . I hope all this will pass away like an awful dream in a short time. We try to do our duty for the time and trust to Providence for the future.

Four days later she added:

The girls continue to devote every moment from morning to evening to active services. . . . Ellen, who is the home worker generally, has come in tonight to give Anne a night out. The poor youth of sixteen in whom she is so interested will scarcely live more than another night— it is thought. I believe I told you his name—W. F. Tresvent, of Columbia, South Carolina—a lovely youth. He took Fanny for his sister today, and was much distressed because she did not kiss him—when she did afterwards— but it would not do. He is delirious and suffering greatly with this amputated limb. We thought we had insured Anne's being in the country—but she will not stay away. . . . We are beginning to feel the inconvenience of short supplies—butter, for instance, we have to give up—of tea and coffee we shall not fail to take up a portion for the use of our dear absent ones. We have to use more than we can spare for these poor sick men.[5]

Rising cost of living drove many women to seek remunerative employment. Judith McGuire had managed to make ends meet for a time, but by the fall of 1863 she was in need:

[Nov. 11] I have just written to Colonel Northrop, Commissary-General, to ask an appointment as clerk in his department. So many of the young men have been ordered to the field that this office has been open to ladies. My cousin, Colonel F. G. Ruffin, of the same office, has interested himself for me. They require us to say that we are really in want of the office—rather a sort of supererogation, I should say, as no lady would bind herself to keep accounts for six hours a day without a dire necessity.

[Nov.] 13. My appointment to a clerkship in the Commissary Department has been received, with a salary of $125 per month. The rooms are not ready for us to begin our duties, and Colonel R. has just called to tell me one of the requirements. As our duties are those of accountants we are to go through a formal examination in arithmetic. If we do not, as the University boys say, "pass," we are considered incompetent, and, of course, are dropped from the list of appointees. This requirement may be right, but it certainly seems to me both provoking and absurd that I must be examined in arithmetic by a commissary major young enough to be my son. If I could afford it I would give up the appointment, but as it is must submit with the best grace possible, particularly as other ladies of my age have to submit to it. . . .

December 12. Today I was examined on arithmetic—"Denominate numbers, vulgar and decimal fractions, tare and tret," etc., etc., by Major Brewer, of the Commissary Department. I felt as if I had returned to my childhood. But for the ridiculousness of the thing, I dare say I should have been embarrassed. On Monday I am to enter on the duties of the office. We are to work from nine till three. . . .

January 3 [1864]. Entered on the duties of my office on the 30th of December. So far I like it well. "The Major" is very kind and considerate of our comfort; the duties of the office are not very onerous, but rather confining for one who left school thirty-four years ago and has had no restraint of the kind during the interim. The ladies, thirty-five in number, are of all ages and representing various parts of Virginia, also Maryland and Louisiana. Many of them are refugees. It is melancholy to see how many wear mourning for brothers or other relatives, the victims of war. One sad young girl sits near me, whose two brothers have fallen on the field, but she is too poor

to buy mourning. I found many acquaintances, and when
I learned the history of others it was often that of fallen
fortunes and destroyed homes. One young lady of high-
sounding Maryland name was banished from Baltimore
because of her zeal in going to the assistance of our
Gettysburg wounded. The society is pleasant, and we hope
to get along very agreeably. I am now obliged to visit the
hospital in the afternoon, and I give it two evenings in the
week. It is a cross to me not to be able to give it more
time; but we have very few patients just now, so that it
makes very little difference. . . .

My occupation at home just now is as new as that in
the office—it is shoemaking. I am busy upon the second
pair of gaiter boots. They are made of canvas, presented
me by a friend. It was taken from one of our James River
vessels, and has been often spread to the breeze under the
"Stars and Bars." The vessel was sunk among the obstructions at Drury's [Drewry's] Bluff. The gaiters are cut out
by a shoemaker, stitched and bound by the ladies, then
soled by a shoemaker, for the moderate sum of fifty dollars. Last year he put soles on a pair for ten dollars. They
are then blacked with the material used for blacking guns
in the navy. They are very handsome gaiters and bear
polishing by blacking and the shoe-brush as well as
morocco. They are lasting and very cheap when compared
with those we buy, which are from $125.[6]

*But it was not all work and no play for the women
of the embattled Confederacy. T. C. De Leon, who was in
Richmond in the winter of 1861-2, noted that*

The people of Richmond had at first held up their
hands in holy horror at the mere mention of amusement.
What! with a war in the land must people enjoy themselves? Never! it would be heartless!

But human nature in Virginia is pretty much like human nature everywhere else; and bad as the war was,
people gradually got used to "the situation." They had
lost friends—a relation or two was pretty badly marked

perhaps—but what glory the tens and hundreds left had gained! There was no fighting now; and the poor fellows in camp would be only too glad to know that their brothers-in-arms were being paid for their toils by the smiles of the fair. The great majority of the strangers, too, were young men who had been recommended to the mercy of the society by these very sufferers in camp.

Gradually these influences worked—the younger and gayer people indulged in the "danceable teas," Wyatt spoke of, after their sewing-circles. Imperceptibly the sewing was left for other times; and by Christmas there was a more constant—if less formal and general—round of gaiety than had been known for years. This brought the citizens and strangers more together, and naturally the result was a long season of more regular parties and unprecedented gaiety. Many still frowned at this, and, as usual, made unhappy Washington the scapegoat—averring that her pernicious example of heartlessness and frivolity had worked the evil. These rigid Romans stayed at home and worked on zealously in their manufacture of warm clothing, deformed socks and impossible gloves for the soldier boys. All honor to them for their constancy, if they thought they were right, and the harmless gaiety wrong; and they fought the good fight, from behind their ABATIS of knitting needles, only with the innocent weapons of tongue and precept. But human nature and inclination still held their own; and there were many defections from the ranks of the elect to those of the more practical—and probably equally well-intentioned—pleasure-seekers.

But parties were by no means the only resource for pleasure-lovers. Anything that combined amusement and put dollars in the treasuries of charitable societies became the rage; and here the rigidly virtuous and the nonelect met on neutral ground. Among the amateurs of the city were some who would have taken high rank in any musical circle, and these gave a series of concerts for the benefit of distressed families of the soldiers. The performers were the most fashionable of the society; and, of course, the judgment of their friends—who crowded to overflowing the churches where the concerts were held—was not to be relied on. But critics from New Orleans and all parts of the South declared the performances creditable to any city. After them the audience broke up into little cliques and had the jolliest little suppers the winter produced, with the inevitable "lancers" until the smallest of small hours.

Then there were charades and TABLEAUX parties; while a few—more ambitious of histrionic fame—got up private theatricals. Altogether, in the gay set, the first winter of the war was one to be written in red letters, for old Richmond rang with a chime of merry laughter that for the time drowned the echo of the summer's fights and the groans of the wayside hospitals. . . .

But the novelty most remarked in the society of this winter was the household of President Davis. Soon after the government was firmly established in Richmond, the state of Virginia placed at his disposal a plain but comfortable house; and here—with only the ladies of his family and his private secretary—he lived with the quiet simplicity of a private citizen.

It will hardly be invading her SACRA PRIVATA to say that the President's lady did everything to remove false ideas that sprung up regarding the social atmosphere of the "Executive Mansion." She was "at home" every evening; and, collecting round her a staff that numbered some of the most noted men and brilliant women both of the stranger and resident society, assured all her varied guests a warm welcome and a pleasant visit. In this circle Mr. Davis would, after the trying business of the day, give himself an hour's relaxation before entering on labors that went far into the night; and favored friends and chance visitors alike here met the man, where they expected the official. . . .

In these informal receptions of his lady, Mr. Davis said

little; listening to the varied flow of talk that showed her equally cognizant and appreciative of social, literary, and sterner topics. For the edification of the gayer visitor, she related odd experiences of her public life, with rare power of description and admirable flashes of humor. She discussed the latest book with some of the small LITTERATEURS with whom she was infested; or talked knowingly of the last picture, or the newest opera, faint echoes from which might elude the grim blockaders on the coast.

Mr. Davis spoke little, seeming to find a refreshing element in her talk, that—as she pithily said of someone else—was like tea, that cheers but not inebriates. Occasionally he clinched an argument, or gave a keener point to an idea by a short, strong sentence.

After all had partaken of the cup of tea handed around informally, Mr. Davis retired to his study and once more donned his armor for battle with the giants without and the dwarfs within his territory.

These informal "evenings" began to grow popular with the better class of Virginians, and tended to a much more cordial tone between the citizens and their chief. They were broken by bimonthly "levees," at which Mr. and Mrs. Davis received "the world and his wife."

But the formal "levee" was a Washington custom and smacked too much of the "old concern" to become very popular, although curiosity to see the man of the hour and to assist at an undress review of the celebrities of the new nation, thronged the parlors each fortnight. A military band was always in attendance; the chiefs of cabinet and bureaux moved about the crowd; and generals—who had already won names to live forever—passed, with small hands resting lightly on their chevrons, and bright eyes speaking most eloquently that old truism about who best deserve the fair.

More than once that winter General Johnston moved through the rooms—followed by all eyes and calling up memories of subtle strategy and hard-won victory. Sometimes the burly form of [General James] Longstreet appeared, ever surrounded by those "little people" in whom he delighted; and the blond beard of [General John B.] Hood—whose name already began to shine with promise of its future brilliance—towered over the throng of leading editors, "senior wranglers" from both houses of Congress, and dancing men wasting their time in the vain effort to talk.

But not only the chosen ten thousand were called. Sturdy artisans, with their best coats and hands scrubbed to the proper point of cleanliness for shaking the President's, were always there. Moneyed men came, with speculation in their eyes, and lobby members trying to throw dust therein; while country visitors—having screwed their courage up to the desperate point of being presented—always dropped Mr. Davis's hand as if its not overcordial grasp burned them.

But the "levees" on the whole, if odd exhibitions, were at least useful in letting the "dear public" have a glimpse of the inner workings of the great machine of government. And they proved, even more than the social evenings, the ease of right with which Varina Howell Davis wore her title of "the first lady of the land." [7]

Social gatherings, at least in Richmond, were not always marked by Spartan simplicity. One lady recorded that in January 1864 she attended a large reception at the Davis home where the ladies looked "positively gorgeous." "We should not," she added, "expect supplies in these times, but we do have them. Champagne is $350 a dozen, but we sometimes have champagne. The confectioners charge $15 for a cake, but we have cake." Another recorded in her diary: "We had for dinner oyster soup, besides roast mutton, ham, boned turkey, wild duck, partridge, plum pudding, sauterne, burgundy, sherry, and Madeira. There is life in the old land yet!" And a Richmond editor wrote that while thousands of the poor had almost forgotten the taste of meat, "upper tendon was as gay as if peace and *plenty blessed the land." There was, he continued, "one continued round of balls and parties and great suppers. . . . Nero fiddled while Rome was burning. There is much fiddling in Richmond, while battle and famine encompass us on every hand." In March 1863 the Richmond* Enquirer *charged:*

This people has been too luxurious. It has not known what it is to want. And the proof that we do not yet suffer what nations usually do in such deadly emergencies, is seen in the fact that it has not yet been found needful to visit every household and to see that it has only a CERTAIN QUANTITY of provisions for its support in a GIVEN TIME; and in the fact that armed mobs have not yet broken into the stores of millers and flour dealers and distributed their contents. . . .

The Confederate people enjoy at this time a high reputation abroad because of the privations which they are supposed to be heroically enduring in their struggle for independence. That reputation is false, and we ought to be ashamed of it. We owe it to the constant Yankee falsehoods about the rebellion being nearly starved out. Northern newspapers, to impose upon Europe and stave off recognition, have assured the world that the people of these states cannot hold out much longer because they have neither food nor clothes. And we have seen Yankee illustrated papers with engravings representing the famishing population of principal Southern cities thronging eagerly around public soup kitchens—high-bred ladies with thin cheeks and the tattered remnants of fashionable dresses—jostling together and rushing over one another, holding out their lean hands for the rations handed to them at the bayonet's point. The Yankee artists do us too much honor. Our resistance has not as yet cost us these picturesque sufferings. And Europeans, lately come over to witness the dreadful scene with their own eyes, are amazed at finding society in the South as well appointed and luxurious as ever. . . .

But is not the time come when luxuries and superficialities are criminal? In this beleaguered land, so hard beset by a savage and powerful foe, harder pressed than ever was a besieged city, and expecting a more terrible doom in case of conquest, has any one man a right to devour the sustenance of four? Has any man a moral right to send the wealth of the land out to the Yankee enemy to purchase fine broadcloth, or jewelry, or artificial flowers? Has any man, not in the army, a moral right to ride or drive sleek horses for show, while the horses that draw our artillery and baggage trains and ambulances are dropping their hoofs off and eating one another's tails for want of proper food? [8]

Judith McGuire agreed:

Some persons in this beleaguered city seem crazed on the subject of gaiety. In the midst of the wounded and dying, the low state of the commissariat, the anxiety of the whole country, the troubles of every kind by which we are surrounded, I am mortified to say that there are gay parties given in the city. There are those denominated "starvation parties," where young persons meet for innocent enjoyment and retire at a reasonable hour; but there are others where the most elegant suppers are served— cakes, jellies, ices in profusion, and meats of the finest kinds in abundance, such as might furnish a meal for a regiment of General Lee's army. I wish these things were not so, and that every extra pound of meat could be sent to the army.

When returning from the hospital after witnessing the dying scene of a brother whose young sister hung over him in agony, with my heart full of the sorrows of hospital-life I passed a house where there were music and dancing. The revulsion of feeling was sickening. I thought of the gaiety of Paris during the French Revolution, of the "cholera ball" in Paris, the ball at Brussels the night before the battle of Waterloo, and felt shocked that our own Virginians at such a time should remind me of scenes which we were wont to think only belonged to the lightness of foreign society. It seems to me that the army, when it hears of the gaiety of Richmond, must think it heartless, particularly while it is suffering such hardships in her defense.

The weddings, of which there are many, seem to be conducted with great quietness. . . . There seems to be a perfect mania on the subject of matrimony. Some of the churches may be seen open and lighted almost every night for bridals, and wherever I turn I hear of marriages in prospect.

> In peace Love tunes the shepherd's reed;
> In war he mounts the warrior's steed.

sings the "Last Minstrel" of the Scottish days of romance; and I do not think that our modern warriors are a whit behind them either in love or war. My only wonder is, that they find the time for the love-making amid the storms of warfare. Just at this time, however, I suppose our valiant knights and ladies fair are taking advantage of the short respite caused by the alternate snows and sunshine of our variable climate having made the roads impassable to Grant's artillery and baggage-wagons.

A soldier in our hospital called to me as I passed his bed the other day, "I say, Mrs. ——, when do you think my wound will be well enough for me to go to the country?"

"Before very long, I hope."

"But what does the doctor say, for I am mighty anxious to go?"

I looked at his disabled limb, and talked to him hopefully of his being able to enjoy country air in a short time.

"Well, try to get me up, for you see, it ain't the country air I am after, but I wants to get married, and the lady don't know that I am wounded, and maybe she'll think I don't want to come."

"Ah," said I, "but you must show her your scars, and

if she is a girl worth having she will love you all the better for having bled for our country; and you must tell her

> It is always the heart that is bravest in war
> That is the fondest and truest in love.

He looked perfectly delighted with the idea; and as I passed him again, he called out: "Lady, please stop a minute and tell me the verse over again, for, you see, when I do get there, if she is affronted, I wants to give her the prettiest excust I can, and I think that verse is beautiful." [9]

Mrs. Chesnut also marked the course of romance in wartime:

Isabella says that war leads to love-making. She says these soldiers do more courting here in a day than they would do at home, without a war, in ten years.

In the pauses of conversation, we hear: "She is the noblest woman God ever made!"

"Goodness!" exclaims Isabella. "Which one?"

The amount of courting we hear in these small rooms. Men have to go to the front, and they say their say desperately. I am begining to know all about it. The girls tell me. And I overhear—I cannot help it. But this style is unique, is it not? "Since I saw you—last year—standing by the turnpike gate, you know—my battle-cry has been: 'God, my country, and you!'" So many are lame. Major [Charles S.] Venable says: "It is not 'the devil on two sticks' now; the farce is 'Cupid on Crutches.'"

General [John C.] Breckinridge's voice broke in: "They are my cousins. So I am determined to kiss them good-by. Good-by nowadays is the very devil; it means forever, in all probability, you know; all the odds against us. So I advanced to the charge soberly, discreetly, and in the fear of the Lord. The girls stood in a row—four of the very prettiest I ever saw."

Sam, with his eyes glued to the floor, cried: "You were afraid—you backed out."

"But I did nothing of the kind. I kissed every one of them, honestly, heartily. . . ."

We have laughed so at broken hearts—the broken hearts of the foolish love stories. But Buck, now, is breaking her heart for her brother, Willie. Hearts do break in silence, without a word or a sigh. . . .

When I remember all the true-hearted, the light-hearted, the gay and gallant boys who have come laughing, singing, and dancing in my way in the three years now past; how I have looked into their brave young eyes and helped them as I could in every way and then saw them no more forever; how they lie stark and cold, dead upon the battlefield, or moldering away in hospitals or prisons, which is worse—I think if I consider the long array of those bright youths and loyal men who have gone to their death almost before my very eyes, my heart might break, too. Is anything worth it—this fearful sacrifice, this awful penalty we pay for the war? [10]

All women were not equally high-minded and patriotic. Many grew tired of the war. They wanted their men back from the army, and some encouraged desertion. Some wearied of standing in line for food and clothing and of paying for it with constantly depreciating money. Some were actually hungry. Their distresses culminated in bread-riots in many Southern cities in the spring of 1863. The most serious occurred in Richmond on April 2. Sallie Putnam was there, and she wrote:

The rioters were represented in a heterogeneous crowd of Dutch, Irish, and free Negroes—of men, women, and children—armed with pistols, knives, hammers, hatchets, axes, and every other weapon that could be made useful in their defense, or might subserve their designs in breaking into stores for the purpose of thieving. More impudent and defiant robberies were never committed, than disgraced, in the open light of day on a bright morning in spring, the city of Richmond. The cry for bread with which this violence commenced was soon subdued, and instead of articles of food the rioters directed their efforts to stores containing dry-goods, shoes, etc. Women were seen bending under loads of sole-leather, or dragging after them heavy cavalry boots, brandishing their huge knives, and swearing, though apparently well fed, that they were dying from starvation—yet it was difficult to imagine how they could masticate or digest the edibles under the weight of which they were bending. Men carried immense loads of cotton cloth, woolen goods, and other articles, and but few were seen to attack the stores where flour, groceries, and other provisions were kept.

This disgraceful mob was put to flight by the military. Cannon were planted in the street, and the order to disperse or be fired upon drove the rioters from the commercial portion of the city to the Capitol Square, where they menaced the Governor, until, by the continued threatenings of the State Guards and the efforts of the police in arresting the ringleaders, a stop was put to these lawless and violent proceedings.

It cannot be denied that WANT OF BREAD was at this time too fatally true, but the sufferers for food were not to be found in this mob of vicious men and lawless viragoes who, inhabiting quarters of the city where reigned riot and depravity, when followed to their homes after this demonstration, were discovered to be well supplied with articles of food. Some of them were the keepers of stores, to which they purposed adding the stock stolen in their raid on wholesale houses.[11]

One of the most notable accomplishments of the women of the Confederacy was their ingenuity in finding substitutes for items no longer available. Shoes were difficult to obtain because of the scarcity of leather, and squirrel and dog skins, canvas, and wood were used in its stead. Kerosene and sperm oil were cut off, and those who stayed

up after dark used candles made of beeswax or other substitutes. Kate Cumming recorded in her diary in March 1863
that "we have no light of any kind, nor even light wood.
I am compelled to retire at dark, which is a great trial
for me, reading being one of my chief comforts." A year
later Mrs. Chesnut noted how easy it was to distinguish
newly arrived persons because of the superior quality of
their clothing. "We were all in a sadly molting condition,"
she said. "We had come to the end of our clothes in three
years, and now our only resource was to turn them upside
down, or inside out, and in mending, darning, patching,
etc." A year before that a Richmond lady recorded that
milk was "very scarce and high," and that white sugar
was beyond the reach of people of moderate means but
that she had learned to use brown sugar for sweetening
her tea. "Before the war," she said, "we would have
scorned it, but now we enjoy it exceedingly, and feel
ourselves very much blessed to have it."

But young girls in Petersburg, like young girls everywhere, were more concerned with wardrobes than with
pantries or larders. Sara Pryor, in January 1864, marveled
at their ingenuity.

My Petersburg beauties were all wearing hats of their
own manufacture, the favorite style being the Alpine with
a pointed crown. For trimming, very soft and lovely
flowers were made of feathers, the delicate white feather
with a tuft of fleecy marabout at its stem. . . . Neatly
trimmed and suitably tinted, these flowers were handsome
enough for anybody, and were in great demand. Cock's
plumes were also used on hats, iridescent, and needing
no coloring. With the downy breast of a goose which came
into my possession I essayed the making of a powder-puff
for my baby, but alas! the oil in the cuticle proved a
perennial spring which could not be dried up by soda or
sunning, and finally I saw my powder-puff disappearing
in a hole, drawn downward by a vigorous and hungry rat.

The young girls who visited me never complained of

their privations in the matter of food, but they sorely grieved over their shabby wardrobes.

"I really think," said one, "if we can only get along until we can wear white waists, we shall do very well. Every time a white waist is washed it's made new—but these old flannel sacks—ugh!"

One day Mary Meade made me a visit. Always beautiful, her face wore on this afternoon a seraphic, beatific expression.

"Tell me, dear," I said, "all about it." I supposed she had heard her lover had been promoted or was coming home on a furlough.

She held up her two hands. "IT'S JUST THESE GLOVES!" said Mary. "I can't help it. They make me perfectly happy! They have just come through the blockade."

The butcher shops were closed and many of the dry-goods stores; but somebody had ordered a large quantity of narrow crimson woolen braid and had failed to accept it. We seized upon it. Every one of us had garments embroidered with it—in scrolls, Maltese crosses, undulating lines, leaves; all of which goes to prove that the desire for ornament is an instinct of our nature, outliving the grosser affections for the good things of the table. The consciousness of being well dressed, we have been told, will afford a peace of mind far exceeding anything to be derived from the comforts of religion.

It had not been many years since every Virginia farm owned a house for a great cumbrous loom, with beams supported against the ceiling. The door of the loom-house was again opened, and the weaver installed upon her high bench. Cotton cloth was woven and dyed yellow with butternut, black with walnut-bark, gray with willow. A mordant to "set the dye" was unattainable—but at last rusty iron, nails, old horseshoes, old clamps and hinges, were found to be effective. Every atom of black silk was a treasure. It was shredded to mix with cotton before carding. Even now the cells of my brain waken at the sight of a bundle of old black silk, and my fingers would fain respond.

Pins became scarce. People walked about with downcast eyes; they were looking for pins! Thorns were gathered and dried to use as pins.[12]

A few months later the wife of a Confederate general wrote a friend in Europe:

There are many little things in which our daily life is changed—many luxuries cut off from the table which we have forgotten to miss. Our mode of procuring necessaries is very different and far more complicated. The condition of our currency has brought about many curious results; for instance, I have just procured leather for our Negro shoes by exchanging tallow for it, of which we have a great quantity from some fat beeves fattened and killed upon the place. I am now bargaining with a factory up the country to exchange pork and lard with them for blocks of yarn to weave Negro clothes; and not only Negro clothing I have woven, I am now dyeing thread to weave homespun for myself and daughters. I am raveling up or having raveled all the old scraps of fine worsteds and dark silks to spin thread for gloves for the General and staff, which gloves I am to knit. These home-knit gloves and these homespun dresses will look much neater and nicer than you would suppose.

My daughters and I being in need of undergarments, I sent a quantity of lard to the Macon factory and received in return fine unbleached calico—a pound of lard paying for a yard of cloth. They will not sell cloth for money. This unbleached calico my daughters and self are now making up for ourselves. You see some foresight is necessary to provide for the necessaries of life. . . .

At Christmas I sent presents to my relations in Savannah, and instead of elegant trifles I used to give at that season I bestowed as follows:—several bushels of meal, peas, bacon, butter, lard, eggs, sausages, soap (home-made), rope, string, and a coarse basket. All of which

articles, I am assured, were most warmly welcomed, and
more acceptable than jewels and silks would have been.[13]

*An Atlanta paper remarked upon the ladies of the Con-
federacy:*

Ingenuity among the female sex was never demonstrated to exist to such a considerable extent as is proven
by a bird's-eye view of the dear creatures as they prome-
nade . . . any pleasant afternoon. . . .

Anyone with an observant eye, in glancing at what
appears to be an elaborate toilet, will detect the marks of
antiquity which is deftly concealed by the artistic fingers
of the remodelers. Look at a dress closely, and you will
find . . . that the skirt has been inverted. The frizzles
that wound about the lower end are now hidden in the
neat folds of the waist. The body you can't see, because it
is worn beneath the neat little net shawl, the work of her
own fingers. Then observe the "set" of the skirt. The full
rotundity—the perfect symmetry of a brand new hoop
skirt is wanting. The shape is goodly, however, for the
dear creature has had it off for the hundredth time, and
hangs it over Dina's or Cuffee's head while she mends
some of the broken ribs. She has bandaged one in half
a dozen places as carefully and neatly as a surgeon
bandages a broken limb. Another that is injured beyond repair is extracted from the skeleton and its place is left
void. Then she has gone over the whole anatomy of her
hoop until it is quite passable, and when concealed beneath her snowy skirts—which, alas, have been turned
upside down—and the folds of her dress, it needs the eye
of a connoisseur to detect that the thing has ever been
mended.

Then look at the hats! into how many comely shapes
do we see the Palmetto woven—and pretty, at that,
especially when they are rigged out with scraps of red,
green, and blue ribbon—resurrected from some dilapi-
dated old band-box—and ornamented with what appears
at a distance to be a white goose. In the manufacture of

plumes, the cock and goose have supplied the function of the ostrich—but it is all home manufacture. Then, again, look at the feet. The stockings are home-knit—store hose are too high—and the shoes are made of some of Pa's old pants, and fit as neatly as a three-hundred-dollar gaiter.[14]

One of the most extraordinary social events of the Confederacy was a dinner given on New Year's, 1865, by the people of Virginia to General Lee's army. The dinner was prepared under the direction of the "King of Caterers," Thompson Tyler. Beef, ham, mutton, venison, shoat, fowl, and sausage were served, and thirty-six thousand loaves of bread were baked at the establishment of Pleasants and Fraser, on Twentieth Street. The night before the feast was to be carried to the trenches, a Richmond editor visited the Ballard House, where the food had been prepared and stored.

The large and commodious bar-room of the Ballard, once filled with liquors, is now filled with the fowl and flesh that has passed through the fiery ordeal of the oven and broiler, and now lie piled into miniature mountains, awaiting the knife of the carver and the pleasure of those for whom they are sacrificed. A guard is constantly stationed here as well as in the cook room, for the savory meats are too tempting to be trusted alone. Gentlemen, members of the separate committees, alternate with each other at night keeping watch and ward and sitting up with the dead turkeys, deceased porkers, departed pullets, and the general hecatomb of slaughtered animals. . . .

It is estimated by good judges of provisions in bulk that enough flesh and fowl is already cooked to feed thirty or forty thousand men; and as additions are hourly being made by purchase and donation of fresh lots, all idea of a lack of anything is dispelled, and it is believed there will be enough to spare, sufficient to send a specimen diet to "Useless" Grant, under flag of truce. . . .

Already there are rumors of the hospitals being depopulated, the laggards and skulkers returning, all hastening to General Lee's lines, to the end that they may partake of a nation's gratitude and a nation's pride in the dinner to the whole army, in which the commonest private will be entitled to the first helping and the best.[15]

This was the last feast the troops were to have. Three months would bring the end. But the devotion of the women, exemplified in this final gesture, was to buoy the hearts of the men of the Confederacy in the still darker days that lay ahead.

VIII: DISCONTENT

Southern soldiers early found that army life was not all glory in battle. Most of it consisted of camp routine, of drill and bad food, of cold and wet—or unbearable heat— of long hours of marching, of sickness, of loneliness, and of unceasing boredom. Many had enlisted for a year or even less, and by the time their terms were up, they had a different outlook on war. Besides, things did not always go well at home. And wives and children had to be supported. Crops had to be planted and fields had to be tended. Congress, forewarned that the army would melt away if left on a volunteer basis, in April 1862 passed

AN ACT to further provide for the public defense.

In view of the exigencies of the country and the absolute necessity of keeping in the service our gallant Army, and of placing in the field a large additional force to meet the advancing columns of the enemy now invading our soil: Therefore

SECTION 1. THE CONGRESS OF THE CONFEDERATE STATES OF AMERICA DO ENACT,

That the President be, and he is hereby authorized to call out and place in the military service of the Confederate States, for three years, unless the war shall have been sooner ended, all white men who are residents of the

Confederate States, between the ages of eighteen and thirty-five years at the time the call or calls may be made, who are not legally exempted from military service. All of the persons aforesaid who are now in the armies of the Confederacy, and whose term of service will expire before the end of the war, shall be continued in the service for three years from the date of their original enlistment, unless the war shall have sooner ended. . . .

SEC. 9. BE IT FURTHER ENACTED, That persons not liable for duty may be received as substitutes for those who are, under such regulations as may be prescribed by the Secretary of War.[1]

This was the first national conscription act ever passed in America, and many patriotic Southerners saw it as a danger signal. To men who regarded the state as sovereign it seemed an unwarranted grasping of power by the central government. To others, who acknowledged its constitutionality, the act seemed unnecessary and unwise—a reflection on the patriotism of the people.

Among those concerned about the conscription act was Governor Joseph E. Brown of Georgia. Not a member of the planter class, Brown had been born in the remote mountain region of north Georgia. From an early life of hardship and poverty, he had educated himself for the law and for politics. In the state legislature he had been an ardent, almost fanatical, defender of State rights. Forceful and independent in judgment, he had been first elected governor in 1857 when he was but thirty-six years of age, and was serving his third term in the spring of 1862. Learning of the passage of the conscript act, he hastily wrote Jefferson Davis.

DEAR SIR: So soon as I received from the Secretary of War official notice of the passage by Congress of the conscription act, placing in the military service of the Confederate States all white men between the ages of eighteen and thirty-five years, I saw that it was impossible for me longer to retain in the field the Georgia state troops without probable collision and conflict with the Confederate authorities in the face of the enemy. I therefore acquiesced in the necessity which compelled me to transfer the state forces to the command of the Confederate general at Savannah. . . . The plea of necessity, so far at least as this state is concerned, cannot be set up in defense of the conscription act. When the government of the United States disregarded and attempted to trample upon the rights of the states Georgia set its power at defiance, and seceded from the Union rather than submit to the consolidation of all power in the hands of the . . . Federal government. The conscription act not only put it in the power of the executive of the Confederacy to disorganize her troops, which she was compelled to call into the field for her own defense in addition to her just quota because of the neglect of the Confederacy to place sufficient troops upon her coast for her defense, which would have required less than half the number she has sent to the field, but also places it in his power to destroy her state government by disbanding her law-making power. . . .

There are a large number of the members of the General Assembly between the ages of eighteen and thirty-five. . . . They, therefore, fall within the provisions of the conscription act. . . . When the members meet at the capitol . . . they might be claimed as conscripts by a Confederate officer and arrested with a view to carry them to some remote part of the Confederacy as recruits to fill up some company now in service. They have no military power and could only look to the executive of the state for military protection, and I cannot hesitate to say that in such case I should use all the remaining military force of the state in defense of a co-ordinate constitutional branch of the government. I can, therefore, permit no enrollment of the members of the General Assembly under the conscription act. The same is true of the judges of the . . . courts . . . and of the secretaries of the executive department, the heads and necessary clerks of the other departments of the state government, and the tax collectors and receivers of the different counties. . . . The same remark applies to the staff of the commander-in-chief. . . . The state's quartermaster, commissary, ordnance, and engineer departments fall within the same rule. The major-generals, brigadier-generals, and other field officers of the militia would seem to be entitled to like consideration.

Again, the Western and Atlantic Railroad is the property of the state and is under the control and management of the Governor. It is a source of revenue to the state, and its successful management is a matter of great military importance both to the state and to the Confederacy. I now have an efficient force of officers and workmen upon the road and must suspend operations if all between eighteen and thirty-five are taken away from the road. I would also invite your attention to the further fact that the state owns and controls the Georgia Military Institute at Marietta, and now has in the institute over 125 cadets, a large proportion of whom are within the age of conscripts. If they are not exempt this most important institution is broken up. I must not omit in this connection the students of the state university and of the other colleges of the state. These valuable institutions of learning must also be suspended if the law is enforced against the students. I would also respectfully call your attention to the further fact that in portions of our state where the slave population is heavy almost the entire white male population capable of bearing arms (except the overseers on the plantations) are now in the military service of the Confederacy. Most of these overseers are over eighteen and under thirty-five. If they are carried to the field thousands of slaves must be left without overseers, and their labor not only lost at a time when there is great need of it in the production of provisions and supplies for our armies, but the peace and safety of helpless women and children must be imperiled for want of protection against bands of idle slaves, who must be left to roam over the country without restraint. . . .

The conscription act gives the President the power to enroll the entire militia of the states between eighteen and thirty-five. . . . It places it in the power of the President to take a major-general of the militia of a state . . . and place him in the ranks of the C. S. Army under the command of a third lieutenant appointed by the President, and to treat him as a deserter if he refuses to obey the call and submit to the command of the subaltern placed over him. . . . I notice, by a perusal of the conscription act, that the President may, with the consent of the Governors of the respective states, employ state officers in the enrollment of the conscripts. While I shall throw no obstructions in the way of the general enrollment of persons embraced within the act, except as above stated, I do not feel that it is the duty of the executive of a state to employ actually the officers of the state in the execution of a law which virtually strips the state of her constitutional military powers, and, if fully executed, destroys the legislative department of her government, making even the sessions of her General Assembly dependent upon the will of the Confederate executive. I, therefore, respectfully decline all connection with the proposed enrollment and propose to reserve the question of the constitutionality of the act and its binding force upon the people of this state for their consideration at a time when it may less seriously embarrass the Confederacy in the prosecution of the war.[2]

Brown was not the only state executive to withhold complete co-operation on conscription. In late summer Davis learned that South Carolina was proposing obstructive measures. On September 3 he wrote the Governor and Executive Council of South Carolina.

GENTLEMEN: I have received from the Adjutant-General a communication addressed to him by Lieut. Col. J. S. Preston, the officer charged with the execution of the law for the enrollment of conscripts in the state of South Carolina. From this communication and its inclosures I learn with profound regret that it is your purpose to promulgate an order "countervailing" that which Lieutenant-Colonel Preston has been instructed to issue, and thus to obstruct the due execution of the conscript law. The issue thus presented to the Confederate government is one which I am unable to avoid without violation of official duty. It is of the gravest character, and I am unwilling to accept it without an appeal to your well-known and fully recognized patriotism and devotion to the common cause. . . . On the 19th of August it was by you "resolved that Col. J. S. Preston be informed that the Governor and Council do insist upon the exemption granted by the state authorities of all persons claimed to be liable to Confederate conscription. . . ."

If I do not misapprehend the meaning of these passages, the right is here broadly asserted that the state of South Carolina may at her pleasure relieve a portion of her citizens from obedience to laws of the Confederate Congress, admitted to be "constitutional laws" by your permitting them to be executed on another portion of the people. The right thus asserted is, to my mind, so devoid of foundation that I hesitate in attributing to you the intention of maintaining it, and still entertain the hope that I may have misapprehended your meaning. It is so very clear that the agreement of the states, as contained in the Constitution, to delegate to Congress the power to declare war and raise armies would be utterly defeated by the exercise of a power on the part of the states to exempt at their pleasure any or all of the citizens from service in the armies of the Confederacy, that I am at a loss how to illustrate so plain a proposition. If a state may free her citizens at her own discretion from the burden of military duty, she may do the same in regard to the burden of taxation, or any other lawful duty, payment, or service. In other words, the assertion of such a right on the part of the state is tantamount to a denial of the right of the

Confederate government to enforce the exercise of the delegated power, and would render a confederacy an impracticable form of government. . . .

The redress of grievances, whether inflicted by legislation or executive usurpation, and the direct conflict of executive authorities presents a condition of affairs so grave and is suggestive of consequences so disastrous that I am sure you cannot contemplate them without deep-seated alarm. On a memorable occasion in the history of South Carolina the state authority nullified an act of Congress because of unconstitutionality, but on no occasion did any portion of her citizens ever maintain the right of that state to modify an order of the General Government. It does not appear either from the resolution of your honorable body or from the letter of the chief of the military department that any other action is contemplated at present than a published order which will deter the citizens from obeying the Confederate laws and render those under them liable to punishment if it should happen that your opinion of their rights to exemption should be held erroneous by the courts. Without adverting to the deplorable effect upon public opinion that must necessarily result from the publication of orders exhibiting a direct conflict between the Confederate and state executives, may I not appeal to your candor for the admission that the rights of the state will be equally vindicated and those of the conscript be secured with less hazard to himself by an appeal to any competent judge for relief from the order of the Confederate officer? [3]

Not only was the constitutionality of the conscription act questioned, but also the effects of its enforcement. Governor John Milton of Florida complained to Davis about an order which required that invalids be brought to camps of instruction for examination. The resulting inconvenience to families was, he said, creating a morale problem. And a group of North Carolina legislators pointed out that there were few slaves in the region of

the state they represented and conscription was creating
a labor shortage there. "If the remaining conscripts," they
wrote, "are enrolled and ordered into camp, it can result
in nothing short of actual starvation among some of [the]
helpless women and children."

As a corollary to conscription Congress had also passed
AN ACT *to exempt certain persons from enrollment for*
service in the Armies of the Confederate States.

THE CONGRESS OF THE CONFEDERATE STATES OF AMERICA
DO ENACT, That all persons who shall be held unfit for military services under rules to be prescribed by the Secretary
of War; all in the service or employ of the Confederate
States; all judicial and executive officers of Confederate
or state governments; the members of both houses of the
Congress and of the legislatures of the several states and
their respective officers; all clerks of the officers of the
state and Confederate governments allowed by law; all
engaged in carrying the mails; all ferrymen on post routes;
all pilots and persons engaged in the marine service and
in actual service on river and railroad routes of transportation; telegraphic operators, and ministers of religion in
the regular discharge of ministerial duties; all engaged in
working iron mines, furnaces and foundries; all journey-
men printers actually employed in printing newspapers;
all presidents and professors of colleges and academies,
and all teachers having as many as twenty scholars;
superintendents of the public hospitals, lunatic asylums
and the regular nurses and attendants therein, and the
teachers employed in the institutions for the deaf and
dumb, and blind; in each apothecary store now established and doing business one apothecary in good standing
who is a practical druggist; superintendents and operatives
in wool and cotton factories, who may be exempted by the
Secretary of War; shall be and are hereby exempted from
military service in the Armies of the Confederate States.[4]

Six months later, the exemption law was amended to
include certain industrial workers, newspaper editors, mu-

nitions makers, farmers who had charge of as many as 500 head of cattle or 250 horses or mules, and an overseer for every plantation having as many as twenty slaves. This last provision became known as the "twenty nigger" law. State laws had already required the presence of a white man on slave plantations in order to provide police protection, as well as to increase production. But the law was detested by the non-slaveholders who cited it as proof that it was "a rich man's war but a poor man's fight."

Military service could also be avoided by securing a substitute who was not eligible for conscription. Thus a way out was provided for civilians who were not included in the exempted classes and who claimed they might make a more substantial contribution to the nation outside of the army.

The exemption acts aroused almost as much opposition as conscription. Many thousands of able-bodied young men sought employment in the deferred classes, or procured a substitute by paying fees ranging up to $5,000. In the summer of 1863 Generals Braxton Bragg, D. H. Hill, Leonidas Polk, and a dozen others wrote the Adjutant General:

SIR: We, the undersigned officers of the Confederate Army, being deeply impressed with the belief that unless the ranks are speedily replenished our cause will be lost, and being thoroughly satisfied that there is enough of able-bodied young men out of the service to accomplish that object, would earnestly implore the President of the Confederate States to take prompt measures to recruit our wasted armies by fresh levies from home. The wisdom of the Executive must decide whether this can better be done by calling upon the respective states for enlarged quotas of troops or by assembling the Congress of the nation so to modify the exemption provision in the conscript bill as to increase the Army without interfering materially with the great interests of the country. The whole system of exemption is based upon a false assumption. It

is assumed that none of the machinery of society, necessary for its comfort and convenience in a state of peace,
is to be disturbed amidst the mighty upheaval of a great
revolution. Thus, for example, we find multiplied rather
than diminished rural post-offices and printing presses,
which add doubtless to the comfort and convenience of
the people but contribute nothing to our success in arms.
In like manner there is an enormous disproportion between
the absolute wants of the people and the number of "shoe-
makers, blacksmiths, tanners, wagon makers, millers and
their engineers, millwrights, skilled and actually employed at their regular vocation in said trades," the
agents and employees of the different bureaus, departments, railroad and telegraph companies, etc.

We have been pained to notice that all those vocations
are crowded which afford exemption, while the ranks of
the army are daily becoming thinner. To their lasting reproach upon their manhood, hearty vigorous young men,
rather than take the field, eagerly seek fancy duty which
could be performed by women or disabled soldiers.

But we especially deplore that unfortunate provision of
the exemption bill which has allowed more than 150,000
soldiers to employ substitutes, and we express our honest
conviction that not one in a hundred of these substitutes
is now in the service. In numerous instances fraudulent
papers were employed, in others diseased men were
presented and accepted but to be discharged; in still more
cases vicious and unprincipled substitutes were bought
up but to desert at the first favorable moment.

Another heavy source of depletion to the Army cannot
be passed over. The friends of timid and effeminate young
men are constantly beseiging the War Department,
through Congressional and other agents, to get soldiers in
the army placed upon details or transferred to safe places.
The aggregate loss to the army from this cause alone is
most enormous.

We do know certainly that the detailed and exempted

men under forty-five exceed a quarter of a million of men; and we think that the army can be increased a quarter of a million without more suffering and inconvenience to the country than is to be expected in such a life and death struggle as we are engaged in. . . .

Lastly, we would respectfully but earnestly urge prompt action. With every inch of territory lost, there is a corresponding loss of men and the resources of war. Conscripts cannot be got from the region held by the Yankees, and soldiers will desert back to their homes in possession of the enemy. Some do so from disaffection, some from weariness with the war, and some to protect their families against a brutal foe. From these combined causes the occupation of our soil weakens us in men as well as in the means to feed and clothe our troops.

Early and vigorous measures to recruit our wasted ranks may save us further loss of men and resources, and possibly the existence of the Southern Confederacy itself.[5]

Governor of North Carolina in 1864 was Zebulon B. Vance, a lawyer from Buncombe County in the western mountains. He had been an ardent Unionist throughout the secession crisis, but when Lincoln called for volunteers to coerce South Carolina he organized a company of which he was elected captain. Promoted to the rank of colonel he fought in the Seven Days campaign around Richmond. He was early associated with W. W. Holden, publisher of the Raleigh Standard, *whose loyalty was already suspect in Richmond and whose early support of Vance caused the Davis government to distrust Vance thereafter, even though Vance advocated and practiced a vigorous prosecution of the war. Vance was a young man at the time—only thirty-four—and his boisterous good humor and frank, blunt honesty made him the most popular man in the state. In February 1864 he wrote Secretary Seddon about a decision State Chief Justice Richmond M. Pearson had just handed down.*

I desire to call your attention most earnestly to the

difficulties and complications arising from the conscription of principals of substitutes in this state.

Chief Justice Pearson has decided recently that the law is unconstitutional, and further that the act of Congress suspending the privilege of the writ of HABEAS CORPUS does not apply to these men. He therefore continues to grant the writ, and the execution being resisted by the enrolling officers by orders from the Conscript Bureau, the result will be a direct and unavoidable collision of state and Confederate authorities. I have taken the ground that the decision of a single judge at chambers does not possess the binding force and effect of an adjudicated case, but it only operates to discharge the individual. It certainly does this much, and until it is overruled it is final and absolute, made so expressly by the statutes of this state. It cannot be overruled except by the supreme court, which does not meet until June next. In the meantime, if the man is discharged I am bound to protect him, and if the process of the court is resisted I am forced by my oath of office to summon the military power of the state to enforce it. There is no escape from this conclusion.

An agreement was proposed by Chief Justice Pearson at Salisbury and accepted by Governor [Thomas] Bragg as counsel for the Government, subject to the approval or disapproval of the same, to remove one case to the supreme court by CERTIORARI, and to bind over all others applying for writs to appear and abide the decision thus to be rendered. This gave general satisfaction and had a quieting effect upon the whole state.

Since it has been understood, however, that the Confederacy would not recognize the arrangement the excitement is becoming very great, and I fear much trouble will result.

Knowing, as I trust you do, my great anxiety to avoid collision with the Confederate authorities and everything else that might tend to hinder its efficiency, yet it cannot be supposed that I am to omit a plain and obvious duty prescribed by my official oath. I therefore earnestly request that you will order a suspension of the enrollment of the principals of substitutes in North Carolina at least until time sufficient be allowed to exhaust all efforts at an amicable arrangement. I do not know a better one than that made at Salisbury, and which, though it would deprive the government of the services of these men until June, would yet give still greater advantages by preserving that peace and harmony between the respective governments without which all our labors will be in vain.

You will observe that I make no comment whatever upon the correctness of the chief justice's opinions. As an executive officer I consider that I have no right to do so; neither, with all due respect, do I consider you to have any such discretion; and however unfortunate it may be to the efficient and equal working of the government that the laws of Congress are at the mercy, so to speak, of the various judges of the various states, I submit that it is not possible to avoid it, in the absence of the supreme court of the Confederacy to give harmony and uniformity of construction. We can only obey the judges we now have, and even this is infinitely preferable to the assumption of judicial power by executive officers, and making their will the law.[6]

State judges like Pearson could nullify Confederate legislation because of the absence of a Confederate supreme court. As has already been noted, the Confederate Constitution provided for such a court, but petty jealousies kept Congress from setting it up. Confederate legislation was, therefore, at the mercy of zealous State rights judges like Pearson.

Conscription was only one of the laws that aroused bitter opposition to the Confederate government. Another was the suspension of the writ of habeas corpus. *Congress had first given Davis power to suspend the writ early in 1862, and had later extended the power until February 1863. But a year later, in February 1864, desertion and treasonable activity in various sections of the country impelled Davis again to ask Congress for the power to suspend. After bitter debate Congress granted the power for a period from February 15 to August 1, 1864.*

Meanwhile, the Georgia legislature had invited Alexander H. Stephens to address it on the progress of the war. An orphan who had been educated for the ministry, Stephens turned to the law, where he made a fortune, and distinguished himself in national politics. He openly opposed secession in 1861, and although Vice-President, he had become by 1862 the leader of the opposition to the Davis administration. His sallow complexion and emaciated body—he weighed less than one hundred pounds —was compensated for by a robust will. On March 16, 1864, he stood before the two houses of the legislature and in a shrill, piping voice said:

I come, now, to the last of these acts of Congress. The suspension of the writ of HABEAS CORPUS in certain cases. This is the most exciting, as it is by far the most important question before you. Upon this depends the question, whether the courts shall be permitted to decide upon the constitutionality of the late conscript act, should you submit that question to their decision; and upon it also depends other great essential rights enjoyed by us as freemen. This act, upon its face, confers upon the President, the Secretary of War, and the general commanding in the Trans-Mississippi Department . . . the power to arrest and imprison any person who may be simply charged with certain acts, not all of them even crimes under any law. . . .

In my judgment this is not only unwise, impolitic, and unconstitutional, but exceedingly dangerous to public liberty. Its constitutionality does not rest upon the idea that Congress has not the power to suspend the privilege of this writ. . . .

It attempts to provide for depriving persons of "liberty without the process of law." It attempts to annul and set at naught the great constitutional "right" of the people to be secure in their persons against "unreasonable seizures." It attempts to destroy and annihilate the bulwark of personal liberty, secured in our great chart to the humblest as well as the highest, that "no warrants shall issue but upon probable cause, supported by oath or affirmation," and "particularly describing the person to be seized." Nay, more, it attempts to change and transform the distribution of powers in our system of government. It attempts to deprive the judiciary department of its appropriate and legitimate functions, and to confer them upon the President, the Secretary of War, and the general commanding the Trans-Mississippi Department, or rather to confer them entirely upon the President, for those subordinates named in the act hold their places at his will, and in arrest under this act are to be governed by his orders. . . . I have no inclination to arraign the motives of those who disagree with me. Great principles are at stake, and I feel impelled by a high sense of duty, when my opinions are sought, to give them fully, clearly, and earnestly. . . .

You have been told that it affects none but the disloyal, none but traitors, or those who are no better than traitors, spies, bridge-burners, and the like; and you have been appealed to and asked if such are entitled to your sympathies. I affirm, and shall maintain before the world, that this act affects and may wrongfully oppress as loyal and as good citizens, and as true to our cause, as ever trod the soil or breathed the air of the South. . . . Whether such was the real object and intention of its framers and advocates, I know not. Against their motives or patriotism I have nothing to say. I take the act as I find it. . . .

Tell me not to put confidence in the President! That he will never abuse the power attempted to be lodged in his hands! The abuses may not be by the President. He will not execute the military orders that will be given. This will necessarily devolve upon subordinates, scattered all over the country, from the Potomac to the Rio Grande. He would have to possess two superhuman attributes to prevent abuses—omniscience and omnipresence . . . !

Who is safe under such a law? Who knows when he goes forth, when or whether he shall ever return? The President, according to the act, is to have power to arrest and imprison whomever he pleases upon a bare charge made, perhaps by an enemy, of disloyalty—the party making the charge not being required to swear it. Who, I repeat, is safe, or would be, under such a law? What were the real objects of the act, in these clauses, as to treason, disloyalty, and the others, I do not know. To me it seems to be unreasonable to suppose that it was to reach real traitors and persons guilty of the offenses stated. For that object could have been easily accomplished without any such extraordinary power. . . . I have heard that one object was to control certain elections and expected assemblages in North Carolina, to put a muzzle upon certain presses and a bit in the mouth of certain speakers in that state. If this be so, I regard it the more dangerous to public liberty. I know nothing of the politics of North Carolina—nothing of the position of her leading public men. If there be traitors there, let them be constitutionally arrested, tried, and punished. . . .

One other view only, that relates to the particularly dangerous tendency of this act in the present state of the country, and the policy indicated by Congress—conscription has been extended to embrace all between seventeen and fifty years of age. It cannot be possible that the intention and object of that measure was really to call and keep in the field all between these ages. The folly and ruinous consequences of such a policy are too apparent. Details are to be made, and must be made, to a large extent. The effect and the object of this measure, therefore, was not to raise armies and procure soldiers, but to put all the population of the country between those ages under military law. Whatever the object was, the effect is to put much the larger portion of the labor of the country, both white and slave, under the complete control of the President. Under this system almost all the useful and necessary occupations of life will be completely under the control of one man. No one between the ages of seventeen and fifty can tan your leather, make your shoes, grind your grain, shoe your horse, lay your plow, make your wagon, repair your harness, superintend your farm, procure your salt, or perform any other of the necessary vocations of life (except teachers, preachers, and physicians, and a very few others) without permission from the President. This is certainly an extraordinary and a dangerous power. . . . Could the whole country be more completely under the power and control of one man, except as to life and limb? Could dictatorial powers be more complete . . . ?

In any and every view, therefore, I look upon this HABEAS CORPUS suspension act as unwise, impolitic, unconstitutional, and dangerous to public liberty.

But you have been asked, what can you do? Do? You can do much. If you believe the act to be unconstitutional, you can and ought so to declare your judgment to be. . . .

Let no one, therefore, be deterred from performing his duty on this occasion by the cry of counterrevolution, nor by the cry that it is the duty of all, in this hour of peril, to support the government. Our government is composed of executive, legislative, and judicial departments, under the Constitution. He most truly and faithfully supports the government who supports and defends the Constitution. Be not misled by this cry, or that you must not say anything against the administration or you will injure the cause. . . . Listen to no such cry. And let no one be influenced by that other cry of the bad effect . . . such discussions and such action will have upon our gallant citizen soldiers in the field. . . .

As a parting remembrance, a lasting memento to be

engraved on your memories and your hearts, I warn you against that most insidious enemy which approaches with her siren song, "Independence first and liberty afterwards." It is a false delusion. Liberty is the animating spirit, the soul of our system of government, and, like the soul of man, when once lost, it is lost forever.[7]

By the autumn of 1864 attrition was depleting the Confederate armies. For some months the possibility of conscripting slaves as soldiers had been informally discussed. Then, on November 7, Davis in a message to Congress proposed the drafting of slaves and rewarding those drafted with emancipation. This recommendation was shocking to many Southerners.

The Richmond Examiner, *edited by the erratic and brilliant J. Moncure Daniel and the caustic and mercurial Edward A. Pollard, had long been an outspoken opponent of the administration. Both men were less than forty years of age at this time, and both were ardent and brilliant defenders of slavery and State rights. Both came to lay the ills of the Confederacy at the feet of Davis. Regarding his proposal to conscript slaves* The Examiner *said:*

The proposal made in the President's message, in so far as it is practical and intelligible, is to double the number of slaves already authorized by law to be impressed for teamsters, laborers, etc., and to employ them in the additional work of "pioneers and engineer laborers." If the message had confined itself to this, and not "invited consideration of the propriety of a radical modification in the theory of the law," there would have been but little to be said. . . .

As it is, Mr. Davis has chosen to open up questions both deep and dangerous which, if Congress do not close them up peremptorily, may gravely disquiet our people and compromise our cause. It is truly astonishing and almost incredible that now in the fourth year of our independence and of a terrible war waged to vindicate that independence—after breaking up the old Federal Union because we would not suffer the Washington Congress to interfere with our state institutions—the President of the Confederate States should "invite" the Richmond Congress to consider a project for emancipating slaves by the Confederate authorities; and should at the same time speak of this emancipation as "a reward for faithful services" as a boon and a blessing, as something which would place these Negroes in a better position than before. Mr. Davis thus intimates his opinion, first, that laws of Congress, or the action of the Confederate executive, can liberate slaves; and second, that slavery is so dire and hideous and evil as to make escape from its horrors a reward and a boon even to an old worn-out Negro at the end of a term of "faithful service". . . .

We have been accustomed to think in this Southern country that the best friends of the Negroes were their own masters. . . . But now the President of the Confederate States opens quite another view of the matter. According to his message it is a rich reward for faithful services to turn a Negro wild. Slavery, then, in the eyes of Mr. Davis, keeps the Negro out of something which he has the capacity to enjoy: it depresses him below the level to which nature has given him powers to attain; it hinders the development of his faculties for good; it forbids his pursuit of happiness. If the case be so, then slavery is originally, radically, incurably wrong and sinful, and the sum of barbarism. This is what [William H.] Seward and [Charles] Sumner say: and this is what Mr. Davis says after them. They invoked the Federal Congress to discourage and discountenance slavery in the territories: he invites the Confederate Congress to consider the expediency of beginning to abolish it in the states.[8]

After months of debate Congress passed an act drafting slaves in mid-March 1865. Meanwhile the Examiner *had other crows to pick with Davis. In mid-December, in discussing an amendment to the exemptions law, it said:*

The bill to limit exemptions, reported by the House

Military Committee . . . ends by a sweeping clause which is to enable the Secretary of War (that is to say, the President) to exempt any other person or persons he, the President, may think proper. . . . He is to exempt such planters, etc., "as he may be satisfied will be more useful to the country in the pursuits of agriculture," and such other persons "as he may be satisfied ought to be exempted . . . on account of public necessity, justice, or equity." It is always HE that is to be satisfied; not the law; not the country. . . . Thus, in passing this act . . . Congress will pretend to designate who should be exempted . . . and then leave it to an irresponsible individual to nullify that law. . . .

We suppose it will be admitted that nobody should be exempted for his own private profit and ease. We suppose it will be admitted that it should not be left to the President to see the public necessity and justice of exempting, for example, his own historiographer, or the mailing clerks and reporters of his own newspaper; and that in the case of any other of his own flatterers, sycophants or political supporters he might perchance be too easily "satisfied" of the expediency of detailing such complaisant persons for agricultural pursuits and the pleasures of the chase.

In short, the grievance and sore evil of the country is, and has been, that the conscription acts have not been executed; and that there are thousands of persons throughout the Confederate States avoiding their military duty to the country . . . by reasons of details which satisfy the President . . . but are not so well calculated to satisfy the general public, and to satisfy General Lee, and . . . those faithful soldiers who have stood in the gap of invasion. . . . Those soldiers know that there are certain laws for putting citizens of fighting age into the army; they know that they are there by virtue of those laws; and they often wonder how and why . . . gentlemen of their . . . neighborhoods, younger and stronger than they . . . can evade their plain duty all this while. . . . They cannot all be planting and hoeing corn. . . . They cannot all be engaged in government works; they cannot all be writing histories of the war. No; but they have all contrived somehow to satisfy that feeling deep in the President's bosom that it is right, or expedient, or at any rate convenient, to detail THEM for domestic duties.

The fact that this system enables the executive to create a large class of personal and political supporters who owe him, perhaps their lives, and at all events their ease and comfort, and who may become ready tools for any enterprise against the liberties of the land, is an evil indeed. . . . The army needs men; and that so urgently as to raise the question of arming Negroes: and the interest at stake is more than life or death; it is independence and prosperity and honor, or oppression, and beggary and shame, for us ALL. Yet we see a large portion of the flower of the land (physically) sedulously avoiding military duty through their influence and interest with somebody or other. . . . How many thousands may have been exempted and detailed by the Secretary of War, "under the direction of the President," is to us unknown. And now Congress, instead of carefully revising its list of exemptions and making them a law and providing that the law shall be enforced, is preparing . . . to abdicate the most important duty it has, and after specifying a few cases of persons who SHALL be exempt . . . to leave all the rest of this vast jurisdiction in the irresponsible hands of the President, who is to satisfy himself—and his friends—and nobody else.

We may be very singular; but we prefer to live under the laws of the land.[9]

It is notable that the men who had been leaders in the secession movement were generally overlooked in the bestowing of high office in the Confederacy. William Lowndes Yancey of Alabama and Robert Barnwell Rhett of South Carolina regarded themselves, and not without cause, as the fathers of secession. Either might reasonably have expected to lead the new government. Yet both were passed over for Jefferson Davis, who was unenthusiastic about secession, and Alexander H. Stephens, who sought to prevent it. When disasters came and the government's shortcomings were revealed, men of ability like Howell Cobb and Robert Toombs who knew Davis for what he was—a patriot who could be both noble and petty and who possessed only moderate ability—and many others went into opposition.

It must be said that Davis, in many ways, aided his opposition. A dignified, impressive, austere man, he was at first more held in awe than loved by the multitude. Surrounding himself with advisers some of whom had mediocre talents, he clung to them with a tenacious stubbornness long after their political capital—if they ever had any—had been exhausted. Much of the criticism aimed at him was unreasonable, but some of it was not. Colonel Lucius B. Northrop, the Commissary-General, was universally disliked and distrusted by generals in the field including even Lee, who rarely spoke disparagingly of anyone. Northrop's was a difficult task—that of providing food for all the Confederate armies and Union prisoners as well. Such an assignment called for a man with exceptional administrative talents, but these Northrop seemed to lack. He was described by contemporaries as "peevish, obstinate, condescending, and fault-finding." He seems to have been supersensitive about interference with his department and was said to be "secretive," and "indirect." Yet Davis refused to remove him until February 1865, when Congress practically forced him to do so.

Even more unpopular was Braxton Bragg, the general who never won a campaign, and who lacked the confidence of his subordinates, both rank and file. Yet, Davis clung to him to the bitter end.

Following the disasters at Gettysburg and Vicksburg, the editor of the Southern Literary Messenger *wrote:*

In all parts of the country there is great depression, and in many states positive disaffection.

To some extent, this is the inevitable result of so many, and so serious disasters. But the root of the prevalent disaffection lies deeper. It cannot be denied that the people have lost confidence in their rulers. Nor can it be truthfully charged that this want of confidence is due to disasters alone. The people do not lack perception, however defective they may be in ratiocination. They see that the failure at Gettysburg differs from the failure at Vicksburg, and this difference measures their estimate of Lee on one hand and Pemberton on the other.

Their inspection does not stop here. They revert to the strange history of the latter general's promotion, and—they sicken at heart—for they see no end to this madness of favoritism. Pemberton's case is not isolated; it is the climax of many similar instances; and the indications are that no change for the better need be expected.

The course of evil is from bad to worse. And the teaching of experience does not encourage the hope of reformation in men of mature years. Desperadoes sometimes undergo a spiritual revulsion which transforms them into devotees and fanatics; but the obstinately moral man, who is wise in his own conceit, knows no change this side of the grave.

Under this conviction we find it almost as hard to prophecy success as to preach charity and forbearance to the evil doer, or to proclaim cheerfulness and confidence which are nonexistent. There are those who seem to think that in time of popular depression, the utterance of a deliberate lie is an excusable if not incumbent act of patriotism. Others are so gifted with sanguine faculties as to see clear skies and fair weather in the midst of tempest and night. Such may follow their instincts and their fallacies, and perhaps do good, God wot. Tis a queer world, this.

For ourselves, we think now, as we thought nearly two years ago, that the South will have to fight two governments instead of one, and its strongest opponent, now as heretofore, is at home. . . . The enemy in our midst is terrible, and he it is who has made the Yankee formidable. This enemy is not the speculator. . . . He is simply a power whose malignant star guides too many of the Confederate armies into quagmires where their strength and valor are wasted—not in open and fair combat with the foe. Almost without a fight they perish or are scattered or captured. . . .

The people see these things dimly; the wise comprehend them perfectly. Hence a twofold trouble, viz.—the wise cannot conscientiously encourage the unknowing in regard to that particular as to which they most need encouragement, and the unwise, incapable of not confounding a cause with its champion, are tempted to abandon the failing and cleave to the successful side. Hence, again, the need of restoring the faith of the wise, and reviving the hopes of the humble masses. Need for some broadly visible manifestation of betterment; some not to be doubted proof of departure from that which is only luckless and Heaven-deserted. But this reversal of the ancient policy, is, as we have already assumed, not predicable upon the peculiar elements of human character with which we have to contend.

Our final success is based not upon men, or the measures heretofore employed and hereafter to be continued by self-sufficient and superstitious rulers. The right means to accomplish right ends we need never look for. Small armies, undisciplined for want of prompt punishment of deserters (including officers absent without leave or otherwise recreant), incompetent generals and chivalry—long ago interred by Mr. [Edmund] Burke—cannot make headway against Yankees ferocious and strong as numbers, cowardice, and . . . absence of sentimentality can make them. Cannonading with feathers is the equivalent of chivalry in this age. Aesthetics in warfare is an obsolete idea.[10]

One of the most vindictive of the anti-administration members of Congress was Henry S. Foote of Tennessee, formerly of Mississippi. He had once defeated Davis for the governorship of Mississippi, and a duel between the two had been narrowly averted when both were serving Mississippi in Washington. In his message of November 7, 1864, Davis had requested power to detail from the army men engaged in essential occupations, among them editors and employees of newspapers. In the debate that followed, Foote said:

Here is what may be expected if Congress should invest the President with the power he desires. Here is an example of how that power would be exercised. The President would discriminate between the editors; he would send some to the field, and those he liked and who flattered him he would permit to stay at home. He would break down the press. There would be no such thing as a free, unshackled press if Mr. Davis should be vested with this extraordinary power. The editors would all have to print what suited Mr. Davis, and if they were not subservient to him he would put them in the army.

The power which is now asked at our hands is not sought for any honest and patriotic purpose. . . . Sir, I tell you and my countrymen everywhere that Mr. Davis will never rest satisfied until he shall have established unconstitutional power. He is every day solidifying his power more and more. His disregard of public sentiment is such as no wise and paternal executive chief has ever before exhibited. He sets at naught, at his own pleasure, our best considered legislative enactments. . . . Others may vote to extend this man's power for mischief; I hold in contempt him and his whole tribe of servitors and minions.[11]

By Christmas 1864 Hood's army was annihilated at

Nashville by General George Thomas, and Sherman had taken Savannah. At this juncture the Richmond Examiner *made a revolutionary proposal.*

There is very general discontent with the present administration of military affairs; and distrust and uneasiness about the result, if the present management be continued. For the assumption that such a futility exists there are but too good grounds. . . . This people is rational, logical, consequent; and while persistless effort and indomitable conflict and defiance come natural to it, yet it requires to feel that it is not befooled. . . . They need to be assured in their own hearts that when they march they are going somewhither; that when they suffer they can see their way to the reward; that when they make sacrifices there is not somebody making a sacrifice of them. It has been with an anxious wish to see the best side of everything . . . that our people have watched the progress of events thus far; but they have met with some rude shocks. Perhaps . . . relieving General Johnston, putting Hood in his place, and then announcing in a public speech that Hood and his army were going to make a tour, and that Sherman had CARTE BLANCHE in Georgia; and now continuing to hold Hood in his place and continuing to hold Johnston out of his place—in the teeth of reason and experience—was the rudest shock of all; they had not believed Mr. Davis, with all his errors, so utterly weak and narrow as this.

It was a misfortune to the Confederacy, as is long since evident, that its first President was, or thought himself to be, a military man. If he had been some worthy planter who never was either at West Point or Mexico and had no special qualifications save a manly, straightforward spirit, then he never would have thought himself competent to plan distant campaigns and interfere with generals in the field. . . . But Mr. Davis unluckily studied at West Point; still more unfortunately, in Mexico he one day formed his regiment of two hundred and fifty Mississippi volunteers into the shape of a V and received a charge of Mexicans À LA FOURCHETTE. . . . The Colonel conceived himself a military genius: we feel its evil effects to this day; and if we are to perish the verdict of posterity will be, Died of a V.

Howsoever that may be, there is a real danger, not only that the military resources of the country, but what is more important, the military spirit of the country may be wasted; the proud resolve to go all lengths in resistance to an infamous invasion—that spirit which would have borne us and our cause triumphantly through to a glorious end, with ordinary sagacity and energy in the conduct of affairs, may grow weary, weary; only stupidity or sycophancy would deny it—and in order that the evil may be remedied it needs that someone boldly point it out and indicate the cause of it and the remedy. In one word, then, we are not afraid of being conquered by the enemy so much as of being defeated by Mr. Davis. He despises all warnings and constitutionally snubs Congress. The press of the country—and we have good reason to know that the army backs the press—calls upon him with an almost unanimous voice to take his hands off, and let General Lee be generalissimo of the forces; he is wholly deaf to such an outcry: calls it "clamor." At last, then, let us try what a Convention will do.[12]

By March Union armies were driving through the Confederacy in all directions and the end was in sight. Only a few remained loyal to Davis. In March 1865 James Chesnut passed through Columbia, South Carolina, and met his wife. She asked her husband:

"Are his critics as violent as ever against the President?"

"Sometimes I think I am the only friend he has in the world. At these dinners, which they give us everywhere, I spoil the sport, for I will not sit still and hear Jeff Davis abused for things he is no more responsible for than any man at that table. Once I lost my temper and told them it sounded like arrant nonsense to me, and that Jeff Davis was a gentleman and a patriot with more brains than the assembled company."

"You lost your temper truly," said I.

"And I did not know it. I thought I was as cool as I am now. In Washington when we left, Jeff Davis ranked second to none in intellect, and maybe first, from the South, and Mrs. Davis was the friend of Mrs. Emory, Mrs. Joe Johnston, and Mrs. Montgomery Blair, and others of that circle. Now they rave that he is nobody, and never was."

"And she?" I asked.

"Oh, you would think to hear them that he found her yesterday in a Mississippi swamp!"

"Well, in the French Revolution it was worse. When a man failed he was guillotined. Mirabeau did not die a day too soon, even Mirabeau." [13]

An agricultural revolution had occurred in the ante-bellum South through the development of cotton culture. In the late eighteenth century, when South Carolina was its focal point, 50,000 bales of 300 pounds each had been the annual crop. From this modest beginning the culture had spread so that by 1860 it was the chief staple from North Carolina to Texas. Decade after decade, production increased in geometric proportion. The crop in 1860 was the biggest ever: that year 4,000,000 bales of 500 pounds were harvested. It was a soil-depleting crop, and in a day when extensive fertilization and crop rotation were uncommon, required new lands for survival. As production increased, the price of cotton declined; even so, there were quick profits to be made from it so long as new land was available. It was cotton that lured settlers from the Upper to the Lower South, and it was cotton that rejuvenated the South's "peculiar institution" at a time when slavery was proving unprofitable in the older section.

Before the Civil War the value of the cotton crop was not only greater than any other exported from the United States but also exceeded the value of all others combined. But when war threatened it was not the money value of the white fluffy staple that loomed largest with Southern politicians. They thought of it as an economic weapon to win diplomatic victories both in the North and in Europe. About one-fourth of the annual crop was consumed in the textile mills of the Northern states, where cotton manufacturing was the dominant industry. Most of the remainder of the crop was shipped to England, where it supplied the Lancashire looms with three-fourths of their raw product and engaged the services of nearly a million operatives. It has been estimated that about one-fifth of England's population at the time was directly dependent upon the cotton industry and that finished cotton goods comprised from two-fifths to one-half of the country's exports. The remainder of the cotton crop was shipped to France and Belgium. It was not nearly so important to their economies as to Britain's, yet France consumed more than 600,000 bales in 1860, most of it imported from America, and stoppage of this supply would bring distress to tens of thousands of workers.

Knowledge of these facts gave Southerners a supreme confidence in the invulnerability of the Confederacy. It was unthinkable that businessmen and statesmen of the world would suffer any interruption of their supply of cotton. If war should come, surely every Southerner could dispose of seven Yanks, but how could war come? Northern businessmen would never permit it. And even if they should fail to prevent war, Great Britain and France would intervene and put a stop to it. The world could not survive without cotton.

The typical Southern viewpoint was that expressed on March 4, 1858, by James Hammond, one of the original South Carolina secessionists. Hammond, a soft-spoken but sometimes bombastic little man, had made his way as an editor and lawyer until he married the daughter of a wealthy Charleston merchant and came into a Savannah River plantation where more than three hundred slaves worked thousands of acres. He supported nullification in 1832-3, and in the 1850 Nashville Convention, after serv-

ing as governor of South Carolina, urged secession if as many as five states acted in unison. Seven years later, at fifty, he was elected to the United States Senate; but by now he had come to doubt the wisdom of secession, convinced apparently that by united action the South could control the Union. When, on March 3, 1858, during the Senate debates over the admission of Kansas, William H. Seward proclaimed the inevitability of the triumph of freedom over slavery, Hammond answered him:

If we never acquire another foot of territory for the South, look at her. Eight hundred and fifty thousand square miles; as large as Great Britain, France, Austria, Prussia, and Spain. . . . With the finest soil, the most delightful climate, whose productions none of those great countries can produce, we have three thousand miles of shore line. . . . Through the heart of our country runs the great Mississippi, the father of waters. . . . Can you hem in such a territory as that? You talk of putting up a wall of fire around eight hundred and fifty thousand square miles so situated! How absurd. . . .

But, sir, the strength of a nation depends in a great measure upon its wealth, and the wealth of a nation, like that of a man, is to be estimated by its surplus production. . . . Last year the United States exported in round numbers $279,000,000 worth of domestic produce. Of this amount $158,000,000 worth is the clear produce of the South; articles that are not and cannot be made at the North. . . .

In addition to this, we send to the North $30,000,000 worth of cotton, which is not counted in the exports. . . . The recorded exports of the South are now greater than the whole exports of the United States in any year before 1856. . . . There is not a nation on the face of the earth, with any numerous population, that can compete with us in produce PER CAPITA. . . .

The South organized separately would [under the present tariff] have about $40,000,000 of revenue. With one-fourth the present tariff she would have a revenue adequate to all her wants, for the South would never go to war; she would never need an army or a navy, beyond a few garrisons on the frontier and a few revenue cutters. It is commerce that breeds war. It is manufactures that require to be hawked about over the world, and give rise to navies and commerce. But we have nothing to do but to take off restrictions on foreign merchandise and open our ports, and the whole world will come to us to trade. They will be too glad to bring and carry for us, and we shall never dream of a war. Why, sir, the South has never yet had a just cause of war. Every time she has seized her sword it has been on the point of honor, and that point of honor has been mainly loyalty to her sister colonies and sister states, who have ever since plundered and calumniated her.

But if there were no other reason why we should never have a war, would any sane nation make war on cotton? Without firing a gun, without drawing a sword, when they make war on us we can bring the whole world to our feet. The South is perfectly competent to go on, one, two, or three years without planting a seed of cotton. I believe that if she was to plant but half her cotton, it would be an immense advantage to her. I am not so sure but that after three years' cessation she would come out stronger than ever she was before and better prepared to enter afresh upon her great career of enterprise. What would happen if no cotton was furnished for three years? I will not stop to depict what every one can imagine, but this is certain: old England would topple headlong and carry the whole civilized world with her. No, sir, you dare not make war on cotton. No power on earth dares make war upon it. Cotton is King.[1]

"Cotton is King!" Southerners believed it was powerful enough to prevent war. Even after the guns boomed at Sumter they clung stubbornly to their belief. William Howard Russell, the distinguished correspondent of the

London Times, *arrived in America in the spring of 1861
to report the crisis that had developed. Upon learning,
on April 12, that a relief expedition was bound for Fort
Sumter, he set out for Charleston. There he met Governor
Francis Pickens, General P. G. T. Beauregard, and other
Confederate leaders. On April 16 he wrote:*

That night I sat in the Charleston club with John Manning. Who that has ever met him can be indifferent to the
charms of manner and of personal appearance, which render the ex-Governor of the state so attractive? There were
others present, senators or congressmen, like Mr. [James]
Chesnut, and Mr. Porcher Miles. We talked long, and at
last angrily, as might be between friends, of political
affairs.

I own it was a little irritating to me to hear men indulge in extravagant broad menace and rodomontade,
such as came from their lips. "They would welcome the
world in arms with hospitable hands to bloody graves."
"They never could be conquered." "Creation could not do
it," and so on.

I was obliged to handle the question quietly at first—to
ask them "if they admitted the French were a brave and
warlike people!"

"Yes, certainly."

"Do you think you could better defend yourselves
against invasion than the people of France?"

"Well, no; but we'd make it a pretty hard business for
the Yankees."

"Suppose the Yankees, as you call them, come with such
preponderance of men and material, that they are three
to your one, will you not be forced to submit?"

"Never."

"Then either you are braver, better disciplined, more
warlike than the people and soldiers of France, or you
alone, of all the nations in the world, possess the means of
resisting physical laws which prevail in war, as in other
affairs of life."

"No. The Yankees are cowardly rascals. We have proved it by kicking and cuffing them till we are tired of it; besides, we know John Bull very well. He will make a great fuss about noninterference at first, but when he begins to want cotton he'll come off his perch."

I found this was the fixed idea everywhere. The doctrine of "cotton is king"—to us who have not much considered this question, a grievous delusion or an unmeaning babble —to them is a lively all-powerful faith without distracting heresies or schisms. They have in it enunciated their full belief, and indeed there is some truth in it, insofar as we year after year by the stimulants of coal, capital, and machinery have been working up a manufacture on which four or five millions of our population depend for bread and life, which cannot be carried on without the assistance of a nation that may at any time refuse us an adequate supply or be cut off from giving it by war.

Political economy, we are well aware, is a fine science, but its followers are capable of tremendous absurdities in practice. The dependence of such a large proportion of the English people on this sole article of American cotton is fraught with the utmost danger to our honor and to our prosperity. Here were these Southern gentlemen exulting in their power to control the policy of Great Britain, and it was small consolation to me to assure them they were mistaken; in case we did not act as they anticipated, it could not be denied Great Britain would plunge an immense proportion of her people—a nation of manufacturers—into pauperism, which must leave them dependent on the national funds, or more properly on the property and accumulated capital of the district.

Two days later Russell wrote:

In the evening I dined with our excellent Consul, Mr. Bunch, who had a small and very agreeable party to meet me. . . .

It was scarcely very agreeable to my host or myself to find that no considerations were believed to be of consequence in reference to England except her material interests, and that these worthy gentlemen regarded her as a sort of appanage of their cotton kingdom. "Why, sir, we have only to shut off your supply of cotton for a few weeks, and we can create a revolution in Great Britain. There are four millions of your people depending on us for their bread, not to speak of the many millions of dollars. No, sir, we know that England must recognize us," etc.

Liverpool and Manchester have obscured all Great Britain to the Southern eye. I confess the tone of my friends irritated me. I said so to Mr. Bunch, who laughed, and remarked: "You'll not mind it when you get as much accustomed to this sort of thing as I am." I could not help saying that if Great Britain were such a sham as they supposed, the sooner a hole was drilled in her and the whole empire sunk under water, the better for the world, the cause of truth, and of liberty.

These tall, thin, fine-faced Carolinians are great materialists. Slavery perhaps has aggravated the tendency to look at all the world through parapets of cotton bales and rice bags, and though more stately and less vulgar, the worshippers here are not less prostrate before the "almighty dollar" than the Northerners.[2]

And Blackwood's *reporter, visiting the South in the autumn of 1861, observed:*

The [Confederate] government have not prohibited the export of cotton except to the Northern states; but self-constituted authorities have, in more than one instance that we know of, made it impossible for ships to load which had run the blockade, and whose owners were desirous of doing so again. The popular feeling which has dictated these violent acts is caused, first, by the desire that the North should be made to suffer for enforcing the blockade, and the apprehension that, if any cotton were to be allowed to leave the country, Massachusetts would manage to obtain it; and, secondly, by the impression that in laying on a general embargo they would incline European governments to recognize the Confederacy. Among the enlightened this latter motive was always repudiated; but there can be no doubt that the prevalent conviction throughout the South is that England cannot do without the "king"; that all cotton, except American, is either too short or too long; and that the medium is the only staple which Manchester cares to have. In vain we would tell them that our manufacturers would soon change their machinery, and adapt it to the necessities of the times; that our government was making great exertions to procure cotton from India and Africa; that it was our interest to foster our own colonies, and to produce it there if possible; and that the longer we were deprived of America as a market, the more strenuous would our efforts be to render ourselves independent of it. But it was no use; they were ineradicably impressed with the conviction that they can command the market at any time; and that the distance from England at which its rivals are placed must always give the Confederacy a great advantage.[3]

Meanwhile, Secretary of State Robert Toombs had early begun labors to secure European recognition of the Confederacy, particularly by Britain and France. Regardless of what material benefits might accompany formal recognition by the great powers, psychologically the rewards would be incalculable. The more sanguine Southerners expected recognition to be followed by armed intervention, if necessary. More conservative Confederates believed recognition would result in refusal by Britain and France to respect Lincoln's blockade, a blockade that was more fiction than fact in the early months of the war.

To secure these diplomatic fruits three commissioners, William Lowndes Yancey, Pierre A. Rost, and Ambrose Dudley Mann were sent to Europe. Reaching London in April 1861, the commissioners presented their credentials, unofficially, to the British Foreign Secretary, Lord John Russell. A month later England, acting in conjunction with

France, issued a proclamation of neutrality which rec-
ognized the Confederacy as a belligerent, but not as a
legitimate government. Further than this Russell would
not go, except to promise the commissioners that, in due
time, he would present the question of recognition to the
Cabinet.

Recognition as a belligerent, while somewhat less than
half-a-loaf, still was not total failure. In the first place it
practically insured that Confederate soldiers captured in
battle would have prisoner-of-war status and would not be
treated as felons. Further, it would regularize purchase of
supplies in neutral countries, and forbid neutrals to aid in
suppressing the rebellion. On the other hand, it did help
clothe the Union blockade with legitimacy and, in time,
came itself to be regarded in the South as an unneutral
act.

By autumn 1861 Yancey went home, discouraged, and
Mann and Rost left London for other European capitals.
Replacing them in London was James M. Mason who,
with John Slidell, an envoy accredited by the Confederate
President to France, figured in an international crisis that
brought England and the United States to the brink of war
in December 1861. Enroute from Havana to Liverpool,
Mason and Slidell had been removed by Captain Charles
Wilkes of the U.S.S. San Jacinto *from the British steamer*
Trent. *Wilkes's act created wild jubilation in Northern*
cities. He was the toast of the hour, and even staid Secre-
tary of the Navy Gideon Welles telegraphed his congratu-
lations.

But the British lion had no intention of submitting to
this tail-twisting. The Foreign Office sent an ultimatum to
Washington demanding an apology and the release of the
prisoners. War drums began to beat in London, and troops
were hurried to Canada. In the face of such a determined
display, the Lincoln government released the envoys and
sent them on their way, but did not make the demanded
apology.

The Mason-Slidell affair aroused great expectations in the Confederacy. For a time it seemed that the event might accomplish the ambassadors' mission without their ever setting foot in Europe. It was with mixed emotions, therefore, that the Davis government learned of the release of the celebrated prisoners and the consequent dissipation of the British-Yankee tension.

The sixty-three-year-old Mason was a grandson of George Mason of Revolutionary War fame. As a United States senator under the influence of John C. Calhoun he had become a strong advocate of State rights. He had read the dying Calhoun's last speech in the Senate, protesting against the Wilmot Proviso, and he was the author of the Fugitive Slave Law of 1850. Although careless in dress almost to the point of slovenliness, he was noted for his courtesy and kindness. On March 11, 1862, Mason wrote to Benjamin, who was now Confederate Secretary of State:

The recent debate in the two houses of Parliament on the question of the blockade clearly demonstrates that no step will be taken by this government to interfere with it. . . .

It came on last night in the House of Lords and is reported in the TIMES of today. You will remark in Earl Russell's reply, at the close, he expresses the hope, if not the belief, that the war will end in three months and looks to its close by a peaceable separation into two states. I was given a seat on the floor of the House, and some two or three of the peers, in conversation with me, construed his meaning to be that the existing separation was final; and such I have no doubt is the settled conviction of the public mind of this country; still the ministry is sustained, and as it would seem, by almost all parties, in its refusal either to question the legality of the blockade or to recognize our independence. Many causes concur to this end.

First, the pervading disinclination in any way to disturb the mourning of the Queen. The loyalty of the English people to their present sovereign is strongly mixed up with an affectionate devotion to her person. You find this feeling prevalent in all circles and classes.

Then, as regards the question of cotton supply, which we had supposed would speedily have disturbed the level of their neutral policy. This state of things manifestly exists. The constantly increasing supply of cotton with a corresponding demand for its fabric for a few years past, it would seem, has so stimulated the manufactories that the blockade found the markets overstocked with fabrics, and very soon the price of the fabric bore a very diminished relative value to that of the raw material. This disproportionate ratio has since continued; the price of the fabric, though constantly rising, still not keeping pace with the rise in the raw material, it would follow, that until prices approached a level, it would not be [to] the interest of the manufacturer to cheapen the latter until the stock of the former on hand should be disposed of. Thus it is that even in Lancashire and other manufacturing districts no open demonstration has been made against the blockade.

True that more than one-third of the mills have been stopped and the rest working only on half time, still the owners find it to their account not to complain, and they silence the working classes by sufficient alms, in aid of parish relief, to keep them from actual starvation. The supply of cotton, however, is now very low, and the factitious state of things above referred to cannot last very long.

The better to keep the public mind quiet, too, on the subject of cotton supply, great efforts have been made, as you are aware, to produce the belief that in any event adequate supplies of this material will be insured by the increase of its culture in India; still, I do not find that much faith is given to such promises by those who ought best to know.

All seem to agree that the hope either of reunion or reconstruction is gone, but that is accompanied by the idea, strongly confirmed by our recent disasters on the Cumberland River, that the South will be forced to yield the border states—or at least Tennessee, Kentucky, Missouri, and Maryland—to the North; and that the government at Washington will be ready in the course of two or three months to agree to the separation on these terms, looking thus to a speedy end to the war, they are the more disinclined to any course which would seem to commit the country to either side. . . .

The late reverses at Fort Henry and Fort Donelson have had an unfortunate effect upon the minds of our friends here, as was naturally to be expected. I assure them that at most they are to be considered only as driving in or capturing outposts by the invading army, and by no means should be taken to foreshadow the result of the general battle which seems impending on our western frontier.[4]

These were realities with which cotton diplomats had not reckoned; and these soon would so weaken the strength of King Cotton as to make future faith in him a delusion.

Meanwhile, arguments for and against recognition of the Confederacy were being coolly calculated by British officials. A division of the American nation with part of it committed to free trade would be welcomed by English industrial and commercial interests. Then, too, a divided America might check the predatory Yankee nation that had swept to the Pacific just a decade before and which had for so many years cast envious eyes at Canada. On the other hand, Britain's primary concern was with Europe, and she must not let herself be drawn into an American war. So long, therefore, as recognition might result in war with the United States, the British government would not move. By the autumn of 1862, however, a series of brilliant military victories by Confederate Generals Robert E. Lee and "Stonewall" Jackson seemed to point toward Union defeat. Concurrently, the delayed cotton famine was striking the Lancashire mills, and distress among the workers there was acute. Recognition now might bring a speedy end to the war without provoking retaliation by the United States. Count Henri Mercier, the French minister in Washington, was urging joint recognition by Britain and France. Lord Russell exchanged notes with the Prime Minister, Lord Palmerston:

Mercier's notion that we should make some move in October agrees very well with yours. I shall be back in England before October, and we could then have a Cabinet upon it. Of course the war may flag before that.

I quite agree with you that a proposal for an armistice should be the first step; but we must be prepared to answer the question on what basis are we to negotiate?

[Russell] [5]

94 Picadilly: September 14, 1862.

My dear Russell,—The detailed accounts given in the "Observer" today of the battles of August 29 and 30 between the Confederates and the Federals show that the latter got a very complete smashing; and it seems not altogether unlikely that still greater disasters await them, and that even Washington or Baltimore may fall into the hands of the Confederates.

If this should happen, would it not be time for us to consider whether in such a state of things England and France might not address the contending parties and recommend an arrangement upon the basis of separation? . . . —Yours sincerely,

Palmerston[6]

Gotha: September 17, 1862.

My dear Palmerston,—Whether the Federal army is destroyed or not, it is clear that it is driven back to Washington and has made no progress in subduing the insurgent states. Such being the case, I agree with you that the time is come for offering mediation to the United States government with a view to the recognition of the independence of the Confederates. I agree further, that, in case of failure, we ought ourselves to recognize the Southern states as an independent state. For the purpose of taking so important a step, I think we must have a meeting of the Cabinet. The 23rd or 30th would suit me for the meeting.

We ought then, if we agree on such a step, to propose it first to France, and then, on the part of England and France, to Russia and other powers as a measure decided upon by us.

We ought to make ourselves safe in Canada, not by sending more troops there, but by concentrating those we have in a few defensible posts before the winter sets in.

I hope to get home on Sunday, but a letter sent to the Foreign Office is sure to reach me.

[Russell] [7]

Broadlands: September 23, 1862.

My dear Russell,—Your plan of proceedings about the mediation between the Federals and Confederates seems to be excellent. Of course, the offer would be made to both the contending parties at the same time; for, though the offer would be as sure to be accepted by the Southerns as was the proposal of the Prince of Wales by the Danish Princess, yet, in the one case as in the other, there are certain forms which it is decent and proper to go through.

A question would occur whether, if the two parties were to accept the mediation, the fact of our mediating would not of itself be tantamount to an acknowledgment of the Confederates as an independent state.

Might it not be well to ask Russia to join England and France in the offer of mediation? . . .

We should be better without her in the mediation, because she would be too favorable to the North; but on the other hand her participation in the offer might render the North the more willing to accept it.

The after communication to the other European powers

would be quite right, although they would be too many for mediation.

As to the time of making the offer, if France and Russia agree—and France, we know, is quite ready and only waiting for our concurrence—events may be taking place which might render it desirable that the offer should be made before the middle of October.

It is evident that a great conflict is taking place to the northwest of Washington, and its issue must have a great effect on the state of affairs. If the Federals sustain a great defeat, they may be at once ready for mediation, and the iron should be struck while it is hot. If, on the other hand, they should have the best of it, we may wait awhile and see what may follow. . . .

Yours sincerely,
Palmerston.[8]

Three weeks later Palmerston, learning of Lee's defeat at Antietam, had reached a decision, and he wrote Russell:
All that we could possibly do without injury to our position would be to ask the two parties not whether they would agree to an armistice but whether they might not turn their thoughts towards an arrangement between themselves. But the answer of each might be written by us beforehand. The Northerns would say that the only condition of arrangement would be the restoration of the Union; the South would say their only condition would be an acknowledgement by the North of Southern Independence —we should not be more advanced and should only have pledged each party more strongly to the object for which they are fighting. I am, therefore, inclined to change the opinion on which I wrote to you when the Confederates seemed to be carrying all before them, and I am very much come back to our original view of the matter, that we must continue merely to be lookers-on till the war shall have taken a more decided turn.[9]

While Russell and Palmerston hesitated in England, the diplomatic fate of the Confederacy was also being decided in France. There John Slidell, the other Trent *captive, was pressing Napoleon III for recognition. A successful New Orleans lawyer and politician, Slidell had been one of the powers behind the throne in the administration of President James Buchanan, whose campaign he had managed. He was too volatile to fit the traditional concept of a diplomat, but he was shrewd, adept at intrigue, and seemed to size up a situation realistically. He was not overly scrupulous in keeping his public and private business separate, as when he negotiated a loan to the Confederacy which made exorbitant profits for Emil Erlanger at the same time arrangements were being made for the marriage of his daughter to Erlanger's son.*

When Slidell walked into the palace of Saint-Cloud for his second audience with the Emperor, his buoyant step and quick eye belied his seventy years. The date was October 28, 1862.

The Emperor received me in a most friendly manner; taking me by the hand, he inquired how I had been, invited me to be seated. He then asked me what news I had from America, and how our affairs were going on.

I replied that we were entirely cut off from the reception of any early news, that we were obliged to take our intelligence from the Northern press, and that he well knew how little reliable it was . . . that since I had the honor of seeing him at Vichy our position had most materially improved, and was now better than at any previous period; that our troops were as numerous and better disciplined than they had ever been; that time and opportunity had developed high military talent in many of our officers, while there was a singular absence of that quality among Northern generals; that while we anxiously desired to see the war brought to a close we had no apprehensions whatever of the final result of the contest; that we had the immense advantage over our enemies of harmonious counsels and a thoroughly united people, ready and willing to make every sacrifice and submit to every privation for the establishment of their independence.

The Emperor replied that he was entirely satisfied of the correctness of all that I said; that he had no scruples in declaring that his sympathies were entirely with the South; that his only desire was to know how to give them effect; that the condition of affairs in Europe was very unsatisfactory, especially in Italy and Greece; that he was obliged to act with great caution, and intimated that if he acted alone, England, instead of following his example, would endeavor to embroil [France] with the United States and that French commerce would be destroyed. He asked what were my views. I said that I had no hope of any friendly action from England until the time should arrive when it would become a matter of indifference to us; that all we asked for was recognition, satisfied that the moral effect of such a step, by giving confidence to the peace party of the North, would exercise a controlling influence; that if it had been taken a few months since it would have secured the election of a majority of the House of Representatives opposed to the war; that recognition would not afford in the eyes of the world the slightest pretext for hostilities on the part of the North; that there were, however, stronger reasons that would bind them to keep the peace. . . . That their navy, of which they boasted so loudly, would be swept from the ocean and all their principal ports efficiently blockaded by a moiety of his powerful marine, and the GLOIRE or the NORMANDIE could enter without risk the harbors of New York and Boston and lay those cities under contribution. . . . And that, mad and stupid as the Washington government had shown itself to be, it still had sense enough not to seek a quarrel with the first power of the world.

The Emperor asked: "What do you think of the joint mediation of France, England, and Russia? Would it, if proposed, be accepted by the two parties?" I replied that some months since I would have said the North would unhesitatingly reject it, but that now it would probably accept it; that I could not venture to say how it would be received at Richmond. I could only give him my individual opinion.

I had no faith in England and believed that Russia would lean strongly to the Northern side; that the mediation of the three powers, when France could be outvoted, would not be acceptable; that we might perhaps, with certain assurances, consent to the joint mediation of France and England; but, knowing as I did the Emperor's sentiments, I would gladly submit to his umpirage. The Emperor said: "My own preference is for a proposition of an armistice of six months, with the Southern ports open to the commerce of the world. This would put a stop to the effusion of blood, and hostilities would probably never be resumed. We can urge it on the high grounds of humanity and the interests of the whole civilized world. If it be refused by the North, it will afford good reason for recognition and perhaps for more active intervention."

I said that such a course would be judicious and acceptable. Indeed, it was one that I had suggested to Mr. Thouvenel [the French Foreign Secretary] when I first saw him in February last; that I feared, however, he would find it as difficult to obtain the co-operation of England for it as for recognition. . . .

The Emperor asked why we had not created a navy. He said that we ought to have one; that a few ships would have inflicted fatal injury on the Federal commerce, and that with three or four powerful steamers we could have opened some of our ports. I replied that at first many of our leading men thought it would be bad policy to attempt to become a naval power, as we had no good ports for large vessels but Norfolk and Pensacola, few steamers, and an inconsiderable mercantile marine; that we would always be essentially an agricultural people, selling freely to all the world and buying in the cheapest markets. We could rely on our peaceful disposition to preserve us from collisions with European powers, while at the same time it would be to the interest of those powers to prevent our only probable enemies from abusing their superiority over us at sea; that we all now saw our error and were endeavoring to correct it; that we had built two vessels in England, and were now building others, two of which would be powerful ironclad steamers; that the great difficulty was not to build but to man and arm them under the existing regulations for the preservation of neutrality; that if the Emperor would give only some kind of verbal assurance that his police would not observe too closely when we wished to put on board guns and men we would gladly avail ourselves of it.

He said: "Why could you not have them built as for the Italian government? I do not think it would be difficult, but will consult the minister of marine about it."

I forgot to mention that King Leopold, in his letter, spoke of his wishes for the success of the French arms in Mexico and the establishment under their protection of a stable and regular government. This gave me an opportunity of alluding to the propositions I had made at Vichy and to hold out the advantages which would result to France from a cordial and close alliance between the countries, not so much depending on treaties and mere paper bonds as resulting from mutual interests and common sympathies. An idea prevails among some of the officers who have gone to Mexico that as troops and ships have been sent there on a scale vastly greater than the apparent object of the expedition requires the Emperor has some ulterior views, perhaps to occupy the old French colony of Santo Domingo, as Spain has done for the eastern portion of the islands. I took occasion to say to the Emperor that however distasteful such a measure might be to the Washington government ours could have no objections to it.[10]

One of the most capable of all Confederate agents sent

abroad was the youthful Henry Hotze. Hotze had been born in Switzerland, but had migrated to America and was on the editorial staff of the Mobile Register *when war broke out. In November 1861, when he was but twenty-seven years old, he was sent to England by the Confederate government to influence public opinion there. Possessed of rare intelligence and an ingratiating and charming personality, he made influential friends. By April 1862 he was writing pro-Confederate editorials for the* Post, *the* Herald, *the* Standard, *and other London papers. A month later he established the* Index, *a Confederate-British journal, which he continued to edit throughout the war. He worked closely with Mason, Slidell, and other Confederate agents in England and on the Continent, earning their complete confidence, as well as that of Benjamin.*

On September 22, 1862, five days after the battle of Antietam, Lincoln issued his preliminary Emancipation Proclamation. An important consideration in his decision to do so was the hope that the Proclamation would allay growing sentiment in Europe for recognition of the Confederacy, and possibly, intervention. The following month Hotze wrote Benjamin:

The Federal emancipation decree, the most important event since I last wrote, has been received by the English press in a manner which leaves nothing to desire. If intended as a bid for European sympathies, the framers have utterly failed, mostly through their own stupidity, which precluded even their ablest defenders from claiming for them the slightest merit of sincerity. Some extracts, on the other hand, from Richmond papers have done harm by producing the impression that the South was in a state of frantic terror at the prospective execution of the decree. I have spared no pains to remove this impression, and not without a degree of success.[11]

Blackwood's *largely expressed the English view that Hotze had reported to Benjamin.*

The past month has brought us to the veritable crisis of the great civil war in America. Brought to bay upon their own soil, the Federals in desperation have invoked to their aid the unutterable horrors of a servile war. With their armies baffled and beaten, and with the standards of the rebel army again within sight of Washington, the President has at length owned the impossibility of success in fair warfare, and seeks to paralyze the victorious armies of the South by letting loose upon their hearths and homes the lust and savagery of four million Negroes. The die is cast. Henceforth it is a war of extermination. The North seeks to make of the South a desert—a wilderness of bloodshed and misery; for thus only, now, does it or can it hope to overcome the seceding Confederacy.

Monstrous, reckless, devilish as the project is, we believe it will not succeed. But it at least marks the crisis and turning-point of the war. It shows that the North has shot its last bolt—the effects of which we do not yet see, but beyond which there is no other. It proves what every one in this country was loth to believe, that rather than let the Southern states be independent, rather than lose their trade and custom, the North would league itself with Beelzebub, and seek to make a hell of half a continent. In return, this atrocious act justifies the South in hoisting the black flag, and in proclaiming a war without quarter against the Yankee hosts. And thus, within the bosom of civilization, we are called upon to contemplate a war more full of horrors and wickedness than any which stands recorded in the world's history.

When a crisis so manifest and so terrible has been reached in this most melancholy of all civil wars, it is natural that at least something like a crisis should arise among the slow-moving minds of her Majesty's ministers. If they cannot yet agree to act upon their opinions, each member of the Cabinet, we should think, must at least have arrived at some definite opinion of his own. Three weeks ago it was rumored that before the end of the month Lord Lyons would return to his post at Washington, bearing with him the definite decision of her Majesty's government. Simultaneously, or immediately in the wake of this rumor, there came Mr. Gladstone's speech at Newcastle, where, amid the applause of his audience, he declared that the people of the Southern states were now to be regarded as a NATION. "There is no doubt," said the Chancellor of the Exchequer, "that Jefferson Davis and the other leaders of the South have made an army; they are making, it appears, a navy; and they have made what is more than either—they have made a nation. We may anticipate with certainty the success of the Southern states, so far as regards their separation from the North. I cannot but believe that that event is as certain as any event yet future and contingent can be. . . ."

The North beheld with rage and chagrin, that all its vast armaments had been unable to accomplish anything; and that, after a year and a half of hostilities, and after incurring an enormous amount of debt, its hopes of success had almost vanished. Discontent was spreading everywhere, and every section of the discontented blamed the government for not embracing its peculiar views of policy. The governors of sixteen of the states which adhere to the Union were to meet at Altoona on the 24th September—a manifest sign of want of confidence in the government—and the whole fabric of the Presidential power seemed ready to give way before a strong gust of popular dissatisfaction. The President felt that something must be done. The people clamored, as they always do in emergencies, for extreme measures; and the only extreme measure which he had left to employ was to proclaim the emancipation of the Negroes. He had previously, with the general concurrence of the people, inaugurated a dictatorship, abolished liberty, and installed Force as the supreme power in the states which still adhered to the Union. He had practically abolished the HABEAS CORPUS Act, and introduced the conscription under the milder name of "drafting." Taxes had been imposed, debt incurred, and paper-money issued, to the fullest amount possible. What more could he do but seek refuge in an emancipation proclamation? On two occasions, within a few weeks before, he had refused to adopt such a measure; but at length he gave way, and on the 22d September—two days before the meeting of the governors at Altoona—he proclaimed the most atrocious act of war-policy which has ever been adopted by a civilized state—adding in his sore bewilderment the honest (we doubt not) but impious saying, "I can only trust in God I have made no mistake!"

A mistake in what? Only nine days previously he had stated to a deputation from Chicago his objection to issue a proclamation of emancipation on the ground "that the whole world would see it to be necessarily as inoperative as the Pope's Bull against a comet." In now issuing it, is the mistake which he dreads that the proclamation be too effective in rousing the slaves against their masters, or not effective enough? With every desire to do justice to Mr. Lincoln as an honest but weak man placed in very trying circumstances, we must believe that his only apprehension as to the effect of his proclamation is not in regard to the awful horrors which it may occasion, but lest, after all, it should fail in accomplishing the conquest of the South. He said himself not long ago—"I will proclaim emancipation entirely, or partially, or not at all, according to whichever of these measures shall seem to me best for the Union."

Mr. Seward, in his dispatch to foreign governments, takes the same view of the matter. He upholds the President's proclamation as "a just and proper military act"— adding, with an effrontery purely American, that he does not doubt that it will be recognized as such by "all the good and wise men of all countries!" We are greatly mistaken in Earl Russell if he allows Mr. Seward to continue in that convenient belief, and if he does not express in strong terms the reprobation by the British government of this atrocious attempt to devastate the South by means of a servile war. . . .

In a moral point of view, there cannot be two opinions in this country as to the President's proclamation. To employ such a means of hostility as a Negro insurrection is simply infamous. In a political point of view we regard it as the greatest mistake which the North has committed. True, the policy of the North has been slowly approximating to this result: it is a natural climax to the mad policy which has animated the North from the beginning. It is the consummation of the mistakes of the North. Union in any shape is now doubly impossible. It remains to be seen, also, whether the temporary accord which the proclamation has established in the North is not on the surface only, and whether the present lull of dissension will not give way ere long to dissensions still more formidable. In the border states of Kentucky, Tennessee, and Missouri, the proclamation cannot fail to excite new and formidable opposition to the Federal government; while the Confederate States, now menaced with untold horrors, will put forth their whole strength to keep the danger at a distance and to roll back the war from their frontiers with the fury of desperation.[12]

Some progress was obviously being made in winning British opinion for the Confederacy. After ten months in England without having secured recognition, however, Mason wrote Benjamin:

I see and hear nothing from the British government, either officially or unofficially. Mr. Slidell has an advantage over me in this, as he sees the ministers frequently, as well as the Emperor. I have sometimes thought it might be due to the dignity of the government under such circumstances that I should terminate the mission here, but I do not feel at liberty to advise it, because, although unaccredited, I find my presence in London as the representative of the government is really important in matters frequently arising where we should not be without some responsible head.[13]

As recognition continued to be withheld, Jefferson Davis addressed the Confederate Congress in January 1863:

During nearly two years of struggle, in which every energy of our country has been evoked for maintaining its very existence, the neutral nations of Europe have pursued a policy which, nominally impartial, has been practically most favorable to our enemies and most detrimental to us. The exercise of the neutral right of refusing entry into their ports to prizes taken by both belligerents was eminently hurtful to the Confederacy. It was sternly asserted and maintained. The exercise of the neutral right of commerce with a belligerent whose ports are not blockaded by fleets sufficient really to prevent access to them would have been eminently hurtful to the United States. It was complacently abandoned. The duty of neutral states to receive with cordiality and recognize with respect any new confederation that independent states may think proper to form was too clear to admit of denial, but its postponement was eminently beneficial to the United States and detrimental to the Confederacy. It was postponed.

In this review of our relations with the neutral nations of Europe it has been my purpose to point out distinctly that this government has no complaint to make that those nations declared their neutrality. It could neither expect nor desire more. The complaint is that the neutrality has been rather nominal than real, and that recognized neutral rights have been alternately asserted and waived in such manner as to bear with great severity on us, and to confer signal advantages on our enemy.[14]

Another fine mind brought to bear on the problem of British failure to recognize the Confederacy was that of Lucius Q. C. Lamar. Lamar was a Georgia-born Mississippian married to the daughter of the humorist Augustus Bald-

*win Longstreet, president of the University of Mississippi.
Lamar was teaching at the University and practicing law
when he went off to war in 1861. In the army he had risen
to the rank of colonel before ill health forced him to retire
in the spring of 1862. That autumn, having recovered, he
was appointed commissioner to Russia. He had arrived in
London when word reached him that the Senate had
failed to confirm his appointment, not through any lack of
confidence but because of the growing conviction that
diplomatic missions were futile. In March 1863, Lamar
wrote to Benjamin from London:*

Though I have been in London but a little more than
two weeks, I have had, through the kindness of Mr.
Mason, unexpected opportunities for obtaining information in regard to the state of public opinion here and
throughout Europe touching American affairs. In this
country the leading contestants for power in both parties,
Conservative and Whigs, supported by the great body of
their respective adherents, are favorable to the success of
the South. Many causes, however, operate to prevent this
partiality from yielding any practical results. Not only the
government party, but even the Conservative leaders are
exceedingly timid in regard to any movement which might
give umbrage to the United States. They seem to consider
that a war with that country would be the greatest
calamity that could befall Great Britain, and they have the
impression that the United States would not regret the
occurrence of a contingency which would justify them in
declaring war. This belief had made a deep impression
upon the mind of England and though it has increased the
willingness to witness the dismemberment of a hostile
power and diffused in a wide circle the sympathy for the
South, yet it has also had a powerful influence in holding
the government to the policy of "neutrality" (so-called) in
which it has taken refuge.

Another cause lies in the peculiar composition of parties
in both Houses of Parliament. You are aware that neither

of the two great parties has such a working majority as will insure its continuance in power. The Whigs can at any moment be ousted, but are equally able, in turn, to eject their successors. This gives to the Radicals, under [John] Bright and others, the balance of power. Although weak in numbers in Parliament, the last-named party has become necessary to the maintenance of either party in power. At least their united opposition would be fatal to any government which might be organized. These men are warm partisans of the United States, and have of late made a series of striking demonstrations by public meetings, speeches, etc. It is well understood, so I am told, that United States gold has been freely used in getting up these spectacles; and although they have been participated in by but few men of any note or consideration, yet they have been sufficiently formidable to exercise a powerful influence upon the leaders of both parties. It was this that elicited Lord Derby's remarkable speech. If the nation were divided solely upon the American question, the overwhelming force of public opinion would be on the side of the South; but inasmuch as it is an issue subordinate to many questions both of domestic and foreign policy and the two parties contesting for power are nearly equal in strength, the Radicals really control the action of the government in regard to American affairs. I do not see any causes now at work to change this state of things. At the same time no one can anticipate the policy of the government on this subject. . . .

Abrupt changes are brought about by a cause which it is difficult for American statesmen to appreciate. The nations of Europe constitute a federative league, a commonwealth of nations, which, though it has no central head, is so intimate and elaborate as to subject the action and sometimes even the internal affairs of each to surveillance and intervention on the part of all the others. No government, therefore, can enter upon a policy exclusively its own, and its action in reference to foreign matters is consequently liable to constant modification. Lord Palmerston is far more deeply engrossed with the conferences, jealousies, and rivalries between the leading powers of Europe than with the fate of constitutional government in America. To thwart Louis Napoleon's policy in Greece or to prevent his ascendancy in European affairs is of far greater importance than to pursue any policy at all with reference to America, which is considered on both sides of the Potomac as alien in European politics. In my opinion, whenever this government shall have entertained the proposition of recognizing the Southern Confederacy, it will have been a result due to influence brought to bear in Europe.[15]

The European political crisis of which Lamar wrote had subsided by the late spring of 1863, and this obstacle to British recognition was temporarily overcome. Then came news of the smashing defeat of Hooker by Lee and Jackson at Chancellorsville. Confederate agents and their British friends determined to press once more for recognition. John A. Roebuck, one of the staunchest friends of the Confederacy, pushed a resolution in the House of Commons requesting the government to open negotiations with the principal powers of Europe for joint recognition. It was common knowledge that Napoleon was eager for joint action with England, but would not move alone.

Before the Roebuck resolution was debated a rumor got abroad that Napoleon had reversed his former position and now opposed recognition. Roebuck then did a questionable thing. Going behind the back of his own government, he went to Paris with William S. Lindsay, a wealthy shipbuilder, and obtained an interview with Napoleon. The Emperor assured them that his view had not changed and that they might say so in the coming debates in Parliament. He promised, further, that he would instruct his ambassador in London so to inform Lord Russell.

In the parliamentary debate that followed, Roebuck indiscreetly stated that the French ambassador had asked

*Britain to join in recognition of the Confederacy. When
Russell denied that any such request had been received
it brought in question the veracity of Russell and Napoleon, on the one hand, and Roebuck and Lindsay on
the other. Oddly enough, all were truthful; for Napoleon
had instructed his London ambassador to seek joint
action, but the ambassador had not done so. The friends
of the Confederacy had been made to appear ridiculous.
On July 11, 1863, Henry Hotze wrote to Benjamin:*

There is . . . no lack of weapons wherewith to take
revenge for the unfair and merciless manner in which the
ministry has pushed its advantage over the discomfited
advocates of recognition.

The whole armory of sarcasm, denunciation, and worst
of all, of ridicule, has been exhausted upon their devoted
heads, and it is not in human nature that they should
forego an opportunity for retaliation. But the cause of the
Confederacy has no longer aught to hope, though still
much to fear, from Mr. Roebuck's motion. All the resources of Southern strategy will be needed to secure a
decent retreat, which the radicals threaten to cut off by
insisting on a division. In Parliament some of the truest
friends of recognition would not vote for the motion,
marred and blurred as it now is by delicate and dangerous
excrescences. Outside the house it is impossible for the
public through the mist and smoke that has been con-
jured up around, to see even the outlines, much less the
real proportions, of the French appeal to England. To the
vast mass of careless observers the step of the Emperor
is not a grave diplomatic measure, imposing a fearful responsibility upon this country, but simply a sort of farce
in which Mr. Roebuck acted a broadly comic part. PUNCH,
which is sometimes singularly felicitous in seizing and
reflecting the passing phase of popular opinion, devotes
itself this week to this idea, ringing the changes upon it
on every page and in every conceivable manner. Against
such a settled current, so long as it flows, no reason or

argument or facts can prevail; gravity or anger only increase the mirth at the expense of the sufferers. I write it with pain and sorrow, but we have lost a great opportunity. The French proposal and the military situation were two levers which might have lifted more weighty obstacles than the present ministry from our path to recognition; instead of removing obstacles, we have succeeded only in rendering that path altogether impracticable. Henceforward to my thinking recognition depends solely on the judgment and courage of Lord Palmerston. In Parliament it will never again receive serious attention, even if a man could be found bold enough to broach it after the experience of the last two weeks.[16]

Benjamin, having learned from Hotze of the ill-fated Roebuck motion in Parliament with its disastrous consequences, wrote Mason:

The perusal of the recent debates in the British Parliament satisfies the President that the government of her Majesty has determined to decline the overtures made through you for establishing by treaty friendly relations between the two governments, and entertains no intention of receiving you as the accredited minister of this government near the British Court.

Under these circumstances your continued residence in London is neither conducive to the interests nor consistent with the dignity of this government, and the President therefore requests that you consider your mission at an end, and that you withdraw with your secretary from London.

In arriving at this conclusion, it gives me pleasure to say that the President is entirely satisfied with your own conduct of the delicate mission confided to you, and that it is in no want of proper effort on your part that the necessity for your recall has originated.[17]

England's refusal of recognition caused resentment to grow against her in the Confederacy. As the war progressed Confederates became understandably sensitive

*over refusal to acknowledge their sovereignty. The con-
duct of British consuls in the Confederacy became particularly irritating. Assigned their posts before secession
through the British Embassy in Washington, the consuls
continued to obey Lord Lyons, the British minister there.
This was bad enough, but to add to Southern frustration
the consuls soon busied themselves with affairs Southerners
considered outside their commissions. One of these was
interference with state and Confederate laws drafting residents who claimed British citizenship. So long as there was
hope of British recognition the Confederacy avoided a
direct conflict over the question. By the autumn of 1863,
however, such a prospect had faded. When Vice-Consul
Allen Fullerton at Savannah challenged Governor Brown's
efforts to force British subjects into the state militia, Fullerton appealed to Benjamin in an arrogant letter setting
forth the British position. To this letter Benjamin replied,
ordering Fullerton and all other Brtish consuls to cease
exercising their functions and withdraw from the country.*

*Meanwhile, as the blockade tightened around the Con-
federacy, Mexico became increasingly important as a
route for circumventing it. Mexican imports from Europe
could be shipped across the border without danger of
Federal capture, and cotton to pay for them could be
shipped out. The Confederacy sent agents to Mexico to
expedite this trade. John T. Pickett was accredited to the
general government at Mexico City and Juan A. Quintero,
was sent to the border states of Nuevo León and Coahuila.
Quintero, a Cuban by birth but a citizen of the Confederacy, had resided many years in Mexico. He was
clever and resourceful and was, with Hotze, one of the
ablest of Confederate agents. He arranged for imports that
probably prolonged for a time Confederate ability to carry
on the war.*

*There was Confederate activity in Canada, also, fur-
tively organized by Clement C. Clay and a one-time Mississippi planter, Jacob Thompson. After a dozen years in*

Congress Thompson had been appointed Secretary of the Interior in Buchanan's Cabinet, but had resigned when Buchanan sent the Star of the West *to the relief of Sumter. He was chief inspector of General John C. Pemberton's Army until it was surrendered at Vicksburg. In the summer of 1864 he and Clay were sent to Canada on a secret mission. In December he wrote Benjamin:*

On my arrival here I heard that there was such an organization as the order of the "Sons of Liberty" in the Northern states, and my first effort was to learn its strength, its principles, and its objects, and if possible to put myself in communication with its leading spirits. This was effected without much difficulty or delay. I was received among them with cordiality, and the greatest confidence at once extended to me. The number of its members was large, but not so great as Mr. [Joseph] Holt, in his official report, represented it to be. Its objects were political. Its principles were that the government was based on the consent of the parties to it; that the states were the parties and were sovereign; that there was no authority in the general government to coerce a seceding state. The [Kentucky and Virginia] resolutions of 1798 and 1799 were set forth as presenting the true theory of the government. Its organization was essentially military. It had its commanders of divisions, of brigades, of regiments, of companies. In the month of June last the universal feeling among its members, leaders, and privates was that it was useless to hold a presidential election. Lincoln had the power and would certainly re-elect himself, and there was no hope but in force. The belief was entertained and freely expressed that by a bold, vigorous, and concerted movement the three great northwestern states of Illinois, Indiana, and Ohio could be seized and held. This being done, the states of Kentucky and Missouri could easily be lifted from their prostrate condition and placed on their feet, and this in sixty days would end the war.

While everything was moving on smoothly to a supposed successful consummation, the first interruption in the calculation was the postponement of the meeting of the Democratic Convention from the 4th of July to the 29th of August, but preparations still went on, and in one of the states the 20th of July was fixed as the day for a movement; but before the day arrived a general council of the order from different states was called, and it was thought the movement on the 20th of July would be premature and the 16th of August was fixed upon for a general uprising. This postponement was insisted upon the ground that it was necessary to have a series of public meetings to prepare the public mind, and appointments for public peace meetings were made, one at Peoria, one at Springfield, and one at Chicago, on the 16th. The first one was at Peoria, and to make it a success I agreed that so much money as was necessary would be furnished by me. It was held and was a decided success. . . . The Springfield meeting came off, but it was apparent that the fire exhibited at Peoria had already diminished. The whole tone of the speakers was that the people must rely upon the ballot-box for redress for grievances. The nerves of the leaders of the order began to relax. About this time a large lot of arms were purchased and sent to Indianapolis, which was discovered, and some of the leading men were charged with the design to arm the members of the order for treasonable purposes. . . .

The Chicago Convention came, the crowd was immense, the feeling was unanimous for peace. A general impression prevailed that a reconstruction could be had and that it was necessary to so far pander to the military feeling as to take General McClellan to secure a certain success. This nomination, followed as it was by divers disclosures and arrests of persons, prominent members, totally demoralized the "Sons of Liberty." The feeling with the masses is as strong as ever. They are true, brave, and,

I believe, willing and ready, but they have no leaders. . . .

Soon after I reached Canada a Mr. Minor Major visited me and represented himself as an accredited agent from the Confederate States to destroy steamboats on the Mississippi River, and that his operations were suspended for want of means. I advanced to him $2,000 in Federal currency, and soon afterward several boats were burned at Saint Louis, involving an immense loss of property to the enemy. He became suspected, as he represented to me, of being the author of this burning, and from that time both he and his men have been hiding and consequently have done nothing.

Money has been advanced to Mr. [Benjamin P.] Churchill, of Cincinnati, to organize a corps for the purpose of incendiarism in that city. I consider him a true man, and although as yet he has effected but little, I am in constant expectation of hearing of effective work in that quarter.

Previous to the arrival of Lieutenant-Colonel [R. M.] Martin and Lieutenant Headly bringing an unsigned note from you, all the different places where our prisoners are confined—Camp Douglas, Rock Island, Camp Morton, Camp Chase, Elmira—had been thoroughly examined, and the conclusion was forced upon us that all efforts to release them without an outside co-operation would bring disaster upon the prisoners and result in no good. All projects of that sort were abandoned, except that at Camp Douglas, where Captain [T. Henry] Hines still believed he could effect their release. We yielded to his firmness, zeal, and persistence, and his plans were plausible, but treachery defeated him before his well-laid schemes were developed. Having nothing else on hand Colonel Martin expressed a wish to organize a corps to burn New York City. He was allowed to do so and a most daring attempt has been made to fire that city, but their reliance on the Greek fire has proved a misfortune. It cannot be depended on as an agent in such work. I have no faith whatever in it, and no attempt shall hereafter be made under my general direction with any such materials.

I knew nothing whatever of the raid on Saint Albans until after it transpired. . . .

The Presidential election has so demoralized the leaders of the order of the "Sons of Liberty" that a new organization under new leaders has become an absolute necessity. This is now going forward with great vigor and success. The new order is styled the "Order of the Star." There is a general expectation that there will soon be a new draft, and the members swear resistance to another draft. It is purely military, wholly independent of politics and politicians. It is given out among the members that Stonewall Jackson is the founder of the order, and the name has significance from the stars on the collars of Southern officers. There is no ground to doubt that the masses to a large extent of the North are brave and true, and believe Lincoln a tyrant and usurper. . . .

Should you think it best for me to return I would be glad to know in what way you think I had best return with the funds remaining on hand. I infer from your personal in the New York NEWS that it is your wish I should remain here for the present, and I shall obey your orders. Indeed, I have so many papers in my possession, which in the hands of the enemy would utterly ruin and destroy very many of the prominent men in the North, that a due sense of my obligations to them will force on me the extremest caution in my movements.

For the future, discarding all dependence on the organizations in the Northern states, our efforts, in my judgment, should be directed to inducing those who are conscripted in the North, and who utterly refuse to join the army to fight against the Confederate States, to make their way South to join our service. It is believed by many that at least a number sufficient to make up a division may be secured in this way for our service before spring, especially if our army opens up a road to the Ohio. Some are now on their way to Corinth, which at present is the point of rendezvous. Also to operate on their railroads and force the enemy to keep up a guard on all their roads, which will require a large standing army at home, and to burn whenever it is practicable, and thus make the men of property feel their insecurity and tire them out with the war. The attempt on New York has produced a great panic, which will not subside at their bidding.[18]

Confederate efforts at recognition never let up. In February 1865, as the country began to feel its death pangs, a desperate President and his Secretary of State sent Duncan Kenner, a Louisiana planter in the confidence of Benjamin, to Paris to inform Mason and Slidell of an astonishing proposal that they were instructed to make to the British and French governments. Mason made his way from Paris to London and obtained an audience with Palmerston. Then he wrote Benjamin:

Last night I asked for the interview by note to Lord Palmerston, which was appointed by him for 12 m. today.

I commenced the conversation by stating that a few days since, while in Paris, Mr. Slidell and I had received dispatches from the Confederate States government, the contents of which it was deemed important by the President should be made known to the two governments of Great Britain and France. As evidence of the importance attached to them by the President, they were sent by Mr. Duncan F. Kenner, of whose character and position I spoke. . . .

I then reverted to that part of the dispatch which reads: "If there be objections not made known to us, etc.," which prevented our recognition, justice demanded that an opportunity should be afforded to meet, and if we could, to overcome them. And in this connection I stated to Lord P. that I was instructed to say that the Confederate States were so fully impressed with the belief that during four years of unexampled trial everything on their part had demonstrated their independence not only as achieved, but that they were able and determined to maintain it, that the President could not reconcile with the existing facts the persistent refusal of Great Britain to recognize us, unless there were some latent objection or hindrance which her Majesty's government had not disclosed, but which yet governed its policy. If such were the case, had we not a right to know it in a matter so momentous to us? That, thus, if it stood a barrier to recognition we might remove it, if in our power to do so; and if not govern ourselves accordingly. . . .

In recapitulation I again impressively urged Lord P. that if the President was right in his impression that there was some latent, undisclosed obstacle on the part of Great Britain to recognition, it should be frankly stated and we might, if in our power to do so, consent to remove it.

I returned again and again during the conversation to this point, and in language so direct that it was impossible to be misunderstood, but I made no distinct proposal in terms of what was held in reserve under the private note borne by Mr. Kenner.

Lord Palmerston listened with interest and attention while I unfolded fully the purpose of the dispatch and of my interview.

In reply, he at once assured me that the objections entertained by his government were those which had been avowed, and that there was nothing (I use his own word) "underlying" them. He then proceeded to review the various points I had made, observing that it was not unnatural that the South should be sensitive, as was the North, in regard to the conduct of a neutral power; that with respect to the blockade, it might be that in the earlier stages of the war Great Britain might have taken exceptions to it, exceptions which she was not disposed to strain, as in future wars she was more likely to be a belligerent than a neutral. . . .

Our conversation lasted for more than an hour, and on

rising to take leave I expressed disappointment, or said rather, that the President would be disappointed to learn that he was mistaken in the impression that there was some operating influence that deterred her Majesty's government from recognizing us which had not been made known to him. As matters now stood, there would remain no alternative but to continue the war until terms could be made with the enemy (probably of the character I had intimated) and from which we had hoped to have been relieved by European recognition. . . .

It will be seen that I made no distinct suggestion of what the President considered might be the latent difficulty about recognition in the mind of the British ministry, construing the private instructions in the letter to Mr. Kenner to require that whilst intimations should be given which would necessarily be suggestive to the Prime Minister, it was for every reason important that an open proposition from us should be avoided, and whilst there was no committal on my part, I do not doubt that Lord P. understood to what obstacle allusion was made; and I am equally satisfied that the most ample concessions on our part in the matter referred to, would have produced no change in the course determined on by the British government in regard to recognition.[19]

But it was now too late—if there ever had been a time —for abolition of slavery to win British recognition. The Confederacy's brief life was near its end, and Palmerston was too wise to embrace a dying cause.

X: THE FIFTH COLUMN

While in general the Southern people went into the war with a remarkable unanimity, scattered here and there were large minorities attached to the Union and openly opposed to secession. This Union sentiment was particularly strong in the Appalachian Mountain region, and in East Tennessee in the summer and fall of 1861 rebellion against the Confederacy flared. Colonel W. B. Wood found himself in command of a detachment of the Confederate troops sent in to suppress insurrection; in November he reported to the then Secretary of War, Judah P. Benjamin:

SIR: The rebellion in East Tennessee has been put down in some of the counties and will be effectually suppressed in less than two weeks in all the counties. Their camps in Sevier and Hamilton counties have been broken up and a large number of them made prisoners. . . .

In a former communication I inquired of the Department what I should do with them. It is a mere farce to arrest them and turn them over to the courts. Instead of having the effect to intimidate, it really gives encouragement and emboldens them in their traitorous conduct. We have now in custody some of their leaders—Judge [David T.] Patterson, the son-in-law of Andrew Johnson; Colonel [Samuel] Pickens, the senator in the legislature from

Sevier and other counties, and several members of the legislature, besides others of influence and some distinction in their counties. These men have encouraged this rebellion, but have so managed as not to be found in arms. Nevertheless, all their actions and words have been unfriendly to the government of the Confederate States. The influence of their wealth, position, and connections has been exerted in favor of the Lincoln government, and they are the parties most to blame for the troubles in East Tennessee. They really deserve the gallows and if consistent with the laws, ought speedily to receive their deserts; but there is such a gentle spirit of conciliation in the South, and especially here, that I have no idea that one of them will receive such a sentence at the hands of any jury impaneled to try them.

I have been here at this station for three months, half the time in command of the post, and I have had a good opportunity of learning the feeling pervading this country. It is hostile to the Confederate government. They will take the oath of allegiance with no intention to observe it. They are the followers and slaves of Johnson and [Horace] Maynard and never intend to be otherwise. When arrested they suddenly become very submissive and declare they are for peace and not supporters of the Lincoln government, but yet they claim to be Union men. At one time whilst our forces were at Knoxville they gave it out that great changes were taking place in East Tennessee and the people were becoming reconciled and loyal. At the withdrawal of the army from here to the Gap and the first intimation that the Lincoln army was like to penetrate the state they were in arms; and scarcely a man, with only a few honorable exceptions, but what was ready to join them and make war upon us.

The prisoners we have tell us that they had every assurance that the army was already in the state and would join them in a very few days; that the property of Southern men was to be confiscated and divided amongst those who would take up arms for Lincoln.

I have to request at least that the prisoners I have taken be held if not as traitors as prisoners of war. To release them is ruinous; to convict them before a court at this time next to an impossibility; but if they are kept in prison for six months, it will have a good effect. The bridge-burners and spies ought to be tried at once, and I respectively request that instructions be forwarded at as early a day as practicable.[1]

Disloyalty, in East Tennessee and elsewhere, a continuing problem for the Confederacy, was, in a sense, part of still another problem, represented in a communication written in July 1862 by George W. Randolph, Benjamin's successor in the War Department, to the governor of every Confederate state:

SIR: Our armies are so much weakened by desertions and by the absence of officers and men without leave, that we are unable to reap the fruits of our victories and to invade the territory of the enemy. We have resorted to courts-martial and military executions, and we have ordered all officers employed in enrolling conscripts to arrest both deserters and absentees and offered rewards for the former. In Virginia the sheriffs, constables, and jailers have also been employed by the permission of the Governor, but still the evil continues, and unless public opinion comes to our aid we shall fail to fill our ranks in time to avail ourselves of the weakness and disorganization of the enemy.

Their resources enable them to repair defeat with great rapidity, and they are more numerous now in Virginia than they were before the recent battles near Richmond.

I must therefore beg Your Excellency's aid in bringing back to our colors all deserters and absentees. If you will authorize their arrest by state officers and bring to our assistance the powerful influence of public opinion in your state, we may yet cross the Potomac before a fresh army is raised to oppose us.

It is desirable that this cause of weakness should be concealed as much as possible from the enemy, but we cannot adopt measures to remove it without risking to some extent a disclosure of its existence.[2]

Sometimes it was the fortunes of war that revealed the underlying spirit of a region or place. After the Confederate retreat from Corinth, Mississippi, in the spring of 1862, Union armies penetrated into North Alabama. Then, when Bragg made his dash into Kentucky in the late summer, the Union troops were hurried north to head him off. Ex-Senator Clement C. Clay was in Huntsville, Alabama, shortly after the Federals departed. On October 24, he wrote to Secretary Randolph.

MY DEAR SIR: There is a great need of prompt action on the part of the government to correct the evil influences of the Yankee reign and of abuses of power of our own agents in North Alabama. The disloyal stand in open defiance of constitutional authority . . . and a large portion of those who are true to the Confederate government are restrained by fear of the return of the Yankees and menaces of greater outrages than they have yet suffered. . . . There is a very general feeling among such that the Confederate government is too weak to protect them or to punish treason or to enforce its laws. Men are here who during the stay of the enemy sold them cotton and bought it for them, acted as their agents, as spies, informers, and depositaries, openly declaiming for the Union and even signing calls for Union meetings, and who are now trading with them at Nashville, passing uninterruptedly between that place and this city. No enrolling agent under the conscript act has been in this section of Alabama, although quite two months has elapsed since the enemy left it, and those who ought to be in the army or to go into it are resorting to every expedient for escaping conscription. Some half-dozen are ensconced in the Niter Bureau office established here. Others are engaging in manufactories or trades or mining, and others are getting certificates of chronic disorders that their neighbors never suspected them of.

The reported retreat of Bragg and the disastrous defeat of [General Earl] Van Dorn have caused general dismay, and many are preparing to abandon their homes and to seek security in the mountains of Middle Alabama so soon as the army of [General Don Carlos] Buell reaches the southern boundary of Kentucky. This city is the place where the Union feeling most prevailed and where it now most exists. It has given tone to the political sentiments of North Alabama. If examples could be made of the leading traitors here, or if they could be restrained from commerce with the enemy, it would have a most salutary effect. . . .[3]

Early in 1863 Governor Brown had received shocking reports of conditions in Northern Georgia. On January 17 he issued

A PROCLAMATION

Reliable information having been received by me that there is at present a very considerable number of deserters and stragglers from the military service of the Confederate States within the limits of this state, who, after having volunteered and entered the service have ingloriously abandoned their country's flag and their brave comrades in arms; and it being represented that numbers of these deserters, encouraged by disloyal citizens in the mountains of Northeastern Georgia, have associated themselves together with arms in their hands and are now in rebellion against the authority of this state and the Confederate States, robbing loyal citizens of their property and threatening to burn their dwellings and do other acts of violence. . . .

I therefore issue this, my proclamation, commanding all persons, as well officers as privates, within the limits of this state, who have been actually engaged in the military service of the Confederate States and who have deserted or are otherwise absent from the respective commands to which they belong without legal furlough or order from the officers having the right to command them, or who have overstayed the time allowed them without providential hindrance, to return to their respective commands immediately after the publication of this notice; and I invoke the pardon of the Confederate authorities for all such who return to their duty within twenty days, but ask that the penalties of the law be vigorously inflicted upon all who refuse so to do; and I call upon the good people of this state to bring to bear the powerful influence of a just public opinion in condemnation of all deserters and stragglers, no matter what may be their position, wealth, or influence.[4]

Six weeks later, the Richmond Enquirer, *aroused by the extent and seriousness of the matter, suggested editorially:*

There is within the limits of this Confederacy, here and there, certain tories and traitors. They consist, first, of cowardly skulkers avoiding military duty and pretending regard for the old Union; second, bandits who abound in all times of war in every country, especially in the remote and mountainous regions; men who own no country and deserve none, but who love a lawless life; third, the most ignorant and illiterate country people of some of our remote districts, who conceive that the secession is a rebellion against Andrew Jackson, and have been taught to expect that each of them is to be presented with a bag of coffee from Washington the moment the rebellion is crushed.

Even worse than this; there is at least one region . . . in which treason is not only practiced by the people but sanctioned and protected by the judges elected by those people. . . .

In these circumstances it once more becomes the duty

of Congress to consider whether it is not needful to act upon the clauses in our Constitution providing for suspension of the HABEAS CORPUS. . . . It is the same thing that has been done twice before from session to session and as the power vested in the President last session has now expired, a member of the House has moved for its renewal. . . .

Undoubtedly it is a hard necessity; and very probably the President will accept the heavy responsibility even more reluctantly than Congress will throw it upon him. It is, of course, well guarded in the bill, being limited to a denial of the HABEAS CORPUS only in arrests made by Confederate authority, and not applicable to . . . state law. . . . The President . . . will be extremely reserved in employing the extraordinary power, and especially careful to prevent its exercise by mere military authorities.[5]

As disaffection spread, an astonishing development in the Alabama Congressional elections, held August 1, 1863, moved Major W. T. Walthall, commandant of a camp of conscripts at Talledega, to write to his superior in Richmond:

The result of the recent elections in this state has developed a degree of disaffection (to use the mildest possible term) which may lead to serious mischief. In this section of the state the elections have been generally carried by an opposition known as the "Peace Party." It is scarcely necessary to remark that (as the present war is on our part a struggle for peace) if a "peace party" has any definite meaning at all, it must mean what it should be treason even to suggest. In the Congressional district from which I write the present incumbent (Mr. [Jabez L. M.] Curry) has been defeated by a large majority, chiefly (from all I can learn) on account of his identification with the government and with what we have been accustomed to consider the established principles of the Confederacy.

In some counties men have been elected to the state

legislature and to other positions of public trust who were not publicly known, or scarcely known, as candidates. These results are mainly attributable . . . to a secret sworn organization known to exist and believed to have for its objects the encouragement of desertion, the protection of deserters from arrest, resistance to conscription, and perhaps other designs of a still more dangerous character. This organization is believed to include some men of intelligence, influence, and prominent position, and there can be little doubt that its leaders are, and long have been, in constant communication with the enemy.

It is not to be supposed for a moment that the opposition above alluded to is entirely, or perhaps that it is even chiefly, composed of disloyal elements; but it is greatly to be feared that this will be the controlling element.

If these considerations were exclusively political it would perhaps be officious or impertinent on my part to present them. But it is a significant fact that hostility to the conscription law has been one of the main elements of the opposition. It is perhaps still more significant that the rank and file of the paroled prisoners of the Vicksburg army, according to my information, contributed largely by their votes to the result of the election. Strength was added also to the opposition by the host of deserters who swarm throughout the country, and who no doubt came forth from their lurking places on the day of the election wherever the polls were not guarded by military force. The disposition is widely prevalent among the population at home to afford shelter and protection to these deserters, and insidious efforts are making to induce the paroled men generally to refuse to return into service.

In this state of affairs it is obviously of the highest importance that the conscription service of the country should be executed not only with vigor, but with discretion.[6]

Elsewhere, with the war more than two years old, conscription officers were having their troubles. From Colum-

bia, South Carolina, Commandant C. D. Melton wrote his chief:

COLONEL: In your communication of the 17th instant my attention is called to a letter from Major A. W. G. Davis, of Greenville, addressed to President Davis, giving information as to the great numbers of deserters in that district. . . . This condition of things is not confined alone to the district of Greenville. In Pickens and Spartanburg the same is found—the disaffection being very much limited to the mountainous portions of those districts along the North Carolina line.

From the districts named, and indeed from these very localities now infested with deserters, were raised some of the best companies in service from this state. The people, however, are poor, ill-informed, and but little identified with our struggle. They have, therefore, been easily seduced from their duty. The mountain coverts have furnished concealment from those sent to effect their arrest. The success of one in securing immunity from service has emboldened others, and the evil has gone on increasing until there can now be found few families which have not a husband, a son, a brother, or kinsman, a deserter in the mountains. The tone of the people is lost; it is no longer a reproach to be known as a deserter; all are ready to encourage and aid the efforts of those who are avoiding duty, and to refuse information to and thwart and even resist those who seek to make arrests. . . .[7]

From North Carolina, a week after Melton had written from South Carolina, an inspector of conscriptions reported to the Superintendent of Conscription.

SIR: When the conscript service was organized the direction that among its duties should be embraced that of collecting and forwarding deserters and skulkers by the use of force was doubtless based on the supposition that such characters would be found lurking about singly, unarmed, acting in no concert, and supported by no local public opinion or party. Even for such work our means at command have been inadequate in many parts of the country, and whatever auxiliary force time may prove to be available . . . cannot be expected to accomplish more than to meet the condition of things above described. . . .

Desertion has assumed (in some regions, especially the central and western portion of this state) a very different and more formidable shape and development than could have been anticipated. It is difficult to arrive at any exact statistics on the subject. The unquestionable facts are these: Deserters now leave the army with arms and ammunition in hand. They act in concert to force by superior numbers a passage against bridge or ferry guards, if such are encountered. Arriving at their selected localities of refuge, they organize in bands variously estimated at from fifty up to hundreds. . . . The patrols sent out from the conscript guard and bringing back a few prisoners each report that they have only captured these by surprise and have been compelled to make good their retreat in returning by circuitous routes to avoid arrangements made to intercept them by superior force.

His Excellency Governor Vance credits official information received by him, that in Cherokee County a large body of deserters (with whom I class also those in resistance to conscription) have assumed a sort of military occupation, taking a town, and that in Wilkes County they are organized, drilling regularly, and intrenched in a camp to the number of 500. Indeed, the whole number of deserters in the latter county is said to be much larger. The reports of our patrols indicate 300 or 400 organized in Randolph County, and they are said to be in large numbers in Catawba and Yadkin, and not a few in the patriotic county of Iredell. These men are not only determined to kill in avoiding apprehension (having just put to death yet another of our enrolling officers), but their ESPRIT DE CORPS extends to killing in revenge, as well as in prevention of the capture of each other. So far they seem to have had no trouble for subsistence. While the disaffected feed them from sympathy, the loyal do so from fear. The latter class (and the militia) are afraid to aid the conscript service lest they draw revenge upon themselves and their property.

The present quiet of such lawless characters of course cannot be expected to continue, and the people look for a reign of marauding and terror, protection against which is loudly called for. Letters are being sent to the army stimulating desertion and inviting the men home, promising them aid and comforts. County meetings are declaring in the same spirit and to hold back conscripts. As desertion spreads and enjoys impunity, in the same proportion do the enrolled conscripts hang back from reporting where there is not force enough to compel them, and the more dangerous and difficult becomes the position of our enrolling officers. All this trouble is of very rapid, recent growth, and is intimately connected with—indeed, mainly originates in and has been fostered by—the newly developed but active intrigues of political malcontents, having the Raleigh STANDARD for their leader, and, it is said, the majority in the [state] capital itself. The resolutions of the several county meetings, central and western, have evidently issued from the same mint, the common stamp being that North Carolina has not received due justice or credit, that she has done more than her share, and that her people ought to contribute no further. I allude to the political aspect only to show that there is danger of marked political division and something like civil war if the military evils reported be not at once met by strong measures of military repression. . . . The balance of physical force is on the wrong side, the loyal having contributed most freely to the army, even their sons still in early boyhood and not liable to serve. So far it does not appear that men of political weight have come forward publicly to any great extent to meet the intriguing demagogues on their own arena and prevent the ignorant masses from following their lead in ovine style.[8]

As desertion and disloyalty increased and spread to all parts of the Confederacy, President Davis himself admitted their existence to Congress in the spring of 1864.

It has been our cherished hope—and hitherto justified by the generous self-devotion of our citizens—that when the great struggle in which we are engaged was passed we might exhibit to the world the proud spectacle of a people unanimous in the assertions and defense of their rights and achieving their liberty and independence after the bloodiest war of modern times without the necessity of a single sacrifice of civil right to military necessity. But it can no longer be doubted that the zeal with which the people sprung to arms at the beginning of the contest has, in some parts of the Confederacy, been impaired by the long continuance and magnitude of the struggle.

While brigade after brigade of our brave soldiers who have endured the trials of the camp and battlefield are testifying their spirit and patriotism by voluntary re-enlistment for the war, discontent, disaffection, and disloyalty are manifested among those who, through the sacrifices of others, have enjoyed quiet and safety at home. Public meetings have been held, in some of which treasonable designs are masked by a pretended devotion to state sovereignty, and in others is openly avowed. Conventions are advocated with the pretended object of redressing grievances . . . but with the real design of accomplishing treason under the form of law. To this end a strong suspicion is entertained that secret leagues and associations are being formed. In certain localities men of no mean position do not hesitate to avow their disloyalty and hostility to our cause, and their advocacy of peace on the terms of submission to the abolition of slavery. In districts overrun by the enemy or liable to their encroachments, citizens of well-known disloyalty are holding frequent communication with them, and furnishing valuable information to our injury, even to the frustration of important military movements.[9]

By this time it was estimated that more than 100,000 men were absent from the armies without leave. Meanwhile, there was another manifestation of deteriorating morale. In mid-April 1864, A. M. Paxton, a War Department inspector in Mississippi, wrote Secretary Seddon:

Under the late act of the Confederate Congress the Secretary of the Treasury is authorized to issue permits to persons to trade beyond our lines. . . . There is in the Yankee lines a perfect mania for trading in cotton, even going so far as to control their military operations, covered under the pretense of getting out Negro men, mules, and supplies of food—in truth, gotten up and being controlled by cotton traders, dividing the profits with superior officers. Witness the late raid into the Yazoo River, and the return to Yazoo City of a steamer for cotton under the French flag; the raid at same date sent into lower part of Hinds County with a military force, government wagons and teams, to procure cotton where they had previously destroyed all the supplies and taken off the Negroes; also the raid into Ouachita and Red River, and the continual trading around Natchez, in all cases the marks being cut off the government cotton and proceeds divided with any woman or man who points it out and makes the outside arrangement, avowedly for the purpose of defrauding their own government by using for private gain Confederate cotton captured, and to which the United States government would be entitled. . . .

The government yet owns a large amount of cotton west of Pearl River, on the entire front from Lake Maurepas to the Tennessee line. This cotton is being hourly stolen and carried to the Yankee lines, and the whole military force of the Confederate States could not stop it. The government has not and cannot procure transportation to move it. As it stands, the whole population is being demoralized, socially, morally, and politically, and the whole social fabric is being destroyed and demoralized, and the country is becoming filled with speculators, deserters, and conscripts—overrun by our own troops and the Yankees. Ladies residing in this region, eminent for wealth, respectability, intelligence, and beauty, make nothing of taking government cotton without authority and traveling in the night to the enemy's lines, as they assert, bribing both pickets, and in return bringing out whisky, calico, and coffee, and have it sold at a large profit. The government should promptly do one of two things—either have burnt every pound of cotton in this region indicated, or make some arrangement to convert it into such articles as the government needs. . . . Our officers are overrun with applications for passports to go to the enemy's lines, and pickets annoyed and corrupted by their attempting to pass without passports. . . . Under the above state of facts it is important that the government should act promptly on the cotton and trading question, and also on the passport question.

Not being known to Mr. Memminger, I address this to you, and if upon consultation it is deemed advisable to procure mules, cast-steel, shoe thread, trace chains, etc., and numerous other articles, by exchange for this cotton, I think I can accomplish it.[10]

A few months after Paxton wrote, an assistant adjutant-general at Jackson, Mississippi, reported that the entire state was demoralized by cotton trading. "Yankee gold," he said, "is fast accomplishing what Yankee arms could never achieve—the subjugation of this people." He charged that Confederate officers and soldiers were bribed to permit the trade. "They have their price," he wrote, "and the blockade runners know well how to pay it. A pair of boots and a bottle of whisky will scarcely ever fail . . . to secure a passage for a load of cotton through the lines."

Illicit trade with the enemy, like disloyalty and desertion, was not confined to any single region or unit of the Confederacy. It seemed that wherever invading armies penetrated there were Southerners ready to turn a hand-

some profit by trade with them. John McVea, a Louisiana citizen, in a letter to General Stephen D. Lee, reported:

MY DEAR SIR: You will pardon the liberty I am about to take with you. I am a stranger to you, but I plead the interest which we both have in our great cause as my excuse for addressing you. The trade between this section and Baton Rouge has been to a considerable extent revived. The usual effects have begun to follow. Our currency has again greatly depreciated and our people become demoralized. There was no necessity, and there never was any, for this trade. The necessity urged in its behalf is that of food and clothing. It never existed. In the fall of 1862 the people in the county were making almost enough cloth to supply the demand. It was cloth of the best quality, such as any gentleman could wear. A large number of looms had been started and more were being put up. Everyone seemed willing to wear homespun, and nearly everyone did wear it. . . . As soon as the trade was permitted with Baton Rouge the looms stopped and homespun went out of fashion. The cloth made in the county sold in our own currency at $5 per yard. People preferred going to Baton Rouge and giving $15.

The disposition to traffic became a mania until a large portion of our people were entirely corrupted. Our currency fell as low as fifteen for one in Federal paper. On the arrival in this department of Colonel J. S. Scott this trade was stopped. Our currency at once went up, and sold at five to one in Louisiana bills, which were then at a premium. Confidence was being re-established and the prices of everything came down. . . . There never was any necessity for the trade arising from a scarcity of provisions. The county could have supported itself. To my own knowledge there has been more meat in it than there ever had been during any two years of peace. The supply of corn and potatoes was most ample. To be sure, there was no flour, or coffee, or canvased hams, or sardines, all of which were bought out of Baton Rouge when the trade revived. In 1863, when the trade was fairly opened, the cry was a want of provisions. Since then we have had an addition to our army here of about 1,500 men. . . . They live on the provisions raised in the county. The necessity for trading with the enemy has been in every instance fictitious and false. The consequences have been desertions, and if it is allowed to continue it will work the ruin of our people. It should be stopped at once, and I appeal to you, in the name of God and our country, to stop it at once. The order should be imperative and peremptory. No discretion should be allowed any officer here, because such are now the falsehood and fraud among the people that the best officers, if allowed any discretion, will be deceived by their representatives.[11]

The inspection reports of Paxton and others led to a cautionary letter from the Secretary of War to the commanding officer in Mississippi, General Richard Taylor.

A number of inspection reports have brought to my notice the existence of very great irregularity and abuse in the administration of your department, and that a reform is imperatively required. These reports refer to facts and circumstances which arose long previous to your assumption of the command of the department, and the consequences from which it will scarcely be in your power wholly to remove. The most important of the matters referred to is the illegal traffic and intercourse with the enemy, and the disloyalty and disaffection that have ensued from it. . . .

The inspection reports show that it has been the habit of the officers of the department to grant licenses to trade with the ports and posts of the enemy, and that the community at large have been seduced by the example into doing the same thing, in total violation or disregard of the acts of Congress. They show that there are a number of impostors—men professing to be agents of the government or licensed by some of its officers to conduct this trade—and that as a consequence of this licentiousness the patriotism and public spirit of the community have seriously diminished.[12]

Desertion continued year after year to deplete the armies of the C.S.A. In November 1864 General John Echols took it upon himself to write to the Secretary of War.

SIR: I deem it my duty to call your attention to the condition of things in Southwestern Virginia, and to urge upon you, and through you upon the other authorities, the necessity of the adoption of prompt and vigorous measures in order to remedy the evils which now exist in that region. . . .

A secret and treasonable organization has been in existence in the department for many months and has lately been increasing in size and importance with great rapidity. It numbers among its members quite a large number of men of some local influence in the respective counties in which they live, among whom are to be found some professional men and officers of the law of the state of Virginia. This organization was formed originally at the suggestion of the Yankee authorities, and has scattered over the country now what are called their initiating officers. Persons who are received into it are bound by the most solemn oaths not to disclose the secrets of the society or order. They are all bound to communicate to the enemy at all times all information which they can convey which may be of value. They bind themselves in the event of the invasion of the country by the enemy to furnish all needed information as to the roads of the country, and to notify the invaders at all times of any approaching danger. In return for these and other services to be rendered it is understood that the Yankee authorities have promised protection to the persons and property of these people. They have adopted a badge by which they recognize one another. They have also adopted a system of signs and grips and passwords only to be communicated to the initiated. The more ignorant classes of the country have been induced to join the organization by the promise of a division hereafter among them of the property of the loyal Southern citizens. . . .

Earnest efforts have of late been made to enlist the soldiers into the order, and it is known that these efforts have been successful to a certain extent. Information has been communicated lately which leads to the belief that a considerable number of the order are now in the Army of the Valley of Virginia, and that some of the soldiers in the army of General Hood, from Virginia, are also members. As a consequence of this a company of Virginia soldiers in this latter army who were on picket are said lately to have gone over to the enemy in a body. Of course the spread or adoption of the doctrines or purposes of this organization by any considerable number of our soldiers would be disastrous to us in the extreme.

This, then, sir, is the condition of the Department of Southwestern Virginia, and some active, energetic measures must at once be adopted to crush out the treason which has rapidly spread itself over that section of the Confederacy. It will be impossible to reach effectually the leading parties by the ordinary processes of law. They are so banded together that in the courts they could and would prove anything which they might desire.

In order to show the spirit which actuates these people it is proper that you should know that in two of the counties of Southwestern Virginia they have recently organized what they call a "new State," for which they elected a governor and lieutenant-governor, etc., and that in this same vicinity there was organized a brigade of deserters, for which was chosen a leader who was denominated "general."

This order has spread itself into East Tennessee and North Carolina. I make this communication, briefly and hurriedly, with the hope that I may have an opportunity of going more into details soon in a personal interview, but if I do not I desire to impress upon the authorities the knowledge of the serious and alarming condition of things of which I have spoken and the absolute necessity of the use of the most decisive measures in relation thereto.[13]

By January 1865 survivors of Hood's Army of Tennessee, shattered at Nashville, had reached Alabama and their lawlessness added greatly to general despondency and encouraged further disloyalty. Up to the last, Confederate authorities struggled valiantly against the wasting away of Confederate strength. Only a month before Lee abandoned Richmond the Superintendent of Conscription wrote to his chief, Breckinridge:

SIR: . . . I assume that the matter of returning deserters to the army is one of the greatest and most pressing necessities now upon the country, the importance of which no terms can exaggerate. That there are over 100,000 deserters scattered over the Confederacy; that so common is the crime it has, in popular estimation, lost the stigma which justly pertains to it, and therefore the criminals are everywhere shielded by their families and by the sympathies of many communities. They form the numerical majorities in many localities.[14]

Thus had morale on the home front deteriorated to the point where armies could not be kept in the field. The thread of life for the Confederacy was almost spun out.

*At the beginning of 1865 Union armies had driven deep
into all parts of the Confederacy. The trans-Mississippi
country had long been cut off. The Shenandoah had
been devastated by General Philip Sheridan. Grant had
fought a bloody path to Petersburg and Richmond and was
extending his left to the southwest to sever the capital's
last rail connection. Sherman had already marched through
Georgia to the sea and was preparing to slosh his way
north through the Carolinas at the time Mary Chesnut at
Columbia, South Carolina, wrote in her diary:*

January 14th—Yesterday I broke down—gave way to
abject terror under the news of Sherman's advance with
no news of my husband. Today, while wrapped up on the
sofa, too dismal even for moaning, there was a loud knock.
Shawls on and all, just as I was, I rushed to the door to
find a telegram from my husband: "All well; be at home
Tuesday." It was dated from Adam's Run. I felt as light-
hearted as if the war were over. Then I looked at the date
and the place—Adam's Run. It ends as it began—in a run
—Bull's Run, from which their first sprightly running as-
tounded the world, and now Adam's Run. But if we must
run, who are left to run? From Bull Run they ran full-
handed. But we have fought until maimed soldiers,
women, and children are all that remain to run.[1]

*As Sherman came north, threatening Lee's rear, and
Grant drew his cordon ever tighter around doomed Richmond, Judith McGuire at her job as a government clerk
knew that the end was near.*

March 10. Still we go on as heretofore, hoping and
praying that Richmond may be safe. Before Mr. Hunter
(Hon. R. M. T.) left Richmond, I watched his countenance whenever I heard the subject mentioned before him,
and though he said nothing, I thought he looked sad. I
know that he understands the situation of affairs perfectly,
and I may have fancied the sad look, but I think not;
and whenever it arises before my mind's eye, it makes me
unhappy. I imagine, too, from a conversation which I had
with Mr. Secretary Mallory, that he fears much for Richmond. Though it was an unexpressed opinion, yet I fear
that I understood it rightly. I know that we ought to feel
that whatever General Lee and the President deem right
for the cause must be right, and that we should be satisfied that all will be well; but it would almost break my
heart to see this dear old city, with its hallowed associations, given over to the Federals. Fearful orders have been
given in the offices to keep the papers packed, except such
as we are working on. The packed boxes remain in the
front room, as if uncertainty still existed about moving
them. As we walk in every morning, all eyes are turned to
the boxes to see if any have been removed, and we breathe
more freely when we find them still there.[2]

*On April 1, 1865, General Sheridan surprised and de-
feated General George Pickett at Five Forks, Virginia,
southwest of the Petersburg lines Lee had held so long.
Lee's right flank was turned. Before daylight the next morning, Union waves smashed over the Petersburg lines. The
South Side Railroad was lost. But Grant withheld a main
assault during Sunday, April 2, and Lee arranged desperately to get his army off to the west.*

*That Sunday dawned clear in Richmond. A dewy mist,
drifting gently up from the James, was soon driven off by*

*the warm spring sun that rose high in a cloudless sky.
Cannon were booming twenty miles to the south, but a
soft, northern breeze prevented the sound from reaching
the capital. Only the musical chiming of church bells
calling the faithful to worship disturbed the Sabbath calm.
Little groups of men and women gathered here and there
on the streets to exchange news or to discuss the latest
rumor, but most people were entering the city's handsome
churches. Sallie Putnam attended services at St. Paul's.
Years later she wrote:*

At St. Paul's Church the usual congregation was in attendance. President Davis occupied his pew.

It was again the regular monthly return for the celebra-
tion of the sacrament of the Lord's Supper. The services
were progressing as usual, no agitation nor disturbance
withdrew the thoughts from holy contemplation, when a
messenger was observed to make his way up the aisle and
to place in the hands of the President a sealed package.
Mr. Davis arose and was noticed to walk rather unsteadily
out of the church. An uneasy whisper ran through the
congregation, and intuitively they seemed possessed of the
dreadful secret of the sealed dispatch—the unhappy condition of General Lee's army and the necessity for evac-
uating Richmond. The dispatch stated that this was inevitable, unless his lines could be reformed before eight
o'clock that evening.

At the Second Presbyterian Church, Dr. [Moses D.]
Hoge, who had received information of the dire calamity
impending over us, told his congregation of our situation
and the probability that never again would they meet
there for worship, and in the thrilling eloquence of which
he is so truly the master bade them farewell.

The direful tidings spread with the swiftness of elec-
tricity. From lip to lip, from men, women, children, and
servants, the news was bandied, but many received it at
first, as only a "Sunday sensation rumor." Friend looked
into the face of friend to meet only an expression of in-

credulity; but later in the day, as the truth, stark and appalling, confronted us, the answering look was that of stony, calm despair. Late in the afternoon the signs of evacuation became obvious to even the most incredulous. Wagons were driven furiously through the streets, to the different departments, where they received as freight the archives of the government, and carried them to the Danville Depot, to be there conveyed away by railroad.

Thousands of citizens determined to evacuate the city with the government. Vehicles commanded any price in any currency possessed by the individual desiring to escape from the doomed capital. The streets were filled with excited crowds hurrying to the different avenues for transportation, intermingled with porters carrying huge loads and wagons piled up with incongruous heaps of baggage of all sorts and descriptions. The banks were all open, and depositors were busily and anxiously collecting their specie deposits, and directors were as busily engaged in getting off their bullion. Millions of dollars of paper money, both state and Confederate, were carried to the Capitol Square and buried.

Night came on, but with it no sleep for human eyes in Richmond. Confusion worse confounded reigned, and grim terror spread in wild contagion. The City Council met and ordered the destruction of all spirituous liquors, fearing lest, in the excitement, there would be temptation to drink and thus render our situation still more terrible. In the gutters ran a stream of whisky, and its fumes filled and impregnated the air. After nightfall Richmond was ruled by the mob. In the principal business section of the city they surged in one black mass from store to store, breaking them open, robbing them, and in some instances (it is said) applying the torch to them.

In the alarm and terror the guards of the State Penitentiary fled from their posts, and numbers of the lawless and desperate villains incarcerated there for crimes of every grade and hue, after setting fire to the workshops, made good the opportunity for escape, and donning garments stolen wherever they could get them in exchange for their prison livery, roamed over the city like fierce, ferocious beasts. No human tongue, no pen, however gifted, can give an adequate description of the events of that awful night.

While these fearful scenes were being enacted on the streets, indoors there was scarcely less excitement and confusion. Into every house terror penetrated. Ladies were busily engaged in collecting and secreting all the valuables possessed by them, together with cherished correspondence, yet they found time and presence of mind to prepare a few comforts for friends forced to depart with the army or the government. Few tears were shed; there was no time for weakness or sentiment. The grief was too deep, the agony too terrible to find vent through the ordinary channels of distress. Fathers, husbands, brothers, and friends clasped their loved ones to their bosoms in convulsive and agonized embraces, and bade an adieu . . . perhaps, thought many of them, forever.

At midnight the train on the Danville Railroad bore off the officers of the government, and at the same hour many persons made their escape on the canal packets and fled in the direction of Lynchburg.

But a still more terrible element was destined to appear and add to the horrors of the scene. From some authority —it seems uncertain what—an order had been issued to fire the four principal tobacco warehouses. They were so situated as to jeopardize the entire commercial portion of Richmond. At a late hour of the night Mayor Mayo had dispatched, by a committee of citizens, a remonstrance against this reckless military order. But in the mad excitement of the moment the protest was unheeded. The torch was applied, and the helpless citizens were left to witness the destruction of their property. The rams in the James River were blown up. The RICHMOND, the VIRGINIA NO. 2, and the BEAUFORT were all scattered in fiery fragments to the four winds of heaven. The noise of these explosions, which occurred as the first gray streaks of dawn broke over Richmond, was like that of a hundred cannon at one time. The very foundations of the city were shaken; windows were shattered more than two miles from where these gunboats were exploded, and the frightened inhabitants imagined that the place was being furiously bombarded. The PATRICK HENRY, a receiving-ship, was scuttled, and all the shipping at the wharves was fired, except the flag-of-truce steamer ALLISON.

As the sun rose on Richmond such a spectacle was presented as can never be forgotten by those who witnessed it. To speed destruction, some malicious and foolish individuals had cut the hose in the city. The fire was progressing with fearful rapidity. The roaring, the hissing, and the crackling of the flames were heard above the shouting and confusion of the immense crowd of plunderers who were moving amid the dense smoke like demons, pushing, rioting, and swaying with their burdens to make passage to the open air. From the lower portion of the city, near the river, dense black clouds of smoke arose as a pall of crape to hide the ravages of the devouring flames which lifted their red tongues and leaped from building to building as if possessed of demoniac instinct and intent upon wholesale destruction. All the railroad bridges, and Mayo's Bridge, that crossed the James River and connected with Manchester on the opposite side, were in flames.

The most remarkable scenes, however, were said to have occurred at the commissary depot. Hundreds of government wagons were loaded with bacon, flour, and whisky, and driven off in hot haste to join the retreating army. In a dense throng around the depot stood hundreds of men, women, and children, black and white, provided with anything in which they could carry away provisions, awaiting the opening of the doors to rush in and help themselves. A cascade of whisky streamed from the windows. About sunrise the doors were thrown open to the populace, and with a rush that seemed almost sufficient to bear off the building itself, they soon swept away all that remained of the Confederate commissariat of Richmond.

By this time the flames had been applied to or had reached the arsenal, in which several hundred carloads of loaded shell were left. At every moment the most terrific explosions were sending forth their awful reverberations and gave us the idea of a general bombardment. All the horrors of the final conflagration, when the earth shall be wrapped in flames and melt with fervent heat, were, it seemed to us, prefigured in our capital. . . .

As early as eight o'clock in the morning, while the mob held possession of Main Street and were busily helping themselves to the contents of the dry-goods stores and other shops in that portion of the city, and while a few of our cavalry were still to be seen here and there in the upper portions, a cry was raised: "The Yankees! The Yankees are coming!" Major A. H. Stevens of the Fourth Massachusetts Cavalry, and Major E. E. Graves of his staff, with forty cavalry rode steadily into the city, proceeded directly to the Capitol, and planted once more the "Stars and Stripes"—the ensign of our subjugation—on that ancient edifice. As its folds were given to the breeze, while still we heard the roaring, hissing, crackling flames, the explosions of the shells, and the shouting of the multitude, the strains of an old familiar tune floated upon the air—a tune that, in days gone by, was wont to awaken a thrill of patriotism. But now only the most bitter and crushing recollections awoke within us, as upon our quickened hearing fell the strains of "The Star Spangled Banner." For us it was a requiem for buried hopes.[3]

A few weeks more, and the end came for Joseph E. Johnston's little army at Durham Station, North Carolina. Two of Kate Stone's brothers had lost their lives in the

Confederate army. From Tyler, Texas, where she had
taken refuge with the rest of her family, she wrote:

May 15: CONQUERED, SUBMISSION, SUBJUGATION are
words that burn into my heart, and yet I feel that we are
doomed to know them in all their bitterness. The war is
rushing rapidly to a disastrous close. Another month and
our Confederacy will be a nation no longer, but we will
be slaves, yes, slaves, of the Yankee government.

The degradation seems more than we can bear. How
can we bend our necks to the tyrant's yoke? Our glorious
struggle of the last four years, our hardships, our sacrifices,
and worst of all, the torrents of noble blood that have been
shed for our loved country—all, all in vain. The best and
bravest of the South sacrificed—and for nothing. . . .
The bitterness of death is in the thought. We could bear
the loss of my brave little brothers when we thought that
they had fallen at the post of duty defending their country; but now to know that those glad, bright spirits suffered and toiled in vain; that the end is overwhelming
defeat; the thought is unendurable. And we may never be
allowed to raise a monument where their graves sadden
the hillside. There is a gloom over all like the shadow of
Death. We have given up hope for our beloved country
and all are humiliated, crushed to the earth. A past of
grief and hardship, a present of darkness and despair, and
a future without hope. Truly our punishment is greater
than we can bear.

Since Johnston's surrender the people in this department
are hopeless. If we make a stand it would only delay
the inevitable with the loss of many valuable lives. The
leaders say the country is too much disheartened to with-
stand the power of a victorious Yankee army flushed with
victory. Still, many hope there will be a rally and one
more desperate struggle for freedom. If we cannot gain
independence, we might compel better terms.

By the twenty-fourth we will know our fate: Submission

to the Union (how we hate the word!), Confiscation, and Negro equality—or a bloody unequal struggle to last we know not how long. God help us, for vain is the help of man.[4]

One of the most dedicated of Southern women was Kate Cumming, a young Mobile girl. In the spring of 1862 she had gone to West Tennessee to become a nurse with the Army of Tennessee. She served loyally throughout the war, and when peace came with defeat, she was still noble and courageous.

To the people of the South I would . . . say a few words in review of our actions during the eventful years just past:

Have the planters given of the abundance of their harvests to the poor women and children of soldiers who were fighting to save their wealth? But I should not say poor; none were poor whose husbands, sons, and brothers offered their lives a sacrifice for liberty.

Have no native Southern men remained at home speculating on what the planters sold them (thus doubly taking the bread from the mouths of these same poor, yet rich soldiers' families) when their country had need of their strong arms?

Have no quartermasters and commissaries robbed these POOR yet RICH soldiers, who walked boldly up to the cannon's mouth regardless of consequences? Many have starved, gone barefooted and ragged, while these delinquent commissaries and quartermasters have lived on the best of the land.

Have the examining surgeons sent none to the field but those who were fit for field service?

Have the conscript officers taken none for the army that the surgeons had discharged as unfit for service, who had they been left at home would have made food for themselves and families?

Have the stewards and foragers in hospitals never

speculated on food sold them much cheaper because it was for the soldiers and the cause?

Have there been no officers to whose keeping mothers have entrusted their young sons—they promising to guide and protect them, but who, as soon as away from restraint, forgot all obligations and took advantage of the position given them by circumstances, to act the tyrant in many ways, provoking many of the men to do what they would otherwise never have thought of?

Have all the young native Southerners who cried SECESSION and WAR to the KNIFE before the war broke out, gone into the field when their country was bleeding at every pore?

Have all the refined and Christian women of the South, who had no other duties needing their attention, gone into the hospitals and prepared little delicacies which no man has ever been able to do, for the poor bedridden soldier who had lost all but honor for his country, and when his hours were numbered stood by his bedside when no mother or sister was there to soothe his last moments and lift his thoughts to the cross and heaven, where all is peace and love?

In a word, have the women of the South done their whole duty, and can the people of the South, as a whole, say they have done their duty? "It is all over with," some may say, "and why bring these things in review before us?" It is not all over with. Men and women of the South, there is much yet to be done.

> What are monuments of bravery,
> Where no public virtues bloom?

What, though we had gained our independence, while all of these sins were crying out against us, could we, as a nation have gone on in them and prospered? Never! We should have worked our own downfall, as we have helped to do it now. Had we been true to our God and country,

with all the blessings of this glorious sunny land, I believe
we could have kept the North, with all her power, at bay
for twenty years.

What I would ask now, is for the Southern people to
look to themselves, forgetting all the wrongs inflicted on
us by our foe, in the knowledge that we have sinned
against each other. I do not mean to forget all we have
suffered, for that would dishonor the glorious dead. I
mean to stop all useless recriminations and look to ourselves. Let us "raise monuments where public virtues
bloom"! [5]

NOTES

I: IT BEGINS

1 *The War of the Rebellion: A Compilation of the Official Records of the Union and Confederate Armies,* 128 vols. (Washington, 1880-1901), Ser. 4, I, 1. Hereafter cited as *Official Records.*

2 Frank Moore, ed., *The Rebellion Record: A Diary of American Events, with Documents, Narratives, Illustrative Incidents, Poetry, etc.,* 11 vols. and Supplement (New York, 1861-8), I, 2. Hereafter cited as *Rebellion Record.*

3 *Official Records,* Ser. 1, I, 443-4.

4 *Official Records,* Ser. 4, I, 101.

5 The Confederate Constitution, from which the following excerpts are quoted, will be found in *Official Records,* Ser. 4, I, 136-47.

6 J. B. Jones, *A Rebel War Clerk's Diary at the Confederate States Capital,* Howard Swiggett, ed., 2 vols. (New York, 1935), I, 36-40. Reprinted by courtesy of Old Hickory Bookshop.

Jones was mistaken about Judah Benjamin's age and place of birth. Benjamin was born in St. Thomas, British West Indies, and was fifty years old when Jones wrote.

His parents moved to Charleston, South Carolina, when he was a child. He settled in New Orleans in 1828 when he was seventeen.

[7] T. C. De Leon, *Four Years in Rebel Capitals* (Mobile, Ala., 1890), 24-8.

[8] *Official Records*, Ser. 1, I, 135-6.

[9] Mary Boykin Chesnut, *A Diary from Dixie* (Copyright 1905, D. Appleton & Company), 32-9. Reprinted by permission of the publishers, Appleton-Century-Crofts, Inc.

[10] *Official Records*, Ser. 4, I, 281-2.

[11] *Official Records*, Ser. 1, II, 911-12.

II: FARMS AND FACTORIES

[1] *The Southern Cultivator*, XIX (Augusta, Georgia, 1861), 9-10, 138-9.

[2] New Orleans *Daily Picayune*, May 25, 1861.

[3] John Q. Anderson, ed., *Brokenburn, The Journal of Kate Stone, 1861-1868* (Baton Rouge, 1955), 18. Reprinted by courtesy of Louisiana State University Press.

[4] *Blackwood's Edinburgh Magazine*, Vol. XC (Dec. 1861), 757-60.

[5] *The Southern Cultivator*, XX (Jan. 1862), 12.

[6] *The Southern Cultivator*, XX (March-April 1862), 168.

[7] *Official Records*, Ser. 4, II, 349-50.

[8] *Official Records*, Ser. 4, II, 468.

[9] *Official Records*, Ser. 1, XXXIX, pt. 3, p. 369.

[10] *Official Records*, Ser. 4, I, 987-9.

[11] *De Bow's Review*, XXXII-XXXIII (1862), 327-33.

[12] *Official Records*, Ser. 4, II, 349-50.

[13] *Official Records*, Ser. 4, II, 1007-8.

[14] J. B. Jones, *A Rebel War Clerk's Diary*, Vol. I, 302. See I, note 6.

[15] *Official Records*, Ser. 4, II, 1012-13.

[16] T. C. De Leon, *Four Years in Rebel Capitals*, 91-2.

III: CHURCHES AND SCHOOLS

1 *South Western Baptist,* quoted in Frank Moore, ed., *The Rebellion Record,* I, 183.

2 *Constitution of the Protestant Episcopal Church in the Confederate States of America* (Columbia, S. C., 1861).

3 *Minutes of the General Assembly of the Presbyterian Church in the Confederate States of America* (Augusta, 1861), Vol. I, 51-60.

4 *The Atlanta Southern Confederacy,* quoted in Frank Moore, ed., *The Rebellion Record,* III, 389.

5 Quoted in Ulrich B. Phillips, "The Central Theme of Southern History," in *American Historical Review,* XXXIV (1929), 32. Reprinted by courtesy of the *American Historical Review.*

6 *Southern Field and Fireside,* Jan. 8, 1862, quoted in Bell I. Wiley, *Southern Negroes, 1861-1865* (New York, 1953), 106.

7 James W. Silver, *Confederate Morale and Church Propaganda, Confederate Centennial Series, Number Three* (Tuscaloosa, 1957), 46-7. Reprinted by courtesy of the Confederate Publishing Company.

8 Edward McPherson, *The Political History of the United States of America, during the Great Rebellion. . . .* (Washington, 1865), 521. The incident of the clergyman giving the gun to the soldier is from the Columbus (Ga.) *Weekly Times,* Dec. 30, 1861, quoted in T. Conn Bryan, "Churches in Georgia During the Civil War," in *Georgia Historical Quarterly,* XXXIII (1949), 289 n. Reprinted by courtesy of *Georgia Historical Quarterly* and T. Conn Bryan. The statement of William Porcher Miles is quoted in James W. Silver, *Confederate Morale and Church Propaganda,* 96. See note 7 above.

9 Edward McPherson, *The Political History of the United States of America, During the Great Rebellion . . . ,* 515.

[10] James J. Marks, *The Peninsular Campaign in Virginia; or Incidents and Scenes on the Battle-Fields and in Richmond* (Philadelphia, 1864), 84-5.

[11] Stephen F. Fleharty, *Our Regiment, A History of the 102d. Illinois Infantry Volunteers* . . . (Chicago, 1865), 132, micro-card, University of Kentucky Library.

[12] *De Bow's Review*, Vol. XXXI (1861), 347-61 *passim*.

[13] John Q. Anderson, ed., *Brokenburn, The Journal of Kate Stone*, 61, 62, 69, 70, 71, 73, 75. See II, note 3.

[14] [Sallie A. (Brock) Putnam], *Richmond During the War: Four Years of Personal Observation*. By a Richmond Lady (New York and London, 1867), 196.

[15] Richmond *Dispatch*, May 6, 1863.

[16] Stephen B. Weeks, "Confederate Text-Books (1861-1865): A Preliminary Bibliography," in *Report of the [United States] Commissioner of Education, 1898-99*, I (Washington, 1900), 1147, 1150.

[17] [Sallie A. (Brock) Putnam], *Richmond During the War*, 188-95 *passim*.

IV: THE MUSES

[1] Quoted in *Southern Literary Messenger*, XXXII-XXXIII (1861), 317-18.

[2] *Southern Literary Messenger*, XXXVIII (January 1864), 63-4.

[3] *De Bow's Review*, XXXIV (1864), 98-9.

[4] *Southern Literary Messenger*, XXXV (Nov.-Dec. 1862), 658-61.

[5] John L. Burrows, *The New Richmond Theatre. A Discourse Delivered on Sunday February 8, 1863 in the First Baptist Church, Richmond, Va.* (Richmond, 1863). Pamphlet in Harvard University Library.

The quotation in the text preceding this document is from *The Southern Illustrated News*, Dec. 20, 1862.

[6] *The Southern Illustrated News*, Feb. 14, 1863.

[7] Richmond *Enquirer,* May 2, 1863.

[8] *The Southern Illustrated News,* Aug. 22, 1863.

[9] Richmond *Examiner,* Jan. 5, 1864.

[10] Richmond *Enquirer,* Aug. 17, 1864.

[11] T. C. De Leon, *Four Years in Rebel Capitals,* 298-301.

V: INFLATION

[1] *De Bow's Review,* XXXI (1861), 327-9.

Robert Toombs' statement in text preceding this document is from the *American Annual Cyclopaedia,* 1861, p. 205.

The estimate concerning taxes raised by the Confederacy is by E. M. Coulter, *The Confederate States of America, 1861-1865* (Baton Rouge, 1950), 182.

[2] *Official Records,* Ser. 4, I, 567-74.

[3] Montgomery *Advertiser,* quoted in *Southern Cultivator,* XX (May-June 1862), 114.

[4] *Official Records,* Ser. 4, II, 309-23.

Governor Vance's statement quoted in the text preceding this document is in the *Official Records,* Ser. 4, II, 181.

Jefferson Davis's statement is in the Richmond *Dispatch,* Oct. 5, 1863.

[5] Richmond *Enquirer,* March 3, 1863.

[6] Augusta (Georgia) *Chronicle and Sentinel,* quoted in Richmond *Enquirer,* March 11, 1863.

[7] *Official Records,* Ser. 4, II, 513-24.

[8] *Official Records,* Ser. 4, II, 1008-9.

[9] *Official Records,* Ser. 4, II, 1012.

[10] *Official Records,* Ser. 4, III, 47.

[11] *Official Records,* Ser. 4, III, 544-5.

[12] *Official Records,* Ser. 4, III, 653-4.

[13] *Official Records,* Ser. 4, III, 689.

[14] J. Harold Easterby, ed., *The South Carolina Rice Plantation As Revealed in the Papers of Robert F. W. Allston*

(Chicago, 1945), (Copyright 1945 by the University of Chicago), 203-4. Reprinted by courtesy of the University of Chicago Press.

VI: INVASION

1 *Official Records,* Ser. 2, II, 1378-9.
2 *Official Records,* Ser. 2, IV, 880-5.
3 John Q. Anderson, ed., *Brokenburn, The Journal of Kate Stone,* 191-201. See II, note 3.
4 *Official Records,* Ser. 2, VI, 776.
5 Richmond *Whig,* Apr. 15, 1864.
6 [Judith White (Brockenbrough) McGuire], *Diary of a Southern Refugee, during the War. By a Lady of Virginia* (New York, 1867), 298-304.
7 Mrs. Roger A. (Sara Rice) Pryor, *Reminiscences of Peace and War* (New York, 1904), 279-83. Reprinted by permission of Macmillan Company.
8 Myrta Lockett Avary, ed., *A Virginia Girl in the Civil War, 1861-1865: Being a Record of the Actual Experiences of a Wife of a Confederate Officer* (New York, 1903), 349-59.

VII: "STITCH, STITCH, STITCH"

1 [Sallie A. (Brock) Putnam], *Richmond During the War; Four Years of Personal Observation,* 38-40, 78-81.
2 *Blackwood's Edinburgh Magazine,* XC (Dec. 1861), 761.
3 John Q. Anderson, ed., *Brokenburn, The Journal of Kate Stone,* 108-110. See II, note 3.
4 Mrs. Burton (Constance Cary) Harrison, "Richmond Scenes in '62," in Robert U. Johnson and C. C. Buell, eds., *Battles and Leaders of the Civil War . . . ,* 4 vols. (New York, 1887), II, 442-5.
5 Sarah Page Andrews to Matthew Page Andrews, Sept. 18, 22, 1862, in Andrews Collection, Duke University Library.

[6] [Judith White (Brockenbrough) McGuire], *Diary of a Southern Refugee during the War*, 244-5, 247, 250-2.

[7] T. C. De Leon, *Four Years in Rebel Capitals*, 148-9, 153-5.

[8] Richmond *Enquirer*, Mar. 12, 1863.

The quotations in the text immediately preceding this document are, in order, from:

[Sallie A. (Brock) Putnam], *Richmond During the War; Four Years of Personal Observation*, 134.

Mary Boykin Chesnut, *A Diary from Dixie*, 268. See I, note 9.

Richmond *Whig*, Jan. 6, 1865.

[9] [Judith White (Brockenbrough) McGuire], *Diary of a Southern Refugee during the War*, 328-30.

[10] Mary Boykin Chesnut, *A Diary From Dixie*, 288-9, 316. See I, note 9.

[11] [Sallie A. (Brock) Putnam], *Richmond During the War; Four Years of Personal Observation*, 208-9.

[12] Mrs. Roger A. (Sara Rice) Pryor, *Reminiscences of Peace and War*, 263-7. See VI, note 7.

The quotations in the text preceding this document are, in order, from Kate Cumming, *Gleanings From Southland* (Birmingham, 1895), 214.

Mary Boykin Chesnut, *A Diary From Dixie*, 218. See I, note 9.

[Judith White (Brockenbrough) McGuire], *Diary of a Southern Refugee during the War*, 257.

[13] Letter from "A General's Wife" to a friend in Europe in *Southern Literary Messenger*, XXXVIII (1864), 382.

[14] Atlanta *Register* quoted in Richmond *Whig*, Jan. 7, 1865.

[15] Richmond *Examiner*, Dec. 31, 1864.

VIII: DISCONTENT

[1] *Official Records*, Ser. 4, I, 1095-7.

[2] *Official Records*, Ser. 4, I, 1082-5.

[3] *Official Records,* Ser. 4, II, 73-5.

[4] *Official Records,* Ser. 4, I, 1081.
   The statement of the North Carolina legislators is in the *Official Records,* Ser. 4, II, 247.

[5] *Official Records,* Ser. 4, II, 670-1.

[6] *Official Records,* Ser. 4, III, 176-7.

[7] Richmond *Whig,* Apr. 14, 1864.

[8] Richmond *Examiner,* Nov. 10, 1864.

[9] Richmond *Examiner,* Dec. 15, 1864.

[10] *Southern Literary Messenger,* XXXVII (1863), 572-3.

[11] Richmond *Examiner,* Nov. 10, 1864.

[12] Richmond *Examiner,* Jan. 9, 1865.

[13] Mary Boykin Chesnut, *A Diary From Dixie,* 360. See I, note 9.

IX: KING COTTON

[1] *Congressional Globe,* 35 Cong., 1 Sess., 961.

[2] William Howard Russell, *My Diary North and South,* 2 vols. (London, 1863), I, 141-3, 169-71.

[3] *Blackwood's Edinburgh Magazine,* XC (Dec. 1861), 762-3.

[4] *Official Records of the Union and Confederate Navies in the War of the Rebellion,* 30 vols. (Washington, 1894-1922), Ser. 2, III, 358-60. Hereafter cited as *Official Records Navy.*

[5] E. D. Adams, *Great Britain and the American Civil War,* 2 vols. (New York, 1925), II, 32. Reprinted by courtesy of Longmans, Green and Company.

[6] Spencer Walpole, *The Life of Lord John Russell,* 2 vols. (London and New York, 1889), II, 349.

[7] Spencer Walpole, *The Life of Lord John Russell,* II, 349.

[8] Spencer Walpole, *The Life of Lord John Russell,* II, 350.

[9] E. D. Adams, *Great Britain and the American Civil War,* II, 54-5. See note 5 above.

[10] *Official Records Navy,* Ser. 2, III, 574-7.

[11] *Official Records Navy,* Ser. 2, III, 566-7.

[12] *Blackwood's Edinburgh Magazine,* XCII (July-Dec. 1862), 636, 639-41, 645.

[13] *Official Records Navy,* Ser. 2, III, 601.

[14] *Official Records,* Ser. 4, II, 343.

[15] *Official Records Navy,* Ser. 2, III, 716-17.

[16] *Official Records Navy,* Ser. 2, III, 839-40.

[17] *Official Records Navy,* Ser. 2, III, 852.

[18] *Official Records,* Ser. 1, XLIII, pt. 2, 930-6.

[19] *Official Records Navy,* Ser. 2, III, 1272-6.

X: THE FIFTH COLUMN

[1] *Official Records,* Ser. 2, I, 845-6.

[2] *Official Records,* Ser. 4, II, 7.

[3] *Official Records,* Ser. 4, II, 141-2.

[4] *Official Records,* Ser. 4, II, 360-1.

[5] Richmond *Enquirer,* Mar. 5, 1863.

[6] *Official Records,* Ser. 4, II, 726-7.

[7] *Official Records,* Ser. 4, II, 769-70.

[8] *Official Records,* Ser. 4, II, 783-5.

[9] *Official Records,* Ser. 4, III, 67-70.

[10] *Official Records,* Ser. 4, III, 282-3.

[11] *Official Records,* Ser. 4, III, 508-9.
     The report of the assistant adjutant-general referred to in the text preceding this document will be found in the *Official Records,* Ser. 4, III, 645-8.

[12] *Official Records,* Ser. 4, III, 688-9.

[13] *Official Records,* Ser. 4, III, 812-14.

[14] *Official Records,* Ser. 4, III, 1119-20.

XI: IT ENDS

[1] Mary Boykin Chesnut, *A Diary From Dixie,* 341. See I, note 9.

[2] [Judith White (Brockenbrough) McGuire], *Diary of a Southern Refugee during the War,* 334.

3 [Sallie A. (Brock) Putnam], *Richmond During the War; Four Years of Personal Observation*, 362-7.

4 John Q. Anderson, ed., *Brokenburn, The Journal of Kate Stone*, 339-41. See II, note 3.

5 Kate Cumming, *Gleanings From Southland*, 236-8.

BIBLIOGRAPHY

GOVERNMENT AND OTHER OFFICIAL DOCUMENTS

Congressional Globe, 35 Cong. 1 Sess.

Constitution of the Protestant Episcopal Church in the Confederate States of America (Columbia, S. C., 1861).

Journal of the Congress of the Confederate States of America, 1861-1865, 7 vols. (Washington, 1904-5).

Matthews, James M. (ed.), *Public Laws of the Confederate States of America.* . . . (Richmond, 1862-4).

Matthews, James M. (ed.), *The Statutes at Large of the Provisional Government of the Confederate States of America . . . and the Treaties Concluded by the Confederate States with Indian Tribes* (Richmond, 1864).

Minutes of the General Assembly of the Presbyterian Church in the Confederate States of America (Augusta, 1861). Vol. I.

Official Records of the Union and Confederate Navies in the War of the Rebellion, 30 vols. and index (1894-1927). Cited in footnotes as *Official Records Navy.*

Ramsdell, Charles W. (ed.), *Laws and Joint Resolutions of the Last Session of the Confederate Congress (November 7, 1864-March 18, 1865) Together with the Secret Acts of Previous Congresses* (Durham, 1941).

Richardson, James D., *A Compilation of the Messages and Papers of the Confederacy, Including the Diplomatic Correspondence, 1861-1865,* 2 vols. (Nashville, 1906).

The War of the Rebellion: A Compilation of the Official Records of the Union and Confederate Armies, 127 vols. and index (Washington, 1880-1901). Cited in footnotes as *Official Records.*

YEAR BOOKS, STATISTICAL AND DOCUMENTARY COLLECTIONS

American Annual Cyclopaedia and Register of Important Events of the Year 1861. Embracing Political, Civil, Military, and Social Affairs; Public Documents; Biography; Statistics, Commerce, Finance, Literature, Science, Agriculture and Mechanical Industry, and volumes for other war years, 15 vols. (New York, 1862-76).

McPherson, Edward, *The Political History of the United States of America, during the Great Rebellion . . .* (Washington, 1865).

Moore, Frank (ed.), *The Rebellion Record: A Dairy of American Events, with Documents, Narratives, Illustrative Incidents, Poetry, etc.,* 11 vols. and Supplement (New York, 1861-8).

CORRESPONDENCE, DIARIES, MEMOIRS

Andrews Collection. Mss. in Duke University Library.

Andrews, Eliza Frances, *The War-Time Journal of a Georgia Girl, 1864-1865* (New York, 1908).

Avary, Myrta Lockett (ed.), *Recollections of Alexander H. Stephens; His Diary Kept when a Prisoner at Fort Warren, Boston Harbour, 1865; Giving Incidents and Reflections of his Prison Life and Some Letters and Reminiscences* (New York, 1910).

Avary, Myrta Lockett (ed.), *A Virginia Girl in the Civil War, 1861-1865; Being a Record of the Actual Experiences of the Wife of a Confederate Officer* (New York, 1903).

Cable, George W. (ed.), "War Diary of a Union Woman in the South," in *Famous Adventures and Prison Escapes of the Civil War* (New York, 1893).

Cumming, Kate, *Gleanings from Southland; Sketches of Life and Manners of the People of the South before, during and after the War of Secession* . . . (Birmingham, 1895).

Dawson, Sarah Morgan, *A Confederate Girl's Diary* (Boston, 1913).

Day, Samuel Phillips, *Down South; or, An Englishman's Experience At the Seat of the American War*, 2 vols. (London, 1862).

De Leon, Thomas Cooper, *Four Years in Rebel Capitals: An Inside View of Life in the Southern Confederacy, from Birth to Death. From Original Notes, Collected in the Years 1861 to 1865* (Mobile, 1890).

Dicey, Edward, *Six Months in the Federal States*, 2 vols. (London, 1863).

Easterby, J. Harold, *The South Carolina Rice Plantation as Revealed in the Papers of Robert F. W. Allston* (Chicago, 1945).

Eggleston, George Cary, *A Rebel's Recollections* (New York, 1897).

"English Merchant, An" [unknown], *Two Months in the Confederate States, Including a Visit to New Orleans under the Domination of General Butler* (London, 1863).

Erickson, Edgar L. (ed.), "Hunting for Cotton in Dixie: From the Civil War Diary of Captain Charles E. Wilcox," in the *Journal of Southern History*, IV (1938), 493-513.

Fleharty, Stephen F., *Our Regiment. A History of the 102d Illinois Infantry Volunteers, with Sketches of the Atlanta Campaign, the Georgia Raid, and the Campaign of the Carolinas* (Chicago, 1865).

Fulkerson, H. S., *A Civilian's Recollections of The War*

Between the States, ed. by Percy L. Rainwater (Baton Rouge, 1939).

Gay, Mary A. H., *Life in Dixie During the War 1861 . . . 1865* (Atlanta, 1897).

Gordon, Armistead C., *Memories and Memorials of William Gordon McCabe,* 2 vols. (Richmond, 1925).

Hague, Mrs. Parthenia Antionette (Vardaman), *A Blockaded Family: Life in Southern Alabama During the Civil War* (Boston, 1888).

Hamilton, J. G. de Roulhac (ed.), *The Correspondence of Jonathan Worth,* 2 vols. (Raleigh, 1909), I.

Harrison, Mrs. Burton (Constance Cary), *Recollections Grave and Gay* (New York, 1912).

Hopley, Catherine C., *Life in the South; from the Commencement of the War. By a Blockaded British Subject. Being a social history of those who took Part in the Battles, from a Personal Acquaintance with them in their own Homes. From the spring of 1860 to August, 1862,* 2 vols. in one (London, 1863).

Hubbell, Jay B. (ed.), "The War Diary of John Esten Cooke," in the *Journal of Southern History,* VII (1941), 526-40.

Jones, John B., *A Rebel War Clerk's Diary at the Confederate States Capital,* 2 vols. (New York, 1935).

Kirke, Edmund [James R. Gilmore], *Down in Tennessee and Back by Way of Richmond* (New York, 1864).

Knox, Thomas W., *Camp-Fire and Cotton-Field: Southern Adventure in Time of War. Life with the Union Armies, and Residence on a Louisiana Plantation* (New York, 1865).

Le Conte, Joseph, *Ware Sherman, A Journal of Three Months' Personal Experience in the Last Days of the Confederacy* (Berkeley, 1937).

Lord, Walter (ed.), *The Fremantle Diary. Being the Journal of Lieutenant Colonel James Arthur Lyon Fremantle, Coldstream Guards on his Three Months in the Southern States* (Boston, 1954).

McDonald, Mrs. Cornelia, *A Diary with Reminiscences of the War and Refugee Life in the Shenandoah Valley, 1860-1865* (Nashville, 1935).

[McGuire, Judith White (Brockenbrough)], *Diary of a Southern Refugee during the War. By a Lady of Virginia* (New York, 1867).

Malet, the Reverend William W., *An Errand to the South in the Summer of 1862* (London, 1863).

Marks, James J., *The Peninsular Campaign in Virginia; or Incidents and Scenes on the Battle-Fields and in Richmond* (Philadelphia, 1864).

Martin, Isabella D., and Avary, Myrta Lockett (eds.), *A Diary from Dixie, as written by Mary Boykin Chesnut, Wife of James Chesnut, Jr., United States Senator from South Carolina, 1859-1861, and Afterward an Aide to Jefferson Davis and a Brigadier-General in the Confederate Army* (New York, 1905).

Phillips, Ulrich B. (ed.), *The Correspondence of Robert Toombs, Alexander H. Stephens, and Howell Cobb,* in American Historical Association, *Annual Report, 1911,* II (Washington, 1913).

[Putnam, Sallie A. (Brock)], *Richmond During the War: Four Years of Personal Observation. By A Richmond Lady* (New York and London, 1867).

Pryor, Mrs. Sara Agnes (Rice), *Reminiscences of Peace and War* (New York, 1924).

Rowland, Dunbar (ed.), *Jefferson Davis, Constitutionalist, His Letters, Papers and Speeches,* 10 vols. (Jackson, Miss., 1923).

Rowland, Kate Mason, and Croxall, Mrs. Morris L. (eds.), *The Journal of Julia Le Grand, New Orleans, 1862-1863* (Richmond, 1911).

Ross, Fitzgerald, *A Visit to the Cities and Camps of the Confederate States* (Edinburgh, 1865).

Russell, William H., *My Diary North and South* (Boston, 1863).

Smedes, Susan Dabney, *A Southern Planter* (New York, 1890).

Spencer, Mrs. Cornelia (Phillips), *The Last Ninety Days of the War in North Carolina* (New York, 1866).

Street, Julian, *A Woman's Wartime Journal; An Account of the Passage over a Georgia Plantation of Sherman's Army on the March to the Sea, as Recorded in the Diary of Dolly Sumner Lunt* (Mrs. Thomas Burge), (Macon, 1927).

Vandiver, Frank E. (ed.), *The Civil War Diary of General Josiah Gorgas* (University, Ala., 1947).

Wright, Mrs. Louise (Wigfall), *A Southern Girl in '61. The War-Time Memories of a Confederate Senator's Daughter* (New York, 1905).

Younger, Edward (ed.), *Inside the Confederate Government: The Diary of Robert Garlick Hill Kean* (New York, 1957).

PAMPHLETS

Burrows, John L., *The New Richmond Theatre. A Discourse Delivered on Sunday February 8, 1863 in the First Baptist Church, Richmond, Va.* (Richmond, 1863). Pamphlet in Harvard University Library.

"Cincinnatus," *Address of the Atlanta Register to the People of the Confederate States* (Atlanta, 1864).

Letter of Hon. Howell Cobb to the People of Georgia, on the Present Condition of the Country [December 6, 1860] (Washington, 1860).

Speech of Hon. L. Q. C. Lamar, of Miss., on the State of the Country. Delivered in the Athenaeum, Atlanta, Ga., Thursday Evening, April 14, 1864 (Atlanta, 1864).

CONTEMPORARY PERIODICALS

Baptist Banner, Atlanta (1860-5)
Blackwood's Edinburgh Magazine
De Bow's Review

Historical Magazine of the Protestant Episcopal Church, XVII (December 1948)

The London Index (1862-5)

Punch, or the London Charivari

Southern Cultivator, A Monthly Journal, Devoted to the Interests of Southern Agriculture, and Designed to Improve both the soil and the Mind; to Elevate the Character of the Tillers of the Soil, and to Introduce a more Enlightened System of Agriculture

Southern Field and Fireside

Southern Illustrated News

Southern Literary Messenger

Southern Punch

South Western Baptist, Marion, Alabama

NEWSPAPERS

Atlanta *Southern Confederacy*

Augusta *Chronicle and Sentinel*

Augusta *Constitutionalist*

Charleston *Courier*

Charleston *Mercury*

Jackson (Miss.) *Daily Clarion*

Macon *Daily Confederate*

Macon *Journal and Messenger*

Macon *Telegraph*

Memphis *Daily Appeal*

Mobile *Advertiser and Register*

Mobile *Evening News*

Montgomery *Advertiser*

Montgomery *Mail*

New Orleans *Delta*

New Orleans *Picayune*

Richmond *Dispatch*

Richmond *Enquirer*

Richmond *Examiner*

Richmond *Sentinel*

Richmond *Whig*

GENERAL AND SPECIAL HISTORIES

Adams, Ephraim D., *Great Britain and the American Civil War*, 2 vols. (London, 1925).

"Affairs of Southern Railroads," in *Reports of the Committees of the House of Representatives*, 39 Cong., 2 Sess., No. 34, Serial No. 1306.

Alfriend, Edward M., "Social Life in Richmond during the War," in the *Cosmopolitan. A Monthly Illustrated Magazine*, XII (1891), 229-33.

Andrews, Matthew P. (ed.), *The Women of the South in War Times* (Baltimore, 1920).

Bettersworth, John K., *Confederate Mississippi, The People and Policies of a Cotton State in Wartime* (Baton Rouge, 1943).

Bill, Alfred Hoyt, *The Beleaguered City, Richmond, 1861-1865* (New York, 1946).

Booham, Milledge L., Jr., *The British Consuls in the Confederacy* (New York, 1911).

Botts, John Minor, *The Great Rebellion: Its Secret History, Rise, Progress, and Disastrous Failure. The Political Life of the Author Vindicated* (New York, 1866).

Bradbeer, William W., *Confederate and Southern State Currency* (Mt. Vernon, N. Y., 1915).

Bradlee, Francis B. C., *Blockade Running during the Civil War and the Effect of Land and Water Transportation on the Confederacy* (Salem, Mass., 1925).

Bragg, Jefferson Davis, *Louisiana in the Confederacy* (Baton Rouge, 1941).

Bruce, Kathleen, *Virginia Iron Manufacture in the Slave Era* (New York, 1931).

Bryan, T. Conn, "Churches in Georgia During the Civil War," in *Georgia Historical Quarterly*, XXXIII (1949).

Chandler, Julian A. C., *et al.* (eds.), *The South in the Building of the Nation . . .* , 13 vols. (Richmond, 1909-13).

Cheshire, Joseph Blount, *The Church in the Confederate*

States; A History of the Protestant Episcopal Church in the Confederate States (New York, 1912).

Cotton Sold to the Confederate States (Washington, 1913), in *Senate Documents*, 62 Cong., 3 Sess., No. 987, Serial No. 6348.

Coulter, E. M., *The Civil War and Readjustment in Kentucky* (Chapel Hill, 1926).

Coulter, E. Merton, "Commercial Intercourse with the Confederacy in the Mississippi Valley, 1861-1865," in *Mississippi Valley Historical Review*, III (1916-17), 275-300.

Coulter, E. Merton, *The Confederate States of America 1861-1865*, Vol. VII of *A History of the South*, Wendell Holmes Stephenson and E. Merton Coulter, eds. (Baton Rouge, 1950).

Coulter, E. Merton, "The Movement for Agricultural Reorganization in the Cotton South during the Civil War," in *Agricultural History*, I, 3-17.

Curry, Jabez L. M., *Civil History of the Government of the Confederate States with Some Personal Reminiscences* (Richmond, 1901).

Davis, Jefferson, *The Rise and Fall of the Confederate Government*, 2 vols. (New York, 1881).

Davis, Jefferson, *A Short History of the Confederate States of America* (New York, 1890).

Davis, William W., *The Civil War and Reconstruction in Florida* (New York, 1913).

Diamond, William, "Imports of the Confederate Government from Europe and Mexico," in *Journal of Southern History*, VI (1940), 470-503.

Dowdy, Clifford, *Experiment in Rebellion* (Garden City, 1946).

Dumond, Dwight L., *The Secession Movement, 1860-1861* (New York, 1931).

Dumond, Dwight L., *Southern Editorials on Secession* (New York, 1931).

Eaton, Clement, *A History of the Southern Confederacy* (New York, 1954).

Fitts, Albert N., "The Confederate Convention," and "The Confederate Convention: The Constitutional Debate," in *Alabama Review*, II, 83-101, 189-210 (April and July 1949).

Fleming, Walter L. *Civil War and Reconstruction in Alabama* (Cleveland, 1911).

Foote, Henry S., *War of the Rebellion; or Scylla and Charybdis. Consisting of Observations upon the Causes, Course, and Consequences of the Late Civil War in the United States* (New York, 1866).

Freeman, Douglas S., *A Calendar of Confederate Papers, with a Bibliography of Some Confederate Publications* . . . (Richmond, 1908).

Gipson, Lawrence H., "The Collapse of the Confederacy," in *Mississippi Valley Historical Review*, IV (1917-18), 437-58.

Hamilton, J. G. de Roulhac, "The State Courts and the Confederate Constitution," in *Journal of Southern History*, IV (1938), 425-48.

Hay, Thomas R., "The South and the Arming of the Slaves," in *Mississippi Valley Historical Review*, VI (1919-20), 34-73.

Hesseltine, William B., *The South in American History* (New York, 1943).

Henry, Robert S., *The Story of the Confederacy* (Indianapolis, 1931).

Hill, Louise B., *State Socialism in the Confederate States of America*, in *Southern Sketches*, Ser. I, No. 9 (Charlottesville, 1936).

Hoole, W. Stanley, "Charleston Theatricals during the Tragic Decade, 1860-1869," in *Journal of Southern History*, XI (1945), 538-47.

Johnson, Robert U. and Buell, C. C. (eds.), *Battles and Leaders of the Civil War* . . . , 4 vols. (New York, 1887-8).

Lonn, Ella, *Desertion during the Civil War* (New York, 1928).

Massey, Mary Elizabeth, *Ersatz in the Confederacy* (Columbia, 1952).

Moore, Albert B., *Conscription and Conflict in the Confederacy* (New York, 1924).

Moore, Frank (ed.), *Songs and Ballads of the Southern People, 1861-1865* (New York, 1886).

Owsley, Frank L., *King Cotton Diplomacy; Foreign Relations of the Confederate States of America* (Chicago, 1931).

Owsley, Frank L., *State Rights in the Confederacy* (Chicago, 1925).

Parks, Joseph H., "A Confederate Trade Center under Federal Occupation; Memphis, 1862-1865," in *Journal of Southern History*, VII (1941), 289-314.

Patton, James W., *Unionism and Reconstruction in Tennessee, 1860-1869* (Chapel Hill, 1934).

Phillips, Ulrich B., "The Central Theme of Southern History," in *American Historical Review*, XXXIV (1929).

Pollard, Edward A., *The Lost Cause; A New Southern History of the War. Comprising a Full and Authentic Account of the Rise and Progress of the Late Southern Confederacy* . . . (New York, 1866).

Pollard, Edward A. *Southern History of the War*, 2 vols. (New York, 1866).

Ramsdell, Charles W., *Behind the Lines in the Southern Confederacy* (Baton Rouge, 1944).

Ramsdell, Charles W., "The Confederate Government and the Railroads," in *American Historical Review*, XXII (1916-17), 794-810.

Ramsdell, Charles W., "The Control of Manufacturing by the Confederate Government," in *Mississippi Valley Historical Review*, VIII (1921-2), 231-49.

Roberts, A. Sellew, "The Federal Government and Confederate Cotton," in *American Historical Review*, XXXII (1926-7), 262-75.

Robinson, William M., Jr., *Justice in Grey; A History of the Judicial System of the Confederate States of America* (Cambridge, Mass., 1941).

Robinson, William M., Jr., "A New Deal in Constitutions," in *Journal of Southern History,* IV (1938), 449-61.

Schwab, John C., *The Confederate States of America, 1861-1865. A Financial and Industrial History of the South During the Civil War* (New Haven, 1913).

Sellers, James L., "An Interpretation of Civil War Finance," in *American Historical Review,* XXX (1924-5), 282-97.

Silver, James W., *Confederate Morale and Church Propaganda,* No. 3 in *Confederate Centennial Studies,* W. Stanley Hoole, Editor-in-chief (Tuscaloosa, 1957).

Simkins, Francis B. and Patton, James W., *The Women of the Confederacy* (Richmond, 1936).

Smith, Ernest A., *The History of the Confederate Treasury* (Harrisburg, Pa., 1901).

Smith, Edward C., *The Borderland in the Civil War* (New York, 1927).

Stephens, Alexander H., *A Constitutional View of the Late War Between the States; its Causes, Character, Conduct and Results. Presented in a Series of Colloquies at Liberty Hall,* 2 vols. (Philadelphia, 1868-70).

Stephens, Alexander H., *The Reviewers Reviewed; A Supplement to the "War Between the States," etc., with an Appendix in Review of "Reconstruction," So Called* (New York, 1872).

Stephenson, Nathaniel W., "The Question of Arming the Slaves," in *American Historical Review,* XVIII (1912-13), 295-308.

Tatum, Georgia Lee, *Disloyalty in the Confederacy* (Chapel Hill, 1934).

Thompson, Samuel B., *Confederate Purchasing Operations Abroad* (Chapel Hill, 1935).

Todd, Richard C., *Confederate Finance* (Athens, Ga., 1954).

Trexler, Harrison, "The Opposition of Planters to Employment of Slaves as Laborers by the Confederacy," in *Mississippi Valley Historical Review*, XXVII (1940-1), 211-24.

Vandiver, Frank E. (ed.), *Confederate Blockade Running through Bermuda, 1861-1865; Letters and Cargo Manifests* (Austin, 1947).

Walpole, Spencer, *The Life of Lord John Russell*, 2 vols. (London and New York, 1889), II.

Weeks, Stephen B., "Confederate Text-Books (1861-1865); A Preliminary Bibliography," in *Report of the [United States] Commissioner of Education for the Year 1898-1899*, 2 vols. (Washington, 1900), I, 1139-55.

Wesley, Charles H., *The Collapse of the Confederacy* (Washington, 1937).

Wiley, Bell I., *The Plain People of the Confederacy* (Baton Rouge, 1943).

Wiley, Bell I., *Southern Negroes, 1861-1865* (New Haven, 1938).

Wright, Gordon, "Economic Conditions in the Confederacy as Seen by the French Consuls," in *Journal of Southern History*, VII (1941), 195-214.

agriculture, 54-63
Alfriend, F. H., 99-101, 105
Anderson, Major Robert, 44, 48-51
Andrews, Sarah Page, 177-8

Baptist Church, 74, 85-6
Beauregard, Gen. P. G. T., 47-8, 229
Benjamin, Judah P.: intellectual powers, 15, 35; sketch of, 41; appointed Secretary of War, 64; replaced by Seddon, 68; banishes English consuls, 255; 234, 244, 253, 254, 256, 260, 263
Blackwood's Edinburgh Magazine: slave morale, 59-61; sewing societies, 171; discusses "King Cotton," 231-2; Emancipation Proclamation, 245
Bragg, Gen. Braxton: loyalty of Davis to, 15, 218; opposes military exemptions, 205; invades Kentucky, 266-7
Bragg, Gov. Thomas, 208
Breckinridge, Gen. John C., 188, 281
Brown, Gov. Joseph E.: denounces conscription, 15; proclamation endorsed, 61-2; sketch of, 198; opposes conscription, 198-201; advocate of State rights, 198; proclamation on desertion, 267-8
Buchanan, James, 44, 256
Burrows, John Lansing, 105-7
Burwell, William M., 101-2, 105
Butler, Gen. Benjamin F., 142-8, 155

Calhoun, John C., 22, 234
Campbell, Charles, 162-3
Cary, Constance, 173, 174-6
Catholic Church, 80, 96
Chesnut, Col. James: at Sumter crisis, 46-9, 51; loyalty to Davis, 223-4; 229
Chesnut, Mary Boykin: sketch of, 46; tells of Sumter crisis, 46-51; of clothing shortage, 191; discusses Davis, 223-4; despair of, 282

Claiborne, Dr. John H., 162
Clay, Clement C., 255-60, 266-7
clothing: substitutes for, 172, 173, 194
Cobb, Howell, 14, 218
Confederacy: geographical area, 13, 17; population, 13; life in, 14; use of resources, 16; source materials on, 18; resentment against England, 255
Congress: responsibility for inflation, 15; passes war resolution, 51-2; urges reduction in cotton and tobacco planting, 62-3; failure to tax, 122; need for taxation, 126-7; passes tax bill (1863), 127-8; suspends *habeas corpus*, 210; enacts conscription, 197-8; and exemption, 204
Confederate Constitution: 26-33; adoption, 26; powers of Congress, 28, 202; veto power of President, 27-8; tariff, 28; internal improvements, 28-9; post office, 29; implied powers, 29; supremacy of, 29; export duties, 30; slavery in, 30-1; new states and territories, 31; amendments, 31-2; ratification, 32-3
Confederate government: division of powers, 27, 213; Executive Department, 27-8; Cabinet, 38-41; financing of, 117-40; State rights, 202, 203; defied by South Carolina, 201-3; conflict with North Carolina, 207-9; need for Supreme Court, 209; foreign recognition of, 232; effect of neutrality on, 233; agents in Canada, 255-6; recruiting in Northwest, 259-60; agents in North, 260; offer of emancipation, 260-2; evacuates Richmond, 283
conscription: wisdom of, 15; centralizing influence of, 16; effect on education, 96; Act of (1862), 197-203; of substitutes, 198; reaction to, 198-203; effect on education, 200; effect on plantations, 200; President's ex-

emption powers, 201; South Carolina opposes, 201-3; Florida opposes, 203; substitutes, 205; exemption difficulties in North Carolina, 207-9; causes friction between state and Confederate governments, 209; resistance to in Alabama, 266; resistance to in North Carolina, 271-3; resistance in South Carolina, 270-1

Copperheads, 257, 259

cotton: wisdom of government policy, 15; influence on Southern economy, 54-5; diversified agriculture, 61; prewar production, 225; effect on slavery, 225; an economic weapon, 226, 228, 231; importance to English economy, 226, 229, 235; importance to French and Belgian economy, 226, 228; embargo, 231; blockade running, 231; in India, 235; diplomatic importance of, 236; trading with enemy, 263-4, 275-8; demoralizing influence of, 275-8

Cummings, Kate, 191, 290-2

Davis, Jefferson: loyalty to friends, 15; interference with generals, 15; stubbornness of, 15, 219-20, 223; elected Provisional President, 26; elected President, 33; description of, 33-4; relations with Cabinet, 38-9; personality and popularity, 39; interest in military affairs, 40; proclaims agriculture battle won, 62; proclamation of fast days, 81; addresses education association, 93; denounces speculators, 122; social life, 182-3; protests South Carolina opposition, 201-3; asks *habeas corpus* suspension, 209-10; proposes drafting of slaves, 214-15; exemption powers, 215-17; charged with favoritism, 217; and secession, 218; enigmatic qualities, 218; opposition to, 209-24; supports Northrop, 218; loses popularity, 219-20, 223-4; and H. S. Foote, 221; removes Joseph E. Johnston, 222; Mexican War reputation,

223; tells of disloyalty, 274; at fall of Richmond, 284; 14, 68, 105, 246, 271, 283

Davis, Samuel, 103-5

Davis, Varina Howell, 182-4

De Bow, J. D. B.: sketch of, 64-5; influence of *Review*, 65; reports on manufacturing growth, 65-8; views on education, 88-90; as Produce Loan agent, 118-19

De Leon, T. C.: sketch of, 37; discusses Confederate officials, 37-44; on Tredegar, 71-3; on music and art, 112-16; on social life in Richmond, 180-4

desertion: reasons for, 197; extent of, 207, 281; states asked to curb, 265-6; in Georgia, 267-8; in South Carolina, 270-1; in North Carolina, 271-3; seriousness of, 274; inspired by illicit trade, 278; in Louisiana, 277-8; in Virginia, 278-81

disloyalty: in Hardy County, Va., 141-2; in East Tennessee, 263-5, 280-1; oaths disregarded, 264; trading with enemy, 266; in Alabama, 267-70; in North Carolina, 271-3, 280-1; in Mississippi, 275-6; in Louisiana, 277-8; in Virginia, 279-81

Echols, Gen. John, 279-81

education, 88-96

Elder, John A., 114, 115

Emancipation Proclamation, 148; British reaction to, 244-5; slave uprisings following, 245, 248; reasons for, 246; Lincoln's inconsistency on, 247; Seward's view on, 247; opposition to in Border States, 248

England: recognition sentiment in, 16, 17, 236, 245, 251-2; cotton in economy of, 226, 229, 235; views of blockade, 235; fear of war with U. S., 236, 250; neutrality proclamation of, 232-3; Russell-Palmerston correspondence, 237-9; plan to negotiate war settlement, 237-8; effect of Confederate victories on, 237; recognition plans (1862), 237; effect of Confederate Navy on, 243; reaction to Emancipation

Proclamation, 244-5; refuses recognition, 248; party politics in, 250; neutrality of, 250; demonstrations favoring U. S. in, 251; effect of Chancellorsville on, 252; resentment of Confederacy against, 255; conduct of consuls, 255; and emancipation offer, 260-2

Episcopal Church: Montgomery Resolutions, 75; Columbia convention, 75-6; statement on faith and doctrine, 76

Estelle, Kate, 109, 111

Fleharty, Stephen F., 86-7

food: scarcity of, 54-6, 135-6, 164-7, 172-8; substitutes for, 170

France: recognition sentiment in, 163; importance of cotton in economy of, 226; and mediation, 238-9; attempts to gain recognition of, 240-3; neutrality of, 243; intervention in Mexico, 243; question of joint recognition with England, 252

fugitives and refugees, 155-67; in Richmond, 155-61; in Petersburg, 161-4; concern for, 155-7; house hunting, 157-61; terror among, 161-3

Grant, General U. S., 187, 282, 283

habeas corpus: conflict over in North Carolina, 207-9; suspension of, 209-14, 268-9; abuses under, 210-12; powers of executive under, 211-12

Hammond, James, 226-8

Hayne, Paul Hamilton, 97, 100

Hoge, Moses D., 162, 284

Hood, Gen. John B., 222, 280, 281

Hotze, Henry: sketch of, 244; operations in England, 244; correspondence with Benjamin, 244, 253, 255

impressment: act of (1863), 129; necessity for, 129-32; speculation and, 129; redundant currency and, 129; operations under law, 130; ineffectiveness of, 130-2, 136-7; farmers protest against, 132-3; commis-

sioners, 133-4; cause of inflation 133-5, 139; evasion of, 136-7; corruption in, 137

inflation: 117-40; effect of government borrowing on, 121; results of, 124; effect of speculation on, 130-1; effect of redundant currency on, 130-1; effect of impressment on, 133-5; effect of on medical fees, 138-9; in Petersburg (1864), 164

Jackson, Gen. T. J., 252, 259

Johnson, Andrew, 263-4

Johnson, L., 93-4

Johnston, Gen. Joseph E., 15, 183, 288

Jones, J. B.: sketch of, 33; *Diary,* 33; secures clerkship in War Dept., 34; discusses Davis and Cabinet, 33-7; and railroad problem, 69; and inflation, 122

Kenner, Duncan, 260-2

Kentucky Resolution, 23, 256

Lamar, Lucius Q. C., 249-52

Lee, Gen. R. E.: regard for Davis, 14; orders removal of Petersburg hospitals, 162; New Year's dinner for army, 196; supreme commander, 223; defeated at Antietam, 239; abandons Richmond, 283

Letcher, Gov. John, 52-3

Leutze, Emanuel, 114

Lincoln, Abraham: calls for volunteers, 51; issues Emancipation Proclamation, 148; accused of tyranny, 246-7, 259; shifts position on emancipation, 247; 74, 256

literature, 97-104

McArthur, Delia, 165-7

McGuire, Judith Brockenbrough: sketch of, 157; housing difficulties, 157-61; and women's war work, 178-80; and romance, 186-8; doubts of victory, 283

McVea, John, 277-8

Mallory, Stephen R., 40, 283

Mann, Ambrose Dudley, 232, 233

Manning, Gov. John L., 47, 48, 229

manufacturing: 63-73; in South prior to 1860, 63-4; of war

material, 64; in Virginia and Carolinas, 65-8; by government departments, 68; increase of, 68; women weaving, 68; domestic, 277

Mason, James M.: *Trent* affair, 233; sketch of, 234; report on Britain and blockade, 234-5; failure of mission, 248; kindness to Lamar, 250; recall of, 254; proposal of emancipation to Palmerston, 260-2; 244

Means, Gov. J. H., 47, 48

Melton, C. D., 270-1

Memminger, C. G.: South Carolina secession convention, 23-4; and L. P. Walker, 35; as Sec. of Treas., 40-1; explains inflation cause, 122-4

Methodist Church, 74

Miles, William P., 47, 48, 85, 229

Milton, Gov. John, 132, 203

military exemptions, 135, 202-7

money: paying for war, 117; specie, 117; bond issues, 118; alarm over redundancy, 122; need to reduce amount of, 123-4; fear of repudiation, 134; repudiation, 140; depreciation of, 277; buried at evacuation of Richmond, 285

music, 112-13

Napoleon III, 240-3; Southern sympathy, 241; views on recognition, 241, 242; and Slidell, 248; joint recognition, 252

Negroes: as laborers, 56-7; worker at Tredegar, 72-3; and music, 113; uprisings of, 148-54; in Petersburg siege, 164; *see* slaves

New Orleans: occupied by Union troops, 142-8; *see* Butler; Walker

North Carolina: legislators complain about conscription, 203-4; difficulties over *habeas corpus*, 207-9; treason in, 212; desertion and disloyalty in, 271-3, 280-1; terrorism, 273

Northrop, Col. L. B., 135, 178, 218

nullification: at Hartford Convention (1814), 22; in South Carolina (1832), 21-3; of conscription, 201-3, 207-9

Palmerston, Lord: denounces Gen. Butler's "woman order," 146; correspondence with Russell over intervention, 237-9; effect of Antietam on, 239; indecision, 240; audience with Mason, 260-2

Paxton, A. M., 275-6

Pearson, Richmond M., 207-9

Pickens, Gov. Francis, 44-7, 229

Pickens, Col. Samuel, 263-4

Polk, Gen. Leonidas, 84, 205

Presbyterian Church, 76-83

Produce Loan, 118-19

profiteers and speculators, 14, 125-6

Provisional Congress, 26, 33, 41-4

Provisional Constitution, 26

Pryor, Sara Agnes, 161-4

Pryor, Col. Roger A., 161

Putnam, Sallie, 189-90, 284-8

railroads, 69-71

religion, 74-87, 174

Rhett, Robert B., 219-20

Richards, George, 149-51

Richmond: hotels cease boarding, 164-7; siege of, 165-7; bread riots, 189-90; evacuation of, 283-8; rioting in, 285-7; 184, 185, 189

Richmond *Enquirer*: denounces Congress for failure to tax, 124-6; criticizes luxurious living, 185; tells of desertion and treason, 268-9

Richmond *Examiner*: criticism of drama, 111-12; denounces Davis, 214-17; proposes stripping Davis of power, 222-3

"Richmond Lady": tells of textbook shortage, 92; discusses education, 95; tells of hardships of refugees, 164-7

Roebuck, John E., 252-3

Russell, Lord John, 232; on neutrality proclamation, 233; blockade, 234; corespondence with Palmerston, 237-9; indecision, 240

Russell, William Howard, 229-31

Russia, 238-9

secession, 22, 41-2

Seddon, James A.: Secretary of War, 68; discusses railroad problem, 69-70; discusses impressment, 129-32; urges allowance for clerks, 132; writes of impressment scandals, 137; 207

Seward, William H., 227, 247

Sherman, Gen. William T., 63, 282-3

slaves and slavery: emancipation, 17; few writings of, 18; inscrutability of, 50; loyalty of, 59-60; treatment of, 59-60; docility of, 61; rioting, 148-54; proposal to draft and emancipate, 214-15; uprisings, 245, 248; proposal to Palmerston concerning abolition of, 260-2; abolition urged, 274; see Negroes

Slidell, John: Trent affair, 233; sketch of, 240; meeting with Napoleon III, 240-3; despairs of English recognition, 241; access to Napoleon, 246; and Duncan Kenner mission, 260; 244

Smyth, Thomas, 83-4

South Carolina: secession convention, 21; State rights belief, 21-2; causes of secession, 23-5; governor denounces truce violation, 44; controversy with Confederate Government, 202-3

Southern Cultivator, 54-7, 61

Southern Illustrated News, 107-11

Southern Literary Messenger, 103, 218-21

Stanton, Edwin M., 63

State rights, 16, 22-3, 274

Stephens, Alexander H.: opposition to government, 14; reluctant secessionist, 15, 218; elected Provisional Vice President, 26; and Vice President, 33; reputation (1861), 39; leader of opposition, 210; denounces habeas corpus suspension, 210-14

Stone, Kate: sketch of, 58; discusses gardening, 58-9; education of brothers, 90-2; tells of escape, 149-54; despair of, 288-90

taxation: constitutional restriction on, 15; popular opposition to, 15; need for, 117, 124-7; to redeem Treasury notes, 120; states to collect, 120-1; tax-in-kind, 127-8

textbooks, 92-5

theater, 105-12

Thompson Jacob, 255-60

Thompson, John R., 97, 100, 114

Timrod, Henry, 97, 100, 108

Toombs, Robert: appearance and intellect, 26; Secretary of State, 36, 39-40; efforts to secure European recognition, 232; 14, 218

treason: in North Carolina, 212; in East Tennessee, 263-5; in Alabama, 266-7; in Georgia, 267-8; in South Carolina, 270-1; in Virginia, 279-81

Tredegar Works: capacity of, 69; importance to railroads, 71; ordnance, 71-2; benefits for employees, 72-3; importance to Confederacy, 73; see manufacturing

Vance, Zebulon: addresses education association, 93; denounces speculators, 122; sketch of, 207; and habeas corpus suspension, 207-9; views on conscription, 207-9; 272

Vernon, Ida, 105, 112

Walker, Alexander, 143-8

Walker, L. P., 34-6, 40, 64

Walthall, Maj. W. T., 269-70

Washington, William D., 114, 115

Wigfall, Louis T., 47-8, 51

women: Gen. Butler's order concerning, 142-3; patriotism of, 168; work on plantations, 168; sewing of, 169, 171; as war clerks, 179; and shoe-making, 180; ingenuity of, 190-4; participate in cotton smuggling, 276

Wood, Col. W. B., 263-5

Wren, Ella, 105, 109-11

Yancey, William Lowndes, 219, 20, 232-3

W